WI

INDIA: LAND OF THE BLACK PAGODA

There are 5,000,000 holy men in India who toil not neither do they spin. They abandon their wives and children, smear themselves with ashes, and ordure of the sacred cow, and wander from shrine to shrine seeking salvation for their souls.

At the top of the caste system are the haughty "twice-born" Brahmins.

LOWELL THOMAS

INDIA: LAND OF THE BLACK PAGODA

Illustrated With Original Photographs
Taken by H. A. Chase, F.R.G.S.,
And by Lowell Thomas

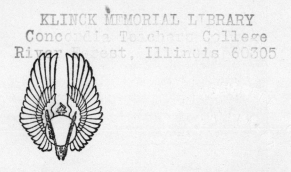

PUBLISHED BY

P. F. Collier & Son Corporation, New York

BY SPECIAL ARRANGEMENT WITH

D. Appleton-Century Co., Inc.

NEW YORK

PRINTED IN THE UNITED STATES OF AMERICA

TO

"Y. B."

CONTENTS

ILLUSTRATIONS

ix

INDIA: LAND OF THE BLACK PAGODA

CHAPTER I

BEFORE THE CURTAIN RISES

AFTER every one else had held forth, the general spoke:
"Yes, gentlemen, you have been to strange places.
But have you ever heard of the Black Pagoda?"

We were with Allenby's army, camped at Deir el
Belah on the edge of the Sinai Desert, just south of the
old Philistine capital of Gaza. I was putting up for the
night at the headquarters of a mounted column and we
were sitting in the mess tent after dinner. The inevitable
toast "To the King!" had just been drunk in Jewish
wine from Richon le Zion, and after the general had
passed around a box of Dutch cigars the conversation
turned to the topic of far countries.

An Englishman, an Australian, and an Irishman
were discussing strange places they had seen. The general was a British officer of the old school, originally of
the Bucks Hussars; the Australian, a major in the Imperial Camel Corps; and the Irishman a captain in the
Hong Kong-Singapore Battery. They were professional
soldiers—had been for most of their natural lives—and
always on the move. They talked in the same off-hand

3

intimate way of Basutoland, Malta, Shanghai, Khartoum, and Mandalay as we might speak of Omaha, Denver or Toledo.

"Right-ho, sir," we all said, "and where and what is the Black Pagoda?" Then we hitched our camp-chairs a bit nearer the general's end of the table and settled ourselves to hear his yarn.

"It was before the war when I was doing my turn in India," continued our host. "Occasionally we would be given a short leave that was hardly long enough for a voyage to England or even for a decent shoot in Kashmir. One winter, while my regiment was stationed at Mhow, I decided to try ocean bathing—for my liver. Getting a bit crotchety, don't you know. I had heard a lot about the wonderful surf at Puri on the Bay of Bengal. And there I went. During my sojourn at this sacred Hindu city the local captain of police took me on the most unusual trip I ever made, and India, as you know, is one country where you can go on an unusual journey any day, or any night.

"Borne on the shoulders of muscular coolies, we bounced along on an all-night journey by palanquin. Just at dawn we arrived at our destination, the Black Pagoda, the weirdest and some say the finest of all the temples in India. Many are the strange sights to be found in Asia, but this temple surpasses them all. Why? Well, for the reason that its sides are covered with images, many of them of life size, that depict human beings in the act of committing nearly every sin in the world.

> 'Strange, weird things that no man may say,
> Things Humanity hides away. . . .
> Cruel things that man may not name,
> Naked here, without fear or shame' . . .

"Of course, there are many British officials in India who know of its existence, but few have ever been there —and those who go do not take their wives."

Then the general gave us such a graphic, detailed description of the Black Pagoda that I returned to my tent there on the plains of Philistia declaring by the whiskers of Samson and Goliath that I would hire me a palanquin and make that midnight journey along the coast of Bengal to the Black Pagoda if my caravel ever touched the shores of mysterious Hindustan.

It was while on a speaking-tour of the world, relating tales of adventures with Allenby and Lawrence, that I caught my first glimpse of India. Here, I realized, was by far the most fascinating of all the countries I had visited. Richard Curle, mining engineer, savant, and friend of Conrad, once wrote a fascinating book entitled "The Shadow Show." I like that title because it has always seemed to me that life on this planet is indeed a shadow show. And when I saw India I knew that I was witnessing the greatest show of all. I had found Australia and New Zealand fascinating, Africa full of

thrills and surprises, and the Far East absorbingly interesting. But India towers as far above them as the
Himalayas tower above the Alps. As a spectacle there is
nothing like it.

Variety, we are assured, is the spice of life. The
country that interests us the most is the one where there
is the most variety. At any rate, so it seems to me. And
India has variety to the nth degree. It is supremely the
land of startling contrast. The southern tip touches the
equator. Central India is in the Temperate Zone and is
not only a land of mighty rivers and fertile valleys, but
also includes vast deserts similar to those of Arabia,
Arizona, and the Sahara. Along the northern border of
India loom those towering mountain ranges, the Himalayas, loftiest of all the peaks of earth, their summits
clad with ice and snow since the dawn of time.

Mark Twain once said that India was the land that
all men long to see, and having seen by so much as a
glimpse, would not trade that glimpse for all the other
sights of the world. He wrote of it as the only land with
an irresistible appeal to alien prince and alien peasant
alike.

After the World War, when the fiery Clémenceau
retired from political life, he announced that there was
one country he simply had to see before he died. Romantic India.

The other day in a book about Napoleon I encountered a mention of a dazzling myth, one of those beliefs,

half superstitious perhaps, that have fascinated men over the span of the centuries. Napoleon was charmed and tricked by it, and held it in the back of all his dreams. Throughout history, in the higher imaginations of statecraft that same beguiling idea appears again and again. Alexander was motivated by some such intuition. The idea is this: Who holds India holds the world. As a theory of world-politics you can pick it to pieces, but you cannot escape its seductive, glamorous persuasion.

Strangest of all the lands of this earth, India is inhabited by peoples who, in outward appearance at any rate, seem to include nearly every race under the sun. They vary in shade from the Untouchables of the south, who are descendants of the black aborigines, to the brown Brahmins, to the Mongolians of the north, and to the Caucasian races that include not only the British rulers but many of the native inhabitants as well.

On top of all this, just to lend more variety and contrast, India is a land of splendor and magnificence far, far surpassing anything to be found in either Europe or America—and at the same time it is also a land of squalor and misery so terrible that the mere memory of it still makes me shudder.

I had thought of India as a country one could see, and be satisfied to come away from, in a month or two. But instead of two months, I stayed for two years. Even then I was not content. I wanted to remain on and on, but unlike Aladdin I had no magic lamp, and one day my chancellor of the exchequer brought me out of my Arabian Nights' dream with the harsh news that my wealth in no way resembled either that of the fabled kings of Golconda, or of a present-day Indian maharajah.

To those of us who stop to think about it there is something impressive in the thought that one out of every four people on this spinning planet of ours is a citizen of the British Empire. And when we get that far in our contemplation, it is interesting to keep on for a moment and ponder over the fact that three out of every four people in the British Empire live in India. A thousand years or so from now, when the Muse of History sets down her verdict as to the success of the greatest empire the world has ever known, she will be obliged to measure that success largely by what the British have accomplished among the Oriental peoples of the vast Asiatic peninsula of Hindustan.

I decided to commence my journey at the extreme southernmost tip of the peninsula, right down near the equator. There is no city there, nor had I ever read of any traveler's visit to that cape. Accompanied by Harry Chase, who had been with me in Arabia, Africa, and Europe during the World War, I sailed down the Red Sea, and then crossed the Arabian Sea and the Indian Ocean to the island of Ceylon. Here we engaged Singhalese fishermen to ferry us across the strait in their primitive catamarans. Then from Cape Comorin we proposed to set forth on our two or three months' journey, a journey that lengthened to two years and took us back and forth across India for a total distance of over sixty thousand miles—more than twice the circumference of the earth at the equator—and over a vast country nearly as large as the continent of Europe and inhabited by more people than there are on the continents of Australia, Africa, and North and South America all combined.

Every traveler from the West who visits India should have a guru, a wise man, to lead him about and explain the strange things he sees and hears. Without a guru the European or American who sojourns for a little while in India wanders in a daze and comes away as bewildered as any Alice in Wonderland. But to find your guru when you get to India, ah, that may not be so easy. Ganesha, the Hindu goddess of luck, smiled on me. She may not have given me the ability to see with eyes of understanding, but she did send me a guru. For I was fortunate enough to have a proper teacher who expounded to me many a mystery and perplexity.

In these western parts the custom of learning is to attend the lectures of a professor in a hall. But in India you sit at the feet of an ascetic hermit in a forest, or accompany a wandering yogi as a humble disciple, and your guru expounds to you the secrets of cryptic wisdom. I, metaphorically speaking, sat at the feet of a guru, a yogi. Incongruous as it may seem my guru was neither Hindu, Mussulman, nor Buddhist monk. He was not even an oriental, at any rate not by place of birth or ancestry. He was an Englishman, and a professional soldier.

"Y.B." was the nickname by which he was known throughout the Indian Army. And most of his fellow officers thought him a bit mad. "Y.B." would take off his uniform, don the picturesque costume of an Afridi, and wander about like a modern Harun-al-Rashid. Then too, he seemed to be genuinely fond of the Oriental peoples around him and seemed to understand them. Also he was an enthusiastic student of the languages and philosophies of the East. All of which somewhat baffled his beef-eating fellow Britons.

Major Francis Yeats-Brown was the younger son of an English diplomat. Against his will—he wanted to be a poet—he was sent to Sandhurst and trained for the army. The Orient called to him and he became a Bengal Lancer, although every turn of his mind was toward scholarship, literature, and philosophy. But he soldiered well and capably, a slashing cavalry officer in the incessant wars along the Indo-Afghan frontier. When the World War came he transferred to the cavalry of the clouds and became an aviator with the British Army in Mesopotamia. During the advance on Bagdad, not long before the fall of Kut-al-Amara, he flew over the Turkish lines on a hazardous mission to cut the enemy telegraph wires. He did so, but was captured, marched across the North Arabian Desert and after months of captivity made his escape, in the plotting of which he had recourse to a desperate expedient. He took up the smoking of opium to gain the confidence of an opium addicted Turkish commandant.

But affairs military were usually subordinate to "Y.B." In India he had plunged deeply into the study of the occult lore of the Hindus, Vedantism, yoga, and gained a knowledge of these mysterious subjects as few save native Indians can hope to do. It was this that caused his brother officers to raise their eyebrows and the finger of astonishment. They all seemed to love "Y.B.", considered him a crack polo player, a gallant soldier, a charming companion, and, as I have said, a bit mad.

Although his charm and drollery are not to be resisted, he is indeed one of the most eccentric fellows alive. And it is his very eccentricity that has resulted in his knowing India as few others do. This is amply demonstrated by a book of his recently published under the title of "The Lives of a Bengal Lancer." It is perhaps the most extraordinary book ever written about India by a westerner. In it he tells of the strange life he lived and something of the strange lessons he learned in the fabulous land of Hindustan.

Any insight that I may have into the ways and ideas of the mysterious land of India I owe to that sapient, whimsical guru, "Y.B." I found him equally at home along the

Coromandel Coast, near the equator, in the mountains
of Waziristan, and in the holy cities of the Gangetic
Plain. He had delved into the lives of the people and
into the hidden knowledge and discipline of yoga. He
was the only western yogi I have ever known.

For months we traveled together, and as scenes of
fantasy and mystery unfolded before us he expounded
the wise, enlightening, and witty ideas of a British yogi.
So whatever of truth and wisdom you find in these pages
should be credited to "Y.B.", the Bengal Lancer who became a yogi.

CHAPTER II

THE FABULOUS CAPE AT THE TIP OF INDIA

FROM our Ceylon fishing-boat we wade ashore near a round black rock over which the rollers of the Indian Ocean throw a lacework of spume and spindrift like the communion-cloth over a high altar. We feel a sense of awe and human smallness. Behind us in V-shape looms the vast peninsula of Hindustan, and in front of us a seemingly endless expanse of sea reaching from the equator to the South Polar ice-cap. To the two hundred million Hindus of the land we are setting out to visit, this is a sacred place—Cape Comorin, the apex of the immense triangular subcontinent that is India.

Between the black rock and the mainland is a quiet pool guarded from the tumult of the waves that sweep up from the Antarctic. Steps cut into the rocky promontory lead below the water's edge, for this is a holy bathing-ghat for pilgrims who assemble in thousands to worship at the shrine of the virgin goddess Kumari. Her shrine stands only a few yards back from the sea, within easy reach of the spray and swept by great winds from the ocean, as befits the temple of a maiden.

13

A Brahmin boy, straight and tall, and naked save for a simple cloth about his well-swung loins, stands facing the sea and wind—reading from the sacred book. It is the Gita, he tells us. But having answered our question he bends his soft eyes to the book again. He has not asked us who we are, nor why we are come. Creatures of an instant, atoms of a moment's space, as we are, he has hardly noticed our arrival from Ceylon, for he has eyes for the eternal mysteries alone.

We turn back a moment to watch him. He stands there leaning against a pillar of the temple, absorbed in the old poetic tale of Sri Krishna and the Charioteer. Stately, graceful, inscrutable, unconcerned, a symbol. . . . Why does he stand so? But that is a question we shall ask at every turn in India, and a question to which we shall so often find no answer.

A short distance inshore we approach a bigger temple. But a turbaned sentry with his bayonet fixed, backed by two surly, scowling Brahmin priests, bars our way. We are foreigners, unclean . . . so back to the sea, the jolly catholic sea, that washes aborigines and Americans, Brahmins and British, saints and sinners, dead men and quick.

Flinging off our clothes, we swim across the bathing-place to the round black rock that is the farthest southern tip of the peninsula and sit there dripping in the sunlight, at the very end of India.

How many eyes, avid for the millions and the

mystery of the East, have seen this cape! The swart Phœnicians saw it, sailing to the tin-mines of Malay. The Roman triremes sighted it when they coasted round it to the kingdom of Madura. Marco Polo called near here at Quilon when his galley skirted these rocks returning from far Cathay. Vasco da Gama and Albuquerque—those old Portuguese for whose ambition this earth was too small—knew Comorin and its pearls. Dupleix and Lally passed here—Frenchmen who held and then loosed the reins of empire in India. St. Francis Xavier, greatest of all international missionaries, voyaged this way in the days when he was carrying the cross of Christ to the idolators of China, Cambodia, and the Coromandel Coast. Then along came boisterous Captain Kidd, and that military marvel, young Clive; likewise Warren Hastings and Elihu Yale. In trireme, galley, frigate, and tea-clipper; pirate, politician, grandee, soldier, missionary, and merchant—in their high-pooped barquentines, Cape Comorin saw these great-hearted buccaneers of the Old World go by in search of the Golden Fleece.

We felt—and who would not?—a sense of awe before the prospect of our journey from Comorin to the Vale of Kashmir, from Bombay to the upper Brahmaputra, and along the wild frontier cirque that crosses Baluchistan, Waziristan, and Afghanistan. Over the various separate sections of Britain's Asiatic empire a thousand writers have gone before us. A thousand brains have evolved apt alliterations for this land of sloth, sensuality, saintliness, squalor, and splendor. A thousand pens have tried to picture the immensity of Hindustan, the teeming population of the Ganges, and India's bewildering complex of religions. But for every thousand pens that have scratched, ten thousand eyes have closed in weariness at bald facts recorded.

The other day we met a man possessing a library of a thousand and five hundred volumes—all on India. He confessed to having read a fifteenth of them. One might be forgiven for thinking that everything to be said about India should be found somewhere in that labyrinth of literature. But every world-traveler and observer who has passed this way has found India an inexhaustible mine with more ore-bearing veins of human interest than any other section of the earth.

India's marvels are all her own. It is impossible to imitate them. She holds the exclusive rights to the caste system, to the mysteries of black magic, yoga, and serpent-power, to Benares and the sacred Ganges, to the car of Jagannath, to the Taj Mahal, to the beauties of the Vale of Kashmir, and to the licentious but exquisite Black Pagoda of Kanarak.

With her three hundred million inhabitants divided into eighty nations speaking eighty languages and worshiping millions of gods, she is, as Mark Twain said, "a country endowed with an imperishable interest for alien prince and alien peasant, for lettered and ignorant. . . .

A land of dreams and romance, of fabulous wealth and fabulous poverty, of splendor and rags, of palaces and hovels, of famine and pestilence. Mother of history, grandmother of legend, and great-grandmother of tradition."

Surely of all the countries of earth, India leads in the staging of the daily human drama of mingled tragedy and comedy. Nor has she lost one atom of her fascination since the days when Britain's freebooters first visited the Great Moghuls. If anything, she presents a more alluring spectacle for the onlooker to-day than ever, because for the first time in history a great nation of Asia—the immemorial home of autocracy—is attempting to supplant her ancient institutions with the democratic theories of the West. What could be more fascinating than a visit to India during the days of this daring experiment?

So to our ox-cart. Let's set forth into the immensity of Hindustan and see this land of contrast and chaos for ourselves. We clamber in and away we bump in our springless cart. With our knees against our chins we crouch under the bamboo canopy, with neither room to sit erect nor room to lie flat. After a few hours of this torture all the romantic memories of our landing at Cape Comorin vanish, and between staccato expletives, punctuated by the bumping of the cart, we curse the day we left our luxurious hotel in Ceylon to invade India.

But look at the miraculous way our driver perches on the pole between his bhails (bullocks). Yet tortures and miracles such as these are the common habits of hundreds of thousands of men and women here. Unnumbered millions, for countless centuries, have sat thus and driven thus down a road that leads right back into the night of primal darkness—yes, this same driver, and these same white bullocks with these same painted horns and neatly tufted tails. And from the very throat of time the "Honk, hai, hai" of the driver seems to come.

Our good white bhails plod onward at a monotonous trot. Far behind us now are the sandy shores of Comorin, with the round black rock covered by the altar-cloth of the sea, and its little shrine to the Virgin, and its bigger temple whose portal we may not pass. To our left there is a line of palms against the evening sky, graceful silhouettes of ebony against the molten gold of sunset. Before us lies the darkness, and—spiritually at least— the Great Unknown.

Materially, however, we are jogging along to the village of Nagercoil, where we shall find alcohol, automobiles, and other abominations of the West, to help us on our way to the country of Travancore. On and on we jog through the night. We doze uneasily. Sights and sounds mingle with the broken meter of the bullock-trot. Then suddenly we are jolted awake. The good white bhails, unyoked, stroll away in the moonlight to the village pond. With difficulty we come to life, stretch our legs, light cigarettes.

Near by is a village shrine lit by a flickering wick. A shrine to Kali, she who drinks the blood of goats, and the blood of men when she can get it (which is rarely, however, owing to the tiresome British Government). We find her here in bas-relief, the terrible four-armed goddess, dancing the wicked Kali dance on the body of her husband. Kali, the black and terrible goddess, dancing with one foot on the thigh and the other on the breast of her helpless helpmate. There is a meaning in this dance, but it is not a thing to tell in print. In one hand she has a human head, in another a dripping knife, with her two others she encourages her worshipers. Her eyes are red, for she is maddened with hemp. Her breasts are besmeared with blood. Her only modesty is a girdle of corpses' hands. Her tongue, like a snake's, protrudes between her teeth. Kali is the chief goddess of Hindustan and her worshipers may be numbered by the hundred million. And why? What atavism of blood attracts her worshipers? What untellable lure has she? To Occidental eyes these things are sealed. We look and look again, with the eyes of travelers from the West, and with such sympathy and knowledge as we possess.

In the flicker of the smoky cresset we see a strange and terrible thing: the four arms of Kali seem to move with signs of menace, as if to elbow out intruders from her mysteries. Her mystery is insoluble for us; try as we will we cannot think ourselves into the mind of the people who come here to worship.

But we are to see far, far more than this, and we are to learn much of the strange religions and the strange ways of these peoples of Hindustan as we journey northward in this bhail-cart—our sarcophagus for three.

We cross the Western Ghats through a forest so dense and a night so black that all we can see are the flickering wicks of oil lamps in huts by the road, faces peering out through piles of mangoes and bananas in dimly-lit shops, and fantastic shapes of palm-trees and twisting banyans outlined against the sky. Just over the crest of the mountain range, where we start on our rapid drop towards the Arabian Sea, we are stopped at the bars of the frontier toll-gate. Even in the faint lantern-light we can see that the men of Travancore are of a different race, and they give us our change in strange, cumbersome coin.

Shortly after midnight we reach the travelers' bungalow in the city of Trivandrum, capital of the equatorial native state of Travancore. This is the second domain we are to pass on our way to the Black Pagoda.

CHAPTER III

IN A LOTUS-EATERS' LAND

NAKED natives are huddling by two and two along the road beneath palm-leaf umbrellas. Rickshaw boys, just back from a slipper-jog to the pier, are wringing out their loincloths. Tall cocoanut-palms bow low before the wrath of the sou'west monsoon that sweeps in from the Laccadive Atolls.

Everything in Travancore looks different from the rest of India that stretches northward from the equator to Capricorn. Here we seem to be in a Christian land of palms and mission churches and black converts. Since St. Thomas started the fashion of missionary enterprise by converting the tree-dwellers of Travancore in the days when St. Paul was enduring the buffetings of Roman prætors and St. James was preaching the Gospel to the devil-worshipers of Nasibin, many Syrian, Portuguese, Dutch, Swedish, French, British, and American missionaries have followed in the footsteps of the Doubting Apostle—accompanied by their less altruistic countrymen. We have dubbed this little-known southwestern shore-line of Hindustan "The Mis-

sionary Coast," because it is the India of the church
magazines and the pictures you saw as a child. There are
churches, images of the Virgin, and crucifixes under the
cocoanut-palms of every island. With its lagoons, inlets,
islands, and bays; with its leaning palms, luxuriant
breadfruit trees, thatched huts, fantastic barges, and
bare-bosomed wenches—it reminds one of the Isles of
the Southern Cross. It is a land of dreams, a haven for
those who are weary of the strenuous West.

The maharajah of this country is a devout and progressive ruler who has achieved efficiency in administration combined with personal popularity. Twenty per
cent of his people are Christians and treated by him with
the utmost benevolence, although he no doubt cherishes
a hope that one day their god may be absorbed in the
great pantheon of the Hindus to share the fate of the
Lord Buddha. He is the most religious prince in India
and a zealot in the practice of the rites of the twice-born.
By his co-religionists of Travancore he is looked upon
as a divinity. Divested of his royal clothes and clad in
the loincloth and sacred thread of the Brahmins, with
the Vishnu trident on his brow and the vision of the
Vedanta in his mind, we may see him any day in the
temple among his people, for he is an ascetic and a
philosopher as well as an enlightened monarch.

Away down here near the equator we notice that the
people look something like the inhabitants of Africa,
excepting that they have not thick lips. They are de-

scendants of the old aborigines, the Dravidians, who lived in India long thousands of years before the first white Aryans came down from central Asia and mingled with them to form the mixture of races that inhabit most of India to-day.

The railway station is three and a half miles away from the city of Trivandrum and the maharajah refuses to allow it to come any nearer. His people say that he prefers not to profane his sandals by crossing the rails when he goes to bathe. But the real reason lies deeper. Trivandrum, as it stands, is a verdant and vivacious little town. The gloomy steam and steel of the West would spoil it. Every one appears contented here . . . we wonder what the secret is of good-tempered Travancore. Is it that it is unhampered by the fetters of a too-rigid administration? And if so, would the rest of India be happier under native rulers with British advisers instead of British rulers with native advisers? Travancore is isolated, old-world, thoroughly well content, green and clean and prosperous. Trains and factories, trams and daily papers—these things have not yet crossed the frowning ghats to the east, nor gained a footing on the harborless shore that forms the western boundary of the state. May they long remain far away!

These cities of the west coast have an individuality that is rich and mellow. They are poles asunder from the irritable aggregations of tired, dusty, gloomy, secretive, neurotic folk that make up so much of the population of

the rest of India. Quilon, the ancient Koilum of Marco
Polo, is one of them, and boasts the oldest European
settlement in India. There is a really first-class dak
bungalow here (everywhere in Travancore the European gets good food and polite attendants) and there is
a fine beach for bathing close at hand. St. Thomas made
this town his headquarters for a time, and the modern
traveler is recommended to do the same. There is nothing much to see in the way of sights, but the backwaters,
which are neither lake nor land, are fascinating regions
with an elusive, pervasive charm. . . .

Since noon to-day we have been afloat in a prehistoric
craft that looks as though it might have been abandoned
as old and unserviceable by Vasco da Gama when he
visited this corner of India four centuries ago. We are
approaching the pier of a tiny island village. But to call
it a pier is to ascribe to it a dignity that it does not possess, for it consists of merely a wobbly plank on a few
shaky poles. The island is so dense with cocoanut-trees
that those lining the shore are obliged to lean out over
the water to get their share of sunlight.

Behind this pier is a thatched hut, and reclining on
a coir mat on the verandah is a bare-bosomed native
woman with a child on her tummy. Around the corner
of the hut two weather-beaten old hags with parchment
faces and wrinkled breasts that look as though they had
been gnawed by rats, are winding cocoanut rope and re-
tailing the village gossip. A large boat built of planks

sewn together with thongs and with prow and stern turning up in graceful elliptical curves is gliding along, poled by sinewy giants whose muscles stand out like lumps of bronze. They are of magnificent physique and in perfect condition. As they bend and turn in poling, the sunlight makes a grill of shadows over their ribs. Grace of the Greeks is in their every movement, and their figures are such as Praxiteles might have modeled.

Alongside now is a tiny thong-sewn skiff full of boys and yellow mangoes. The boys keep it balanced with their spoon paddles and all the while chant the praises of their mangoes. One member of our party is down below reveling in the favorite pastime of the Travancore coast at this season—mangling mangoes. He has the habit in an acute form. When a man falls victim to mango-madness he goes loco whenever he sees one. To hold a ripe one before his eyes produces an effect identical with that of dangling a wienerwurst before the nose of a dachshund or a watermelon before the eyes of a pickaninny. Until he has tasted a Tranvancore mango no man knows "Paradise regained."

Recently we spent two days on an estate where there was a large mango-orchard. All the trees were classified and every mango numbered. At night a watchman stood on guard. If one mango was stolen he would have to pay his employer a rupee. He drew a salary of ten rupees a month, so that the nervous tension was something awful. Here on the Travancore coast during the height of the season, mangoes can be bought five for a penny, and they are dear at the price, so one of us thinks—while the other would mortgage his soul for them in a moment of mango-mania.

On and on we steam in our placid tug through the romantic islets and lagoons of the Missionary Coast.

To our left, behind the setting sun, roar the breakers of the monsoon. But in this backwater all is peace. We are gliding through a fairyland of blue water and green palms. Sometimes we are on a broad rippleless expanse dotted here and there with fishing-boats. Then the perspective narrows to an avenue of palms. We are shut into the vast fecundity of the forest, and a great uneasiness, a claustrophobia, a horror of being imprisoned beneath the over-arching palms, creeps over us. There is beauty in these backwaters, but it marches hand in hand with terror. One shuts one's eyes, one opens them again, still the never-ending forest ahead, behind, all around us—the trees, the strangling creepers, the invading moss. To be marooned here would be more awful than to be lost in the desert. There is no air here, no view or wind, no light but the undersea green that comes to a diver in deep waters. All round is swarming life and huge decay. The great temples of this people, with their piles of gods on gods trampling on men and beasts, have their origin here in the dead trees, the fallen flowers, and the fierce struggle of a life that is ever renewed and eternally defeated. Life that is fertilized only to decay as the lingam of Siva is emblem of that procreation without which there can be no death.

At last the avenue broadens again; we are in another lagoon, but the obsession of death follows us. Here men are destroyers, fish the victims. All round as far as the eye can reach fishermen have spread their lines and nets. Below, glittering in the hyaline water, the fish spawn and die by the nets or by bigger fish. Ten thousand, twenty thousand years ago, there were the same lagoon, the same fish, the same nets and canoes. Perhaps the man who paddled the canoe was hairy and more beetle-browed. Perhaps the saber-toothed tiger and the plethiosaurus splashed in the reeds where that cross now stands—else all was the same.

CHAPTER IV

THE CITY OF BLACK AND WHITE JEWS

AT dusk we reached the end of the first stage of our voyage through the romantic backwater lagoons and inlets of the Malabar coast. A crowd of brown boys gathered at the jetty, shouting, "Allerpey!"

We got out and sorted our baggage. Then the brown boys saw visions of baksheesh. Nor were they alone in demanding toll. There was the man who took our tickets, and the man who watched the man who took our tickets to see that he didn't swindle, and the boy who brought the bullock-cart, and the man who brought the boy who brought the bullock-cart.

"Baksheesh! Rickshaw! Allerpey!" clamored the brown coolies. But alas! Allah didn't pay. We were the victims who had to produce!

In these out-of-the-way parts of India the nervous traveler is apt to get rattled by the constant demands for baksheesh. But it is the custom of the country. He is a foolish man who tries to pay only for services rendered. It is the undeserving who demand baksheesh and get it too, if the traveler is in search of smiles and peace.

After all, the privilege of visiting this country is worth a lot of the fat coppers of Travancore!

It is a moonless night. Our beds are in the garden by the road, where a breeze is floating through the sentinel palms. The voice of the mosquito is heard in the land and the time of the brain-fever bird has come. But we lie safe inside our mosquito-nets and relax in the tepid air, pondering dreamily on the life about us. A bullfrog croaks for a moment, then lapses into sudden silence. By the garden gate pass silent figures sheeted like the Roman dead. A bat looms by. There comes to us the agonized wail of some beast in pain. Then again a sudden silence, as if a throat had been choked. The powers of evil are abroad. A million tiny lives are born only to die again. By fang and foot the tragedy is played. Then from far away comes to our sleepy ears a sound of worship, the murmur of a multitude, the bugling of conches—the people of Brahma are at prayer.

Allerpey is on the backwater from Quilon to Cochin, a flourishing city so unknown to the outer world that even Murray's voluminous guide-book doesn't name it.

At Cochin, the pepper port, we are again in touch with the West, for British Cochin is a big and growing commercial center where cocoanut-fiber, spice, "and all things nice" are exported to an annual value of three and a half millions sterling. There are roughly three towns at Cochin—British Cochin, Jew Town, and Ernakulam. The latter is on the land side of the bay that forms a natural harbor, and is the terminus of the railway. It is a clean and prosperous city, with no historical associations but good accommodation for travelers. British Cochin and Jew Town rank among the quaint places of the world.

Two thousand years ago Chinese pirates taught the Cochinese a peculiar way of fishing. They still prefer it to modern methods. There is a contraption of string and bamboo by the quay-side on which a long pole is hinged, with one end inland and the other over the sea. From the sea end is suspended a kite-like affair. This is the net. The other end of the pole is weighted, for the convenience of the fishermen, who lower the net slowly into the sea and then withdraw it with its freight of fishes. The cords and stones with which these machines are hung, and the curious old creatures who work the levers and stare into the net with googly eyes, are like Heath Robinson's and Rube Goldberg's cartoons come to life, and are a strange contrast to the Pierce Leslie factory a hundred yards away. From time immemorial this fishing has continued, and until recently at Cannanore, farther up the coast, half the catch of sharks' fins and one fish were the perquisites of the rajah's cat, as a curious form of state tax.

Towards the club we come to St. Francis's Church, shut and locked after the unfortunate Church of England fashion. It is a gray, unimpressive building both within and without, yet venerable for its associations.

This was the first Christian church in India. Here Vasco da Gama was buried on Christmas Day, 1524.

Those who believe that the caste system, India's social cancer, will ever be rooted out, should visit Cochin. Here there are as many subdivisions among the Christians as there are among the Hindus, and the lines between them are almost as sharply drawn.

According to tradition, the first Christian converts were made nearly two thousand years ago when the Apostle Thomas came to the Malabar coast. Since then climate and tradition have been at work on Christianity, with the result that to-day there are three divisions of the Roman Catholics using the Latin liturgy, but who do not worship together and who are differentiated by name—"The Three Hundred," "The Five Hundred," and "The Seven Hundred." Then there is another Catholic sect that uses the Church of Rome liturgy in the ancient Syrian language instead of in Latin. There are also the Chaldean Syrians, who obey the "Patriarch of Babylon," and the Jacobite Syrians, who recognize the leadership of the "Patriarch of Antioch," and the St. Thomas Syrians, who disregard the rule of both Rome and Antioch and elect their own bishop.

The last-named are the "religious Bolsheviki" of Cochin. They call themselves St. Thomas Syrians on the ground that they are the only Christians in India who adhere to the ritual of the apostolic age. They believe in neither confession, absolution, fasting, invocation of the saints, veneration of relics, masses for the dead, nor baptismal regeneration.

As a result of century after century of dispute these sects have petrified into castes, and to-day intermarriage between castes is as uncommon among them as it is among their Hindu neighbors.

In addition to these seven groups there are others who adhere to various Protestant faiths. But by far the most interesting community we find in Cochin is in Jew Town, a quarter reminding us of the ghettos of Warsaw, Constantinople, or New York. But such is the effect of India on invading religions that even the Jews are split up into three separate castes, known as the "Whites," the "Browns," and the "Blacks."

As we drive in our rickshaws toward Jew Town we are confronted by the curse of Cochin. A plague hangs over their city, the plague of death by deformity. One out of every ten of the people we pass suffers from elephantiasis, one of the most terrible diseases known to medical science, for it not only destroys the human frame but first distorts it into a thing of ridicule. The disease causes a swelling of the ankles and knees until the legs are the size of bolsters. It is a common sight to see men walking around in what are apparently brown top-boots, their flesh being thus travestied by this hideous affliction. It is cured in several different ways, one of which is for the victim to have the accumulated fat pared down until his legs are of normal size. But not

many can afford the operation, or the necessary trip to
the distant metropolis of Madras. The afflicted often
live and work to late middle age, but their limbs grow
bigger and bigger until they reach the limit of elasticity,
and the periodic attacks of fever that accompany elephantiasis grow more frequent until at last the sufferers
are relieved of their "too too solid flesh." Fortunately, English bacteriologists have isolated the mi-
crobe—a water-borne germ.

A Brahmin, with the gaudy, diabolic-looking trident
of Vishnu on his forehead, who is employed as a clerk
by the wealthiest Jew shopkeeper, leads us through a
maze of crooked thoroughfares until we find ourselves
in a narrow street among a stately silent people dressed
in long tunics of rich color, waistcoats buttoned tight
around the neck, baggy white trousers, wooden sandals,
and skull-caps. It is easy to distinguish them from the
other inhabitants of Cochin by the locks that hang down
in front of their ears.

The two-storied houses on either side of the street
are of a style foreign to India, and the faces looking
out at us from the shuttered windows remind us of the
Rebeccas and Jezebels of Jerusalem. At the head of the
street we come to a synagogue, with its tower and the
old Dutch clock that has told off the lazy, listless hours
of life in this Indian ghetto since the day when the merchant buccaneers from Amsterdam protected these Jews
from the horrors of the Portuguese Inquisition.

No one seems to know just when these people settled in southern India. The history of the early days of the colony is shrouded in the mists of obscurity. The Black Jews, who look much like the native Muhammadans except for their locks, stoutly uphold their tradition that they arrived first. According to one of their legends, the Apostle Thomas landed on the coast of Malabar in the year 52 A. D., and they came seventeen years later.

Some writers believe that the Children of Israel have been in touch with this portion of India since the ships of Solomon came here for their "precious cargoes" one thousand years B. C. Sir W. Hunter, a historian of wide repute, tells us that Roman merchant triremes sailing between Myos Hormuz on the Red Sea and the ports of Arabia, Ceylon, and Malabar, found a Jewish colony in southwestern India in the second century A. D.

But the historians and the antiquarians are unable to agree. Some hold that the Black Jews were the first, while others believe that the White Jews preceded them. The former have a tradition that they are descendants of the Judean-Arabians who are still found at Sanaa in the Yemen, and at Aden. The White Jews laugh at this story and declare that the Black Jews are merely the descendants of slaves whom they bought and afterwards converted and liberated.

One of the rabbis of the White Jewish community told us that Nebuchadnezzar, the haughty monarch who carried the Children of Israel off to Babylon in captivity, extended his empire all the way to Cape Comorin, the southernmost tip of India, and then exiled the tribe of Manasseh to this extreme corner of his realm. He firmly believed that his people were the descendants of this tribe. A few have names like David Castile (David the Castilian), and this has been responsible for the rumor that they may be descendants of the Jews who were driven out of Spain during the reign of Ferdinand and Isabella.

For centuries these people lived in peace and contentment with their Hindu and Muhammadan neighbors. But with the arrival of the representatives of the first great Christian power to invade the Orient—the Portuguese—their era of persecution began. Great rivalry existed between the Portuguese and the Dutch. The buccaneer dons suspected the Jews of helping their enemies, so they burned their settlements and chased them into the mountains. It was during this time that the records that might have revealed their origin were destroyed. Later on, when the Dutch defeated the Portuguese, the Jews came out of the jungle and with the assistance of their protectors rebuilt their homes and synagogues in Cochin.

The Black and the White Jews worship separately. The floor of the synagogue belonging to the latter is paved with priceless old china-blue tiles. The rajah of Cochin had them imported from China by the Dutch. He intended them for his palace. When the White Jews saw the tiles, they decided that here was exactly what they needed for their new synagogue. So a delegation of graybeards waited on the gullible rajah and gravely confided to him that bullock's blood had been used in the manufacture of the tiles. This so incensed the devout Hindu potentate that he begged them to take away the tiles, so that he might never see them again. Such profane use of the blood of the sacred bullock was deeply offensive to his religious sensibilities. With alacrity the Jews obeyed the royal command, and since then the tiles have been the pride of their synagogue.

But the relic of relics that has caused more controversy among the Jewish communities of Cochin than anything else, is a charter of the emperor of Malabar to one Joseph, the rabbi. The date on the copper plates corresponds to the year 378 A. D. It gave the Jews the right to carry silk umbrellas and lighted lamps on certain occasions, also to use "trumpets, shawms and dulcimers and other musicks," to fire salutes with mortars, to collect taxes, to ride on elephants, and to do many other things indicating that they were a favored community. The White Jews have possession of this charter. But their dusky brethren are the only ones who now make use of its privileges in their various ceremonies, and the Black Jews say the copper plates were originally given to them and then fell into the hands of the White Jews at the time of the Portuguese invasion.

The Black and the Brown Jews number about one thousand. The White Jews have dwindled down to a community of two hundred, and hold themselves aloof, refusing to intermarry with the members of the two darker castes.

For fifteen hundred years the members of this little community have lived apart, keeping their racial characteristics uncontaminated and unchanged throughout the centuries. What they live on is something of a mystery, for very few of the White Jews engage in trade or financial operations. Most of them are very poor, and the only two prosperous families in the little community of two hundred and fifty souls have heavy calls made on their charity.

The Black Jews, no less than the White, run true to type, with the strongly marked features, erect bearing, and congenital good-health which, the world over, are typical of the vitality of a race that endures, without a nation, over all the earth, as the Chosen of the Lord.

To the original settlers, Malabar must have seemed a second Heaven. To the small, harried band of Israel's children, driven before the wrath of the king of Babylon and across the bleak and burning deserts of Arabia, shady Cochin must have seemed bliss indeed! . . . And how delightful it must have been to find themselves among docile Dravidians after the sullen Assyrians and the arrogant Arabs of the Captivity! Yet Cochin was a city with a curse. Soon the little colony began to learn the truth.

Into the houses they built, fever began to find its way —fever, disease, and death. For long years, undaunted, they have clung to their "ghetto." Though built and re-built no doubt since the time of the early settlers, it is still reminiscent of a medieval village in Europe, and is a standing proof of their tenacity and endurance.

Among both groups the Feast of the Tabernacles is the most important event of the year. During this festi-val a temporary pandal with a flat roof covered with plaited leaves of cocoanut-palm and decorated with tropical flowers is erected outside each house. The fami-lies gather in these huts to observe the feast.

As we start back to British Cochin in our rickshaws young Rachel passes us bearing a mess of pottage. Obed over there has his long nose buried in a volume of Leviti-cus, just like his Canaanitish ancestors in the days before they wept by the waters of Babylon.

They are dying out, these White and Black Jews of Cochin, although they still keep their pride of race. How different their lot to that of the Rothschilds and the Guggenheims who wandered off to London and New York instead of leaping out of the frying-pan of Hit into the tropical fires of southwestern Hindustan!

Cochin is a growing port, with a great trade in spices, bananas, and cocoanut-fiber. Big ships call here for cargo, and when the present arrangements are complete, the town will be the center of the Malabar trade. Brokerage, finance, the chandling of ships, and cognate activities will attract an ever-increasing population, and it would seem at first blush as if the Jews would be among the first to benefit by an accession of trade. But not the Jews of Cochin. They are too old a branch to flourish again, unless indeed the doctors who are studying elephantiasis can graft new health upon their failing stem.

But the probability is that their time is done. For a few years, ten, twenty perhaps, they will remain in their picturesque old quarter, under palms and shady banyan-trees. After that, no one will speak of the Jews of Cochin, save as a name and a memory, and a backwash of the tide of race-migration will have dried up and disappeared.

CHAPTER V

MOPLAHS OF THE MALABAR COAST

❧

OVER all the Malabar coast the names of "Da Gama," "Cabral," and "Albuquerque" still live in the descendants of the jolly old Portuguese who wined and wived and killed and died so picturesquely in the land of their adoption. The cold-blooded Dutch and the materialistic English have left no living record of their occupation to compare with that of the Portuguese, for their specialties have been bricks and mortar instead of flesh and blood. Even the Protestant faith has a precarious tenure, whereas the missions of the Jesuits prosper and abound.

However faint the mark of British occupation, there can be no doubt that British commerce is flourishing in Calicut, the metropolis of the Malabar Moplahs. Calicut is a large seaport town, and the center of the warlike race of hillmen of southwestern India, who in recent years have converted many of their peaceful Hindu neighbors to the faith of Islam by forcing them to repeat the Kalimah and to undergo a certain physical operation.

Calicut derives its name onomatopoetically from "colicodu," the crowing of a cock. The legend is that in the Middle Ages all the land within the hearing of a cock's crowing was given to the Zamarin of the coast by the emperor of Malabar of that day, Cheruman Perumal.

It is a bustling town, with wide, well-kept streets. Its citizens have the cosmopolitan, bold-eyed look of traders in a seaport town. There is little to remind one of the former grandeur of Calicut except perhaps the palace of the Zamarins, a barren place littered with relics of the past. But with little effort of the imagination we can people it with those bold sea-pirates who long held their own against all the buccaneers of the age of discovery. In sight of this fort Vasco da Gama anchored his galleass on May the eleventh, 1498, six years after Columbus planted the flag of Spain on the island of San Salvador in the Indies of the Western Hemisphere. Five years later Pedro Alvarez Cabral landed here and fought with the Zamarin. At the end of that same year the Zamarin was defeated finally by Alphonso d'Albuquerque in alliance with the rajah of Calicut, thus ending the sea-power of India, probably forever.

It is interesting to visit Calicut, not only because of its romantic past, but also to study the Moplah types, and to ponder over the fact that these men and their relatives quite recently engaged in a rebellion whose object was nothing less than the subversion of British power in the East. Germany's 1914 to 1918 experiment with the same object in view made no impression on these wild and fanatical hillmen. For close on a hundred years rebellions have been smoldering in Malabar, and in every generation there has been a flare of revolt among the Moplahs.

They are fiery Muhammadan zealots, these Moplahs, and of a stalwart appearance that would hardly warrant Sir Richard Burton's scathing criticism, "bastards got by Arab sires on India dams." From earliest times—when they traded apes and ivories to the Tyrian triremes of King Solomon—they have been the brigands and merchant adventurers of the Malabar coast.

In the revolt of Manjeri, in 1896, when the Moplahs advanced to attack they were shot down at a distance of seven hundred yards. None got nearer. Yet they continued to advance, and every man wounded had his throat cut by his nearest friend in order to insure that he should die fighting the infidel and thereby secure the martyr's crown of Islam.

The chronic restlessness of the Moplahs under British rule has been due partly to the circumstances under which they held their land, but chiefly to their dislike of being dominated by a Christian power. In 1921 this unrest was worked up by seditionists and Khilafat agitators, and by the propaganda of Mr. Ghandi, who aroused their sympathies over the supposititious woes

of Turkey. In April of 1921, at their religious strong-
hold of Tirurangadi, discontent broke out into open
rebellion. A railway station was wrecked, railway lines
were cut, British and Indian officials were murdered,
thousands of Hindus were forced to repeat the Moslem
formula of faith (the Kalimah), and a Khilafat kingdom was set up.

Troops were hurried into the country to assist the
police, but the terrain in which they had to operate was
mountainous and thickly wooded, so that it was a long
time before even a semblance of order could be restored. In the less accessible districts some of the leaders
proclaimed their independence as local kings. Then
they levied blackmail on the Hindu population and
flaunted the ascriptions of royalty, even to the establishment of law courts and the issue of their own paper
money.

Whether the fires of insurrection were encouraged by
Bolshevik gold we do not know. The president of the
Third International admitted publicly in Moscow that
three million gold roubles ($3,500,000) had been sent
to fan the flames of revolution in India. Doubtless most
of this got stuck on its way across central Asia and Afghanistan, and it may have dwindled to a dribble before
it reached the ministers of the "Khilafat kingdom" in
the hills of Malabar. But it seems probable that the general campaign of the Khilafat agitators was timed to
coincide with the Moplah rising, and aimed at the sub-

version of British power, and at Islamic dominion over India.

No one knows or ever will know the full particulars of the reign of terror in the hills back of Calicut and Cannanore, but a distinguished Indian leader who spent more than four months investigating conditions in connection with Malabar relief, gave us a few of the grim stories that came to his ears, stories that he had confirmed on the spot.

The fiery spirit who did the most to arouse the religious frenzy of his clan was a Muhammadan priest, a mulah named Chamarsher Thangal. One day while reading a passage from the Koran to his followers in the mosque, he looked up at the blue dome of the sky above the haram and burst into a hysterical laugh. When asked the reason of this hilarity, he pointed to the heavens and said that he saw the doors of Paradise standing open and the "hurs" welcoming those killed that day to the pleasures of the heavenly garden of delights. "Mad fellows," said he, "go and attack the Gurka camp and after being killed sit in the company of hurs." Whereupon the company took this as a divine command, and five hundred Moplahs dashed recklessly into the near-by camp of the Gurka soldiers and were either shot or bayoneted.

But the most terrible episode was the well massacre, where several thousand victims were marched to the edge of the well, decapitated, and their bodies pushed

over the brink. The man who brought back this story
was one of the few lucky ones who escaped with their
lives. To-day he lives in Calicut, but his neck will be
deformed for life. He declares that a number of others
like himself were struck and pushed into the well alive,
and that as he clambered up the wall, some hours later,
men in a half-conscious condition appealed to him for
help that he hadn't the strength to give. The Moplahs
later declared that the originator of the plan was the
same Chamarsher Thangal who saw the gates of Paradise ajar.

Then there was a skull that had been cut with a saw,
said to have belonged to one Kalkal Narain, whom the
Moplahs sawed into two pieces when he refused to repeat the Kalimah.

Hundreds of homes were burned and many Hindu
temples ravaged. We were told that not a house in the
town of Horaham Sham had escaped, and that the in-
mates were skinned alive and their skins hung over the
idols in their temples. The Moplahs used one temple as
a barracks and a slaughter-house where the sacred cows
of the Hindu community were killed and their hides
placed on the images of the goddesses. The little pig-
tails, or chotias, that Hindus wear as an emblem of their
faith, were cut off and strewn about the shrines, and
one sayyad, a Moplah named Abdullah Thangal,
boasted of having "converted" twenty of his unwarlike
neighbors, which he had been told by leaders of the up-

rising was the proper way to bring about Hindu-Muslim unity in India!

Lately the situation has been more or less in hand. However, there are still bands unapprehended, gangs still unbroken. One of these groups we passed at the railway station on our way from Calicut. There were some sixty swarthy, semi-nude peasants squatting on the platform in groups of four. They sat silent and sullen. An armed guard stood over them. What crimes these men had committed we do not know. Perhaps they too skinned their Hindu neighbors alive. At any rate there is little doubt that each of them had taken his toll of the Philistines like the Jews of old, and had the blood of at least one Hindu on his conscience. Yet one could not help feeling a little sorry for these fanatical hillmen, who were looking for the last time for several years at the busy world they had tried to convert forcibly with their bludgeons and blunderbuses and knives.

A ghastly stain on the annals of British rule in India occurred during the course of the last Moplah rebellion. The stain was nobody's fault, or at any rate not directly the fault of those in high authority. But in the East a king is judged by results, not by his good intentions, and in the eyes of the people there can be no palliation for the train tragedy of Podanur.

A party of one hundred Moplah prisoners were being entrained at Tirur station. Their destination was a central jail some distance inland. They were in the charge of a British sergeant and they were packed rather tightly, although without any inhumanity, into a covered goods wagon. Each man had enough room to sit down. The doors of the van were padlocked. At various stations on the journey the prisoners were heard moaning and wailing for water. No notice was taken of their cries, according to the evidence given before the commission of inquiry.

At Podanur, seventy-seven miles from Tirur, the padlocks were removed and the doors of the van opened. The prisoners neither spoke nor moved. There was utter silence. It was the silence of death; fifty-six had perished from asphyxiation and the remainder were all unconscious. Eight more died soon after their admission to the hospital.

A thrill of horror ran through India, and the shudder reached far-off Europe. On the very day the tragedy happened the viceroy ordered an inquiry. Unfortunately the president of the commission of inquiry was the I.C.S. officer who had been for some time the special commissioner in charge of Malabar affairs. The native papers of India made considerable capital out of this fact, contending that this official must be both *de facto* and *de jure* responsible for all that had happened in Malabar and therefore technically responsible for the train tragedy. The British rulers of India, however, had no difficulty in proving to their own satisfaction that this was a quibble designed to embarrass the admin-

istration. Official regret was expressed for the disaster
and compensation was paid to the relatives of the deceased. Meanwhile the inquiry proceeded. After ex-
haustive proceedings, which extended over several
months, the commission made its report. By that time
the world had forgotten about the Moplahs and their
train tragedy. But the Moplahs and their friends had
not forgotten, nor are they likely ever to forget.

Some one had blundered, but who? At the inquiry
the British sergeant admitted that he had heard the
cries of the prisoners, but stated that he hadn't a suffi-
cient guard along to run the risk of opening the doors in
the disturbed state of the district through which they
were passing. Naturally he did not know that the prisoners were dying of slow torture, owing to the fact that
the ventilating apparatus at the top of the wagon had
been blocked by paint. Still, somebody has a lot to answer for.

Lord Curzon's memorial stands in Dalhousie Square
for all the world to mark where one hundred and
twenty-three Englishmen died in the Black Hole of
Calcutta. Memories such as these are apt to rankle.
Possibly some Moplah in the far-distant future will
erect a tablet or a stone replica of a covered goods
wagon in Calicut, to the memory of those of his race
who were suffocated in the Podanur train tragedy.

But what of the Hindus who were butchered by the
fierce Malabar followers of the Prophet? And what

possibility is there that Gandhi's Utopian dream of Hindu-Muslim unity will be realized as long as there are races in India who practise conversion by massacre, by skinning their neighbors alive and hanging the skins over the grinning idols of the victims?

CHAPTER VI

RELIGION AT 100 FAHRENHEIT

THERE are over two hundred million people in this world who, from the day they are born to the day they are roasted on the funeral pyre, pray only to misshapen little red things—abortions in stone—like Hanuman, the monkey god, and Ganesha, the idol with the elephant's head. These two hundred million people are under the sway of the cleverest priestcraft that has ever existed, men who believe they are half gods and half men, and that at the age of ten years they are reborn to a spiritual life beyond the common herd. Twice born, sacrosanct, above the monarchs of the earth, the Brahmin exercises his priestly rule in mysterious India undiminished after three thousand years of change and conquest and conflicting creeds.

The Brahmin system was codified at about the time of the Christian era. The first principle is that the Brahmin is the best man on earth. To sit down beside one is to incur the penalty of having the sitting-down part removed. To strike a Brahmin is to incur a thousand years of hell.

The Brahmins divided the Hindus of India into castes—thousands of different castes. Now many of these are again subdivided into subcastes, which are split up into sects, and the most curious of all the sects that we encountered during our two-year journey through southern Asia was a Vaishna sect called the "Vallabha." Their tilak, or forehead-mark, is a trident. The descendants of Vallabha, the founder of the sect, are known as maharajahs, and are worshiped as gods. They believe that desires can best be extinguished not by austerity and prayer, but by immediately satisfying them. In addition to complete freedom of intercourse with every member of the clan, they have the following sources of income: For homage by sight, 3 rupees; for homage by touch, 12 rupees; for the honor of washing the maharajah's foot, 18 rupees; for the credit of swinging him, 24 rupees; for the joy of sitting with him, 36 rupees; for the bliss of occupying the same room, 30 to 200 rupees; for the performance of the circular dance, 60 rupees; for the delight of eating betel-nut spat out by the maharajah, 10 rupees; for drinking the maharajah's bathwater, 11 rupees.

Some one has said that India is not a country but a religious controversy. If you ask an Indian what he is, instead of replying that he is a Bengali or a Madrasi or a Punjaubi, he will tell you that he is a Hindu or a Muhammadan or a Parsee or a Jain or a Buddhist or a Sikh or a Theosophist, or some other of India's one thousand and one religious persuasions. But more than two thirds of the people are included in one or the other of the two thousand-odd subdivisions of Hinduism.

Now Hinduism, as expounded by the Brahmin pundits, is a history of religions rather than a religion; a compendium, not a creed; a library of travel stories in the trackless paths of speculative inquiry rather than a guide-book to bliss. Hence to attempt to review the literature of the Brahmins here is about as easy as it would be to summarize all the Baedekers on earth.

One fifth of all the people who live on this planet reside in India. Hence if you are interested in world-affairs you must become acquainted with the peoples of Hindustan, and to do this it is essential to know something of the ancient and wonderful system of the Brahmins. Their books, the Vedas, are the oldest scriptures in the world, dating from at least a thousand years before Christ. They embrace every department of human activity, every hope and inquiry, every love and lust.

From the loftiest conceptions of the human mind to bestialities past belief, from the Bhagavad Gita to the Tantras, the religious system of the Hindus runs the gamut of belief.

Briefly, the Vedas teach that there was a Primal Cause, He who cannot be discussed, the Unknown God of the Athenians. Brahm is his name, immobile, impersonal, sunk in sleep—essentially the god of 100° Fahrenheit—a hot-weather dream of divinity, and not to be confused with his offspring or collateral, Brahma, the Father of the Gods. From Brahm sprang Brahma, Siva, Vishnu—the last two being the gods of the two principal Hindu cults of the present day, the Vaishnas and the Sivites.

In addition to these there were the Vedic or elder gods of Nature, such as the Storm-God and the Fire-Light-Heat God. Of these some, such as Surya and Agni, are worshiped still, as well as a multitude of minor offshoots from the great Elemental Powers.

It must be remembered that for the Hindu every action and reaction, and every phenomenon of the conceptual universe, from stones to suns, and from the manner of tying a loincloth to the composition of interstellar space, have been discussed and defined by the Brahmins; and that standing or sitting, awake or asleep, the Hindu has a religious sanction and an appropriate deity for every act of daily life. He eats, drinks, bathes, dresses, and sins religiously. There are thirty-three million gods, goddesses, and demons in the Hindu pantheon. And yet, as Max Muller says, "even in the invocation of their innumerable gods, the remembrance of *a* God, one and infinite, breaks through the mist of an idolatrous phraseology like the blue sky that is hidden by passing clouds."

Educated Hindus do not believe that their gods are more or less than vehicles or mediums of expression of the divine principle. They remember the ancient Aryan concept expressed in the oldest word in the world, *Dyaus-pitr,* Jupiter, Our Father which art in Heaven, and seek in the modern eclectic systems (followed by many of their best thinkers of recent times, such as Pandit Bhagawan Dass, Lala Rajpat Rai, and the Theosophists) to show that God's dealings with man have varied with varying religions according to man's need— underlying all being one divine wisdom. But to follow these ideas to their origin is impossible here. The fact remains that the educated Hindus are in a microscopic minority.

Hinduism divides society into four classes: the priests or Brahmins, the kings and captains or Kshattriyas, the merchants or Vaishyas, and the men who do the dirty work—Sudras or slaves. No one must change his caste or marry out of it. If you are in a low caste you can console yourself by reflecting that under the law of Karma, or reincarnation, you might have been a pig instead of a Sudra. And if you are a hard-working Sudra, who doesn't appear where his untouchable presence isn't wanted, there is no reason at all why you shouldn't be born eventually among the people who are privileged to lend money to the ruling race—that is, when you are born again into this transitory world.

Now in England there was a certain noble marquis, not unknown to fame, who divided the world into the classes and the masses. The classes were the king and the noble marquis; the masses, the remainder of the population. He was one of the typical Brahmins of the West, and he offered to the masses the comfortable words of the catechism about doing their duty "in the state of life unto which it has pleased God to call them," instead of the exciting Aryan idea of reincarnation.

In England's colonies caste is paramount. Black skins are barred. So also Asiatics are excluded from the United States. Can we blame these old Brahmins for insisting on their race-distinctions? Should we not rather admire them for sticking to their pride of birth through all these long years? After all, Europeans are doing the same thing in much the same way at this moment.

The word for caste is "varna" in the Vedas, and "varna" means color. Against the savage Dravidians of three thousand years ago the white race of the Aryans raised the barriers of caste, and against the colored races of to-day there is just the same barrier. Idealists may rant, but they can't prove that black is white, or break down the deep-rooted instinct of a people. There is much loose talk of "brotherhood," but how many white men would willingly see one of their womenfolk married to an Asiatic? This is a thing that should be faced frankly. So why not avow our caste principles, like the old Brahmins, instead of trying vainly to disguise them? We deceive no one but ourselves by burying our heads in the sands of prejudice. Why blame the Brahmin when we are nearly as bad ourselves?

As to caste's breaking down, because of Western civilization and railways—it will happen when the Ganges flows backwards from Calcutta to Kedarnath. There are Brahmin families in India who were converted to Christianity by the Portuguese in 1650 who still maintain their caste traditions and will only intermarry with other Brahmin families converted at the same date! The Ethiopian cannot change his skin. The leopard is extremely proud of his spots: nothing would induce him to change them.

The two chief gods of the Hindus are Siva and Vishnu. Siva is the Destroyer of mankind. He who terminates each kalpa or era of the earth by exterminating gods and men by a ray from his central eye. He generally skulks about in graveyards. His wife has many names, such as Uma, Parvati, Haimavati (daughter of the Himalayas), Durga, Kali (the black), and Bhairavi (the terrible).

Calcutta derives its name from Kalighat, where there is a noted temple of Kali. She is represented as a black woman with four arms. In one hand she has a weapon, in the second the head of the giant she has slain. With the two others she encourages her worshipers. For earrings she has two dead bodies. She wears a necklace of skulls. Her tongue is between her teeth. In the ancient texts it is laid down that the flesh "of the antelope and the rhinoceros give her delight for a thousand years," but nowadays her temples swim in the blood of goats.

The mantra or password to the initiates of Siva, is "Si-va-na-va-ma." Their caste-mark is three perpendicular lines on the forehead.

Vishnu is a god co-equal but not co-eternal with Siva, for he is destroyed at the end of the kalpa. He has avatars or incarnations, first a fish, then a tortoise, then a bear, then a man-lion, then a man-with-an-axe, then the beautiful Rama, then Krishna, then Buddha. The tenth and last incarnation of Vishnu is not to appear until the end of this age, when he will come clothed in thunder in the heavens, riding a white steed of the Apocalypse. Until Mahatma Gandhi was thrown into prison by the Government of India and then failed to walk out miraculously through the walls, tens of thousands of his followers believed him to be the tenth and last incarnation of Vishnu.

Surely these incarnations of Vishnu are no more nor less than a story of mankind in parable? The ninth or Buddha incarnation is worthy of note because it shows how the Brahmins absorb every creed into their system. After bitterly opposing the doctrines of Siddhartha, the prince who knew no passion, and who is known to adoring multitudes to-day as the Lord Buddha, they found that it was simpler to swallow his doctrines than to deny them. So they made him an incarnation of Vishnu.

Any man can become a god in India, or at any rate a deity to be propitiated. Some time ago a British officer met with a violent death near Travancore. He was afterwards worshiped as a demon, and brandy and cheroots, which he had loved during his lifetime, are still brought to his shrine by the kindly natives.

There are many strange Hindu sects, such as the Vallabhacharis, who drink each other's bath-water. But the Vallabhacharis are no more representative of the religious life of the Hindus than the Holy Rollers are of Christianity. They are a sect, and mentioned only because they demonstrate the Hindu tendency towards the worship of the abnormal. *Power* is worshiped in every form. If a man be a great saint or a great sinner, or a great king, he will be worshiped. Queen Victoria and John Nicholson, and the big brass gun at Bijapur, and the goddess of thieves, and a bootless, hatless, long-haired American globe-trotter, each have their several votaries. The reproductive principles, under the form of the lignam and the yoni, the male and female organs, are also worshiped.

Offerings to the gods consist of marigolds and jasmine, the leaves of the wood-apple, fruits, rice, little candles, milk, and money.

The three cardinal tenets of Hinduism are the preservation of caste, the sanctity of the Brahmins, and the holiness of the cow. Everywhere we find cows wandering about the streets and sitting on the sidewalks.

It is easy to scoff at the system of the Brahmins; but that is done only by people with a little knowledge and a great conceit. The fact remains that the Brahmins have

preserved religion in the hearts and homes of Hindustan. They have given the people the gods that they
require. As the intellectual standard is raised, so will
the Brahmins provide higher concepts from their treas-
uries of thought. But always these concepts will be such
that the masses can understand them. Ethics for the
educated, idols for the ignorant. Heirs of all the ages of
the Aryan philosophy, and custodians of the people's
conscience, they are awake to the forces that are astir
in the land to-day. In the time appointed they will pass
on to the people what the West is giving to them—a new
concept of service and sacrifice for others, like that
shown forth in the life of Christ. We tell ourselves that
we must not be too easily contemptuous or cock-sure on
this journey of ours to the distant Black Pagoda.

CHAPTER VII
AT THE SHRINE OF THE FISH-EYED GODDESS

ONE hundred and fifty thousand people have come to the holy city of Madura to celebrate the nuptial feast of their saint-patroness, Minakshi, with the great god Siva. She was married a few days ago, Minakshi, the fair Brahmin girl with fish-eyes, and now she and her husband have been left alone in their jeweled shrine. But to-day, to-night, is Minakshi's golden hour. For to-day, to-night, amid the heaped flowers and the incense of their thousand-year-old shrine, Siva and Minakshi are met. In peace and love the priests have left them with $500,000 in jewels as their playthings. Through this night of May, when the moon is at its full, Siva can see into the emerald and the amethyst of Minakshi's eyes. . . .

To-morrow the great concourse in the bed of the River Vaigai will be held. The incident it celebrates seems trivial enough, yet there will be a quarter of a million people there to celebrate it, as there have been a quarter of a million people there since history began, to enact this pageant of the Disgruntled Wedding Guest. Here is the story, as it happened:

Once upon a time Minakshi was a queen of Madura who had subdued all earthly princes and heavenly deities. Born with three breasts, when she met Siva her third breast vanished. So this must be her future husband, for an angel at her birth had stated that her third breast would vanish when she found her lord and master. Marriage preparations were at once begun, and an enormous number of people were invited. As was only natural, one of the first to be asked was Alagar, the brother of Minakshi, who lived (and still lives) in a village about eighteen miles from Madura. By some mischance the message sent to him got garbled, so that when he came sailing down the Vaigai in great state, in the equivalent of a morning-coat and beaver hat, in the expectation of speeches and champagne, he found that the marriage had already taken place. Naturally he was furious. He retired in high dudgeon to the far bank of the Vaigai, so that he should not set even a foot in the unsisterly city of Madura. Since that far time, year after year, Alagar comes in gilded state and hears how churlishly he has been treated, and retires in a huff.

That is the story which the gathered thousands will commemorate to-morrow. All night long we hear them pass, on wheels, and donkey-back and afoot. Ox-nose to tail-board of the cart ahead, by file and company and troop, the pilgrims come without pause or intermission; a river of pilgrims such as Chaucer saw, with a "joyous garde of children." At dawn the scene is still the same, but now it is like a stream of ants. . . .

The sun flames over the sea-mists of the East: of a sudden it is full day. In the dust and glare we see strange and sad sights: children leading blind fathers, and fathers leading blind children, and the halt, and the leprous, and the lost, and old, old women who seem to sum up in themselves all the horror of the body's decay.

Besides the hundred and fifty thousand who came yesterday, and the fifty thousand who passed last night, there is high holiday in all Madura. Not a soul in the city. Business is at a standstill. The Great Temple is empty. But down in the river-bed of the Vaigai more than a quarter of a million people are assembled to do honor to the great god Alagar with prayer and praise and jollity and junketing.

From the bridge above we look down on a wonderful, moving, mixing, rainbow crowd. [The white clothes of the men, and the red and yellow of the women's saris, the blue of elephants and water, the green of trees and turbans, the glinting gold of the processional car, the swaying fans, the merry-go-rounds, the joy-wheels, the hurly-burly and helter-skelter, and the brightly tinseled dancing-men, plumed with white and crimson—all this changing color in the dazzle of the sunlight and under an arch of perfect turquoise almost blinds the eyes with overbrightness.

One must linger on the bridge a moment or two and adjust one's senses to the scene below. One has seen crowds as big, pageants more impressive, perhaps. But never a sight like this! We are children, children by the hundred thousand, back in a gigantic nursery of ages past. And we are children at prayer, with the simple faith and the unclouded eyes of the springtime of the world. We must leave aside the toys of our own middle age, our pocket-books and cameras and fountain-pens, and leave aside the hard heart of ambition and the haughty mind of little learning, before we mix with the throng below, and are one with them in spirit. What a gorgeous scene it is for nursery eyes! Were ever children happier than these?

Going down to the river we pass a street full of tents and booths and shrines, thronged to bursting and wedged and jammed so that the passengers are immobile in places where a clever juggler or a holy "saddhu" arrests the attention of the holiday-maker.

One saddhu, so thin that he seems to have no inside, lies in the dust on his back, and holds a baby above him. He rolls over, and over on to his back again, always holding the baby above him. A girl collects coppers in a cocoanut-shell from the watching crowd. The baby watches the crowd who are watching him, and he smiles as he sees the coppers go into the cocoanut-shell, and he sucks his thumb dispassionately while his proprietor (for he is a bought baby, no doubt, and will be made into a freak or a deformity by his master) rolls over and over, as if the rocking motion were rather agreeable than otherwise.

Then there is the legless man, who has flippers about six inches long and casual toe-nails growing from them here and there. He scrabbles in the dust with these flippers. . . . The crowd thinks these freaks tremendous fun, and so they are if we jettison our prejudice and see them with the eyes of the crowd.

In the river-bed southern India is enjoying herself in the mass, in the multitude, by the hundred thousand. There is every variety of caste and trade, beauty and deformity, untouchable and elect. The "average man" is slightly below medium height, of a bright brown color, clean-shaven, and bald-pated except for a patch at the back from which a topknot grows, giving him an effeminate appearance that his habits of life do not belie. A more sensual and effeminate-looking man it would be difficult to find. Yet he also looks clever: he is not brutish, as his women sometimes are. For clothes he wears two white cloths, one about his loins, the other over his shoulders, like a shawl. Below the loin is a tiny triangular strip of linen. He walks with dignity, especially if of the Brahmin caste.

The "average woman" also wears two cloths, always colored, and generally of red-and-yellow check: one is the loincloth, the other the body-cloth, so arranged that the trunk from the hips to the base of the breasts is left

bare. Very attractive her figure is, a slim column of
burnished copper, with chevelure of polished ebony,
and a heavy collar of gold that sets off admirably the
warm beauty of her skin. The young women are loaded
with gold; gold on wrist and ankle, gold collars, and
huge ear-rings of gold, so huge that they drag down the
lobe of the ear until it touches the shoulder. The old
women have the same extended lobes, but no ear-rings
in them, for they are either neglectful of themselves,
or neglected by their families—God knows which. The
adolescent girls are the most beautiful: the maturer
graces of womanhood are generally lacking. The young
girls have bodies of brown velvet, eyes of infinite tenderness, and mouths—so soon to grow thick and brutalized
—with the bowed lip of Aphrodite, which is one of the
distinctive features of the Aryan. Splendid creatures of
the sun they are, these girls with the kiss of so much
gold against their young and glowing skin.

But their beauty is brief. Married women (chiefly of
the lower classes) have a ruby or a diamond fixed in
their left nostril, which increases the "something animal" that has grown in their eyes, and that shows in
their flaccid lips. Married before their teens and
mothers at fourteen, they deteriorate rapidly, growing
limp and weary, so that the upper cloth of their dress
no longer hangs on the twin contours of their body, but
sags apart, and reveals them prematurely old.

Every woman in India (and this is as true as any

generalization can be) is "old at thirty," but sometimes there is a great tenderness and a great grace in the motherhood of Hindustan. The world over motherhood is a holy thing, and in India, as elsewhere, and especially at the great fairs and festivals of Ganges land and the Carnatic, you may see the ineffable beauty of a mother with her baby child. Thus looked, thus walked, the Galilean girl to whom the churches pray. Thus laughed the Child in its Mother's eyes, and thus He clung to her shoulder in the flight to Egypt.

The festival of Minakshi, the fish-eyed goddess of Madura, is a family feast. So many babies and brothers and sisters and fathers and mothers and grandparents and great-aunts—so many generations of the sons of Japheth in their respective family groups—you never saw gathered together in one place.

And in all the crowd no one is drunk or disorderly or vulgar. The great throng has a great heart of happiness and prayer and praise.

CHAPTER VIII

THE ANGER OF ALAGAR

LET us suppose that you are a pious Hindu. You have come to Madura to celebrate the feast of Alagar in the river-bed of the Vaigai. . . . First you scrape a hole in the sand, about a foot deep: this soon fills with water, for there is an underground current. In this hole you and your family drink and wash and wash and drink. Then you get a barber to scrape your head with his razor until it is innocent of hair. Meanwhile the ladies and the babies of your family have been indulging in further intimate ablutions in the puddle. Finally, when you are all shaved and washed and purified, you wander out to see the old car of Alagar high on the river-bank. The god is resting for the moment, in his perfumed tent, and it is impossible to get very near him because of the thousands that press around the Presence. Nearest the chariot is a throng of men with large mat fans inscribed with the Vaishna trident: a "U" in white with a red line down the center, representing the two legs of Vishnu, and the symbol of his wife. The fans are all in motion, and no doubt the god needs air in the thick of all that hot humanity.

We cannot get near the god, so we wander among the crowd. The people at the roundabouts and swings here are much the same as the people at the roundabouts and swings anywhere else, except for this, that they are brown and naked and very gentle in Madura. Otherwise there is not much difference between Madura and Coney Island or Hampstead Heath. Dress them as clerks, costers, flappers, servant-girls, gipsies, schoolmasters, thieves, and you might be at a bank holiday in England or a Saturday carnival in America.

The clerkly caste is very prominent, however. The Brahmins of the Vaishna sect, tall, well-set-up men with intellectual heads, have the trident of their Lord Vishnu marked on their brow, and it is extraordinary how wicked this painted monogram makes them look. With their shaved heads and forked white eyebrows, and a streak of red between the eyes, they stalk through the crowd like so many Mephistopheleses among the simple villagers. Mingling with them are the lower castes, soldiers, merchants, and slaves, all the pageantry of an age of pilgrims, miracles, and saints. We turn back the pages of history and see before our eyes, not in print but in moving limb and crying mouth, the hosts of the Crusades and the swarming multitude of the devout who flocked to the shrines of the Renaissance.

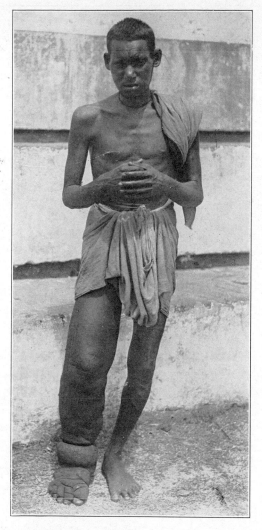

Cochin is called "The City with a Curse." One out of every ten inhabitants suffers from a monstrous disease that causes legs and arms to swell up until they are as big as bolsters.

Ascetics about to lie down for an afternoon siesta on their feather beds—of sharp iron spikes.

Back to the chariot of Alagar. . . . Here are the tumult and the thronging of thousands who have come to worship. Here are the detonation of mortars and the bugling of conches that herald Alagar's approach. The Vaishna fans of those about his person sway back to let the godhead pass. Before the image marches a posse of police. High on his gilded car, which is set on the backs of terrible steeds with enamel eyes, the god comes out, borne upon the shoulders of a hundred men. The temple elephants make obeisance. Men, women, and children touch their finger-tips together and bend the head in reverence. The cries of fractious babies are stifled by their mothers. No dog barks. The merry-go-rounds have stopped and their riders are worshiping, with hands joined in the ancient gesture of prayer and praise. The murmurs of all this host are hushed.

The god passes up the bank to his next resting-place. Then wheels go round, children cry, and the voice of the crowd resumes its droning key.

From dawn to high noon the festival continues. Six times the god moves along the river-bank through the adoring multitude of his worshipers.

But the heat is becoming furnace-like. The breeze has dropped. Women draw their saris across their tired eyes. Children wilt and droop. The crisp terra-cotta babies of the morning have become lumps of putty on the shoulders of their parents. Even the god is drowsy,

and remains in his marquee amid the fumes of frankin-
cense, which are stirred gently past his jeweled nostrils
by the fans of devotees.

By tens and twenties the crowds melt away to such
shade as they can find by tent and tree. Life gasps in the
torrid noon of May. Beasts and men are still. Even the
mina birds stay limply under the shade of eaves and
pant there with open beak. . . .

When we go out again the sun has long passed its
zenith and is slanting behind a storm that is gathering
in the west. The air is thick with thunder.

Through the narrow streets of the bazaar we wend
our way towards the Great Temple. Suddenly it hulks
above us, the pyramidal entrance of richly carved stone
and stucco, known as a "gopuram." What strange people they must have been who built these gopurams!
Row after row of gods, goddesses, griffins, gargoyles—
strangely graceful, subtly lewd, four-headed, five-
armed, fish-eyed—things made by minds quite alien to
these Western eyes that look on them. Great pyramids,
high walls, a welter of carving—terrific labor of brawn
and brain, and tiny result in beauty—that is the first
impression this temple makes on Western minds. The
next is that of respect, and of a nameless fear.

Inside, across the open court, there is a maze of dark
carved corridors, where male images and female images
and hemaphrodite idols and beast idols are writhing,
interlocking, trampling upon their foes. This is char-

acteristic religious imagery of which we will find a supreme example at the Black Pagoda.

There are bats also in these corridors, and an elephant strolling to his stable, and a sacred cow nosing for banana-skins under the idols. And the never-ending crowd : the same crowd that we saw this morning at the river has now gathered among this medley of divine and bestial forms, in the eternal twilight of the corridors, for the rite of evensong to Siva and Minakshi, the happy lovers.

Already the lamps are lit in the temple, although it is broad day outside, for this is a place where daylight does not come.

A gong strikes close to us—so close that it makes one tremble. Surges of men and women crowd to a doorway, a doorway all worn and glistening with the rubbing of the millions of bodies that for a thousand years have sweated and struggled in the portals of the shrine. There is a terror in this devotion half seen, half guessed, of this panting naked people that are pressing all round us. We are part of a consciousness we can no longer understand. We have swung back through the ages to an elder day. And of all the traveling we have done, there is none so strange as this journeying back through centuries to find the life of other times, still sentient, still aquiver with desire and fear. It is like catching a mummy at its prayers.

There are a hundred priests in the temple at Madura,

a hundred dancing-girls for the pleasure of the god, and treasure untold. The personal jewelry alone of the god and the goddess is valued at about a million dollars.

And in the town of Madura not a mile away there is another temple, a temple of healing, a plain two-storied spotlessly whitewashed house. It is the American Medical Mission, and owes its inception to Dr. Van Allen, who worked in Madura for thirty years, giving all that he loved and life itself for the sick in India. And this hospital, like the Great Temple at Madura, has been built and is supported by Indians. Not a penny of Western money went into its building. It was built by the natives of the country, because they loved Dr. Van Allen of Yale, and because in India the Holy Spirit is not dead, and saints still walk the earth, and the Indians can recognize them when they see them.

In all romantic India there is no more romantic and splendid life than that of the medical missionary—the man or the woman who carries the science of the West as well as the banner of Christendom into the wild and outer marches of empire.

Medical missionaries have gone everywhere in India. Among the aboriginal tribes of Bengal and Assam there are millions of animists who drink the blood of human sacrifice (when they can get it) and indulge in orgiastic rites that have put them almost outside the pale of humanity. In the south there are Dravidians whom long centuries of slavery have reduced to a level of morals and mentality little better than that of the beasts. And among the strange Semitic tribes that have haunted the hills and harried the plains of the northwest frontier since Indian history began, there is no law but that of the strongest and no mercy but the mercy of sleep and death. . . . Into these lands, and unto a strange diversity of creatures, the soldiers of Christendom have gone, and gone further and fixed their conquest more securely than any other conquerors of the past, for their kingdom is not terrene, but in the hearts of the people.

Many have questioned the value of missionary work in India. But no one who knows the country and has met all sorts and conditions of men there, in all sorts and conditions of weather—any one in short who does not get his opinions from blue-books or bureaucrats—will admit that the medical missions in India have done more than their share toward keeping the Indian Empire reasonably contented in the past.

The Indian is not especially grateful for administrative or judicial perfection: these things are apt to be uncomfortable in reality, however imposing they may appear in reports. It is the heart of love of the missionary, the brotherly sympathy of a poor man living among poor men, that wins the confidence of the great voiceless "public" of Hindustan—the two hundred and fifty millions who live in the childhood of ignorance and superstition.

Purely spiritual missions are apt to arouse sectarian

animosities, but when, as at Madura far in the south, a prosperous Christian hospital under a man like Dr. Van Allen carries on a work of healing that no other organization has dared to attempt, and when, as at Bannu, three thousand miles north, the fame of Dr. Pennell, another American, spread from Peshawar to Kabul, then indeed we may assert that the cross of the West stands higher than the crescent of the Muslim or the trident of the Vaishnas in the estimation of Hindustan.

Dr. Van Allen and Dr. Pennell, now, alas, no more, laid down their lives for these people, but the hospitals they founded continue their work. Dr. Van Allen's medical mission has made its influence paramount in Madura, and is now entirely supported by funds subscribed by the wealthy Hindus of the district, so that this Christian organization does not have to ask for a penny of outside help. From surgical ward to dispensary, and from Bible room to football ground, the whole institution is economically justified by the most rigid tests that a Henry Ford could devise. In spite of their love for the mysticism and weird rites of Hinduism, the people of Madura want this mission, and they want it so much that they are prepared to pay for it!

These medical missionaries have something of the soul of St. Paul, who went out across the world, to win souls by faith and works, carrying nor scrip nor staff.

CHAPTER IX
RUBIES, PRIESTS, AND SACRED BULLS

"TRICHY," where the cheroots come from, is celebrated for its canopied bazaar, its Gibraltar-like rock, and its pigeon's-blood rubies. The rubies of Trichinopoly are to be seen in a score of stalls in the main bazaar—dazzling piles of them in yellow paper packets, ranging in price from two rupees for a spinel to two lakhs for a pigeon's-blood. It is the biggest ruby-market in the world.

Under the bamboo arcades of the bazaar, past the shops of the ruby merchants, we ride through an endless concourse of semi-nude citizens on our way towards the Rock, which dominates the city from every point. Nature shrugged this pile of stone 273 feet above the plain in some prehistoric shiver. The temple on its summit is approached by four hundred and thirty-four steps. If the visitor funks these, he may see other temples but nothing quite like this. We yield to its spell . . . it is the time of evening prayer. It is twilight in the city below. But here in this old cave-temple the shafts of sunset linger, so that we can see dimly the sculptures of the gods worn and polished with the sweat of centuries. A silent priest passes before us and we catch a red look in his eyes—as red as the rubies of the town, a look of hate and contempt. His lips move silently. Is it a prayer or a curse? We are fain to ask him a question, but he has vanished silently and mysteriously into the darkness of an inner shrine.

We walk gingerly down the steep face of the Rock in the growing gloom, remembering that these steps are haunted by the shades of five hundred devotees who were trampled to death by their co-worshipers during a panic.

Here also died Bishop Heber of Calcutta, he who wrote the unfading words of the missionary hymn:

"From many an ancient river,
From many a palmy plain,
They call us to deliver
Their land from error's chain."

The author of "From Greenland's Icy Mountains to India's Coral Strand" died of apoplexy in a swimming-bath at the fort, after having delivered an address from the steps of the Austrian mission church of Dr. Schwartz.

The wee white church of Dr. Schwartz still stands spick and span near the Temple of the Bull in Tanjore, its walls decorated with the elegant epitaphs of the early nineteenth century. A few hours' run lands us at

the great temple of Siva in Tanjore—of Siva, the god
of birth and death, who has been pictured in vivid
verse by Sir Alfred Lyall:

"I am the god of the sensuous fire,
  That moulds all nature and forms divine,
  The symbols of death and of man's desire,
  The springs of change in the world are mine,
  The organs of birth and the circlet of bones,
  And the light loves carved on the temple stones."

Here you may see the "light loves," not in stone, but
as comely Davidasis, or temple-girls, who are dedicated
to the rites of Siva and who dance during the full moon
of April. Here also is Nandi (the Happy One), the
bull that Siva rides. This is a gigantic Nandi. He
weighs eighty tons, and has a polished, urbane appearance, for he is anointed every day with gingelly oil.
There was once a toad inside him, so that he kept growing and growing until it was feared that he would out-
grow the temple. A nail was therefore driven into the
nape of Nandi's neck that killed the toad and kept
Nandi of reasonable size and weight—a mere eighty
tons and only eight feet around the collar. Nandi is a
strange, attractive idol with gentle, sensual, inscrutable eyes, like the eyes of some of Siva's worshipers.

Pierre Loti in his delightful book, "India Without
the English," described everything that he saw in Hindustan excepting the British burra sahibs of Calcutta,
the British bureaucrats of Delhi, and the rest of the one

hundred thousand-odd Anglo-Saxons and Celts who are the ruling race of the country. Pierre Loti completely and purposely disregarded the British Raj and all its works and devoted his pages to descriptions of an older and more intimate India.

We too have followed in the footsteps of the immortal Frenchman, but we have visited two portions of India to which the title of Pierre Loti's book could be more appropriately applied—Pondicherry and Goa.

India is so vast, its people so apathetic to the introduction of new things and by tradition so antagonistic to Western theories of life, that it is difficult for one to visualize what the results of British rule have been-- until one compares them with the methods of administration in French and Portuguese India. Between Nordic and Latin colonial methods, in this part of the East, there is a chasm wider than the Grand Canyon of the Colorado.

There may be corruption in British India. The Anglo-Indian newspapers hint that there is! Investigating committees clog the files at Delhi and Simla with mountainous reports about it. Even the most casual observer can see evidences of it—and then does his own little part toward encouraging the disease. But the man in the train who told us all about India's Latin colonies, told us that the problem there is not one of petty graft but of wholesale loot.

In "Le Matin" we saw that a complaint had been

filed in the criminal court of Paris against the two dep-
uties of French India, and also against the mayor of
Pondicherry. Far be it from us, however, to throw
stones from the glass house of this peculating peninsula.
Pondicherry may be a corrupt city, or it may not, but
it is certainly a very charming one.

"Little old town; living on tradition, living because
she has lived, systematically isolated from the rest of
India by her hostile neighbors, and with no port or
roadstead on the Gulf of Bengal where her ships can
shelter. No hurry and bustle here, as at Calcutta or
Madras. No strangers either, no tourists, for the traveler does not pass by Pondicherry—and who would
come here for the sake of coming?

"By the sea, a garden where the band plays in the
evening, and where, with the setting sun, wan babies
gather, some from France, others born in exile. . . .

"Oh, the sadness of arriving here, in this ancient far-
off charming place, between whose moss-grown walls
sleeps a whole great past of France! Little streets, like
French streets in the heart of some quiet province, little
straight streets, with low houses, century-old houses,
very white on the red soil from which they rise: garden
walls hung with garlands of creepers and tropical
flowers: barred windows through whose grill one sees
the pale faces of creoles, or of half-castes, who seem almost too beautiful, with the mystery of India in their
eyes. . . .

"Besides the officers and civil officials of the colony, there are some creole families here that arrived in the heroic age of French India, and have become quite Pondicherrian after four or five generations. Old ladies with gentle, rather old-fashioned manners. Old salons of a melancholy charm with their eighteenth-century sofas, and their Empire clocks that came adventurously by the Cape of Good Hope . . . and that have counted the hours of so many languid lives, told the minutes of so much agony of exile. . . ."

Thus Loti mourns, in that inimitable way that takes us with him, sadly but surely, into the ruined grandeurs of the past.

Let us get back to the present, however, and step off our train.

"Cou Soundiramallée, An 1913," whoever he may be, has erected a very charming bronze of an Egyptian girl, just outside the railway station. She is modern, but instinct with the art of the Latins. She upholds the common telegraph wires. At her feet is a stand-pipe where the living bronzes of the Pondicherriennes fill their gourds and cooking-pots in rivalry with the graceful poise and limber hips of the delicate statuette above.

This is France. We have found France immediately, at the exit to the station. A perfectly black policeman comes with a customs' form and says, *"Signez ici, s'il vous plait, m'sieu."*

We drive through picturesque and filthy streets. The

citizen sweepers of enlightened Pondicherry are liable
to transfer their votes if they are unduly hustled. But
they are not hustled at all. No one is hustled. It is a
happy, happy-go-lucky place. At every house-front
there is a cow. The cows are there because it is early
morning and they are waiting to be milked, waiting
placidly, while their calves stroll about nibbling at the
piles of garbage at the street-corners. Natives are doz-
ing in the street, sleeping off the effect of too much
toddy and bonhomie, or rubbing their eyes and staring
and scratching. . . .

At the British Consul's house we enjoy a British
breakfast, and thank our stars we are with him and his
delightful wife, instead of at the Hôtel de l'Europe or
the Hôtel de Londres et de Paris, for these establish-
ments, by all accounts, do not live up to their names.
But they are interesting because they are often the re-
sorts (quite against the wish of the proprietors, be it
understood) of gentlemen fleeing from justice in British India.

After breakfast we drive out to the square, in the
fascinating conveyance called a *"pousse-pousse,"* which
is like a bath-chair on four wheels. Pondicherry is a
symbol of the French mind in that it is laid out method-
ically. The governor's house, the mayor's house, the law
courts, the hospital, barracks, club, museum, are all
central and easy to reach. Out on the sea-front the statue
of Dupleix looks seaward—Dupleix, who dreamed of

empire, Dupleix, to whom the carved colonnades that now stand around his statue were given to embellish the palace of a viceroy of France, a palace that was never built. . . . He stands there in his full-bottomed wig and Georgian waistcoat and top-boots, hot and bareheaded in the Indian sun. Here for once the Latin genius caught some infection from the Victorian taste of British India. The statue was erected in 1869. M. Clémenceau, when he came out to India before he died, placed a palm-leaf at the feet of Dupleix.

We drive out along the Cuddalore road, where Clive and his merry men once marched, through scenes of tropical luxuriance and villages nestling in the palm-groves. We watch the graceful well-workers, drawing water by walking the length of a pole suspended above their well, which is perhaps the most graceful irrigation-system in the world. They are paid the magnificent sum of two cents a day, so it is not surprising that they are thin and emaciated. We watch the women grinding their corn, and see the grove where the great god Ayyanar lives, guardian of the villages, with his five clay horses, on which he rides through the paddy-fields o' nights slaying demons or incautious villagers who ought to be in bed.

There is less activity, less "bundobust," fewer village officials, in French territory than in British India, but there is more contentment, more "graft," and a good deal less sanitation.

Back through the native town, we see many Indo-French, who bear themselves with the pride of citizens of a great empire, especially the children—young Gauls in garb, Indians in soft grace of movement. Everywhere the delicious tongue of France comes fluently to Indian lips.

Before the Cathedral of Nôtre Dame stands a statue of Joan of Arc, lately erected by a prominent citizen. We enter the ever-open doors of the House of God, and all is peace and colored lights there. A corporal of the Armée Coloniale kneels before one of the stations of the cross, a splendid and soldierly figure. We watch him a moment, in reverence and admiration, for here is France on her knees . . . a France we hardly know. . . . A shaft of red light strikes across his white uniform and on the square yellow beard that brushes the ribbons of the World War that he wears. He kneels erect and still, with joined hands, like a knight before the Grail: a symbol of the old France of Dupleix, of the new France that held Verdun. And now this scarcely seems to be the Land of the Black Pagoda.

CHAPTER X

AN IRISH HIGH PRIESTESS IN INDIA

⚜

MADRAS is the doyen of the British cities of the East Indies, dignified, delightful, and "somehow different." The black Tamil men with their long, straight hair gathered in a bunch at the top of their heads, carry umbrellas and fulfil to a nicety one's notions of the mild Hindu. The less opulent Tamils have noses like the beaks of birds. Their cheekbones are sharp. Their elbows are sharp. Their knees are sharp. Their bodies are mostly vein and bone, minus muscle and meat. They chew betel-nut, which makes their teeth black and their lips red. They drink rice toddy, which makes them forget, temporarily, the nightmare that their lives must be.

But high-caste Madrasi people and prosperous untouchables become sleek in appearance and oval in shape, especially the women. Their dress consists of a long strip of cloth draped gracefully about the figure, showing their perfectly molded torsos from hip to breast like a column of burnished copper. They are

A joyous Hindu religious festival is in progress. The merrymakers are nearly all men, and they gleefully throw red paint at each other, symbolic of the blood of women.

Some 250,000 people come to Madura to attend the Festival of the Fish-eyed Goddess.

hung, and placqued, and laden with gold. If Ghengis Khan had seen the population of Madras nobody could have restrained him.

The burra sahibs, the captains of industry of Madras, are contentedly rich. They haven't the money-fever of Calcutta or Bombay. Every white man in Madras lives like a gentleman, with a "flivver" and a share in a sailing yacht. It is a city of great distances and a great many clubs. The Madras Club is one of the finest in Asia and their sheep's-head curry is a dish for Lucullus. Then if Lucullus desires he may repair to the Golf Club to correct his liver.

There also is a boat club, a gymkhana club, and the Adyar Club. What with bathing, boating, tennis, polo, golf, dancing, and dining at his five clubs, the "white man's burden" is very cheerfully borne here.

Every traveler should pay a visit to the Victoria Institute, where he will find excellent and moderately priced examples of the indigenous industries of a province where master craftsmen survive and art is still a living reality. Every province has now an exhibition of arts and crafts, but none is better managed than that of Madras.

The climate of Madras is certainly sticky, but it has never, during our three visits, been so bad as the orchid-house moisture of Bombay. There is plenty to see. Georgetown, Elihu Yale's church, the Cathedral of St. Tomo, and the High Court, built in the Hindu-

Saracenic style of thirty years ago, are all "worthy of inspection," as the painstaking guide-book says.

But it is at evening on the Adyar that the true spirit of the city speaks. The rippling river, the graceful palms against the evening sky, the cool breeze from the sea, the greenness, the peace of this suburb, are unrivaled in any of the great cities of India. The traveler will like Madras although he may not fancy Bombay and Calcutta, the other two presidency cities.

By a window overlooking the Adyar River sits an aged woman with silvery white hair. She sits crosslegged, in Eastern fashion, on a masnad. Behind her is an embroidered bolster. Over the masnad is spread a Persian rug. She is dressed in white shawls with a border of royal purple, and the surroundings are as unmistakably Indian as her appearance is Irish.

Why does she sit here, like an Eastern queen? The answer to this question is a romance difficult to parallel in this materialistic age. This woman, who has long passed threescore years and ten, is an authoress, editor, orator, political leader, and the head of a religious movement whose forty thousand adherents are to be found in every quarter of the world.

As an authoress she has made her mark wherever the wisdom of the East is studied. As an editor, she has, through her paper, "New India," a faithful public. As an orator she holds great audiences wherever she goes. Among the learned bodies she has addressed is the grave and ancient Sorbonne. As a political leader she has bitter enemies, and followers who idolize her.

More than half a century ago, when scarcely out of her teens, she was the wife of an Anglican clergyman. She became a Roman Catholic, and left him. Then she became an agnostic and for several years worked in close association with the English reformer, Charles Bradlaugh. During this time she was an energetic materialist. Then she met Madame Blavatsky, the Russian spiritualist, and with characteristic courage threw her old opinions overboard. From earnestly believing nothing she came to believe almost everything, with equal enthusiasm! She gave up her work in London, where she had gained a reputation as an able speaker and a trenchant writer on social problems, and sailed for the East. From that time she has been a loyal disciple of Blavatsky.

In India she had to make her life anew. First she settled in Benares. Later she moved to Madras, and on Colonel Olcott's death she was elected the second president of the Theosophical Society, a post which she has held from that day to this, having been twice reëlected.

This is her life-story in baldest outline. To tell of her trials and successes, of her friends and enemies, would need a volume. She is Irish and—saving her presence—she enjoys a fight. But she wouldn't admit this for a moment. Always she tries to turn the other cheek, but at times the ancient Eve will out. . . . She is a very gentle lady. There is nothing small about her. She never did a mean thing in her life, we feel quite sure.

Of the wisdom of her activities there has been much question; of the purity of her motives, none. Nor can her ability be disputed, even by her enemies, of whom she has aplenty. Annie Besant is a world-figure.

At a time when big-whiskered undergraduates were wondering whether they dared follow Newman or not, a little slip of a girl (oh, the madman her husband must have been not to realize the treasure he held!), brought up in sheltered surroundings, gave up home and faith and husband, to follow the light of Truth, as she saw it. She had hardly any money. She earned her living by writing for the newspapers. Through slough of despond and over uplands of hope she followed the light she saw, until at last, after many ups and downs, it has brought her here, to Adyar.

She is a tireless worker. When the Indian dawn is breaking over the Bay of Bengal, she is to be found sitting here just as we found her, cross-legged, surrounded by her work, writing, planning, dealing with the letters her secretary brings her, giving instructions to the officers of the Theosophical Society, giving advice to aspirants to the "kingly wisdom" and "kingly mystery," administering affairs that not only circle the earth, but "step from star to star."

Mrs. Besant has none of the false modesty of the unknown. She has seen too much of the world to object
to facing the camera. Yet she has none of the airs of
a high priestess, none of the moods of a mystic. She is
simple and direct, a person of singular charm. Her
favorite mottoes probably are: "For God, for King
and Country," and "There is No Religion Higher
than Truth": for these two adorn the walls of her room.
Every one who knows her, not Theosophists only, will
tell you that she has lived these ideals throughout her
strenuous and striking career. Among her followers
(many of whom, by the way, believe her to be an incarnation of the famous Italian philosopher, Giordano
Bruno) she is believed to be rather a despot (and they
surely need to be galvanized with the fear of God
occasionally, for like all such bodies this one contains
a proportion of people that the world would call
cranks, or something harsher), but to us outsiders, she
is a delightful, soft-spoken, cultured old lady. And in
her bright brown eyes there is a hidden fire.

The objects of Mrs. Besant's colony at Adyar, and
of Theosophists at large, are described to us as both
spiritual and practical. The spiritual side is rather
difficult to explain in a paragraph, but briefly it is (a)
to promote the brotherhood of man, (b) to study com-
parative religion and philosophy, and (c) to explore
the hidden powers latent in man. Practically, members
can believe what they like. They can be Hindus or

Holy Rollers, Buddhists or Baptists. "There is a good deal of difference of opinion on matters of doctrine," said Mrs. Besant, "and I think that this is a very healthy sign. Unless we have differences of opinion on matters of doctrine we shall inevitably become a church or sect. It is not our business to become either, for we are a society of students, and if all students agree there will be a very poor advance."

But the common denominator for the average Theosophist seems to be a belief in Karma. Karma is "the good law," whereby every action in this world has its inevitable consequence, or reaction. In other words, in this life or succeeding lives, each shall reap as he has sown. Gradually through the experience of countless births, the soul learns the lessons of Karma and attains to the "kingly wisdom and the kingly mystery of the unborn, undying, unbegun." It then leaves the earth, to seek expression in some other flesh. . . .

As to the inner or esoteric section, their beliefs may be crudely summarized as follows, by outsiders who are not initiated into their secrets: Each age of the world, from the æon-long past of the Lemurians, who lived on the banks of the Mediterranean, and the Atlanteans, whose civilization sank beneath the ocean waves in far centuries of geologic time, has had a Manu, or typical Man, who sets the example to humanity for the race that is to come and strikes the keynote of its religion. The Manu of this age, say these

Theosophists, is the Lord Gautama Buddha. But they believe the world to be now on the threshold of a new age. The new world-teacher, the successor to Buddha, is soon to come, to give light and leading to the world. The day of the Messiah is at hand. Already a herald of the great teacher has come in the body of a Brahmin youth, young Krishnamurti, known to the elect as "Alcyone." His is a thoughtful, beautiful face, with the eyes of a mystic.

A gentle-voiced American, in horn-rimmed glasses, takes us to see the practical work that the Theosophists are doing in Adyar. His costume, consisting of a purple skull-cap, a white shirt worn with the tail out, and a white loincloth, makes it difficult for us to believe that he was a resident of Madison, Wisconsin, not long ago, and an instructor in the university there. All the Occidentals at Adyar—British, American, French, Scandinavians, and others—adopt the cool and comfortable garments of Hindustan. Many have taken high university degrees in Europe, but they wear dhoties none the less.

On our way to the Theosophical Publishing House, we pass Mrs. Besant's Rolls-Royce—the gift of an Indian maharajah—waiting to take her to the city offices of her daily paper, "New India." At the Publishing House we see learned Sanskrit works, and well-bound books in English, which are being distributed to the four points of the compass. We continue our stroll around the two hundred and sixty acres of the domain, which contains some two hundred Theosophists. We pass Leadbeater Chambers: the Seva Ashrama, which is the headquarters of the Order of the Brothers of Service—a sort of *corps d'élite* of Theosophists, vowed to poverty and obedience, and numbering twenty-five members who have renounced all worldly possessions to work for their order: the Annie Zoroastrian Home: Miss Bell's bungalow: the Olcott bungalow, where the first president lived: the Masonic Temple: the workshop: the power-house: the dairy and students' quarters, where a successful agricultural school has been started: and the Vesanta Press, where a monthly and a weekly magazine and many books are printed.

Then back to headquarters. Still we have seen nothing of education. The society maintains five schools in England, three in Scotland, and a thousand pupils in Ceylon. Locally, the Olcott-Panchama schools were pioneers in the work of educating the depressed classes of Madras Presidency and continue to do an immense amount of good.

There are some fifteen hundred branches of Theosophists scattered throughout the world. Even Iceland has its lodge, named "Jolabladid." In Java a group of devout Dutchmen meet for the purpose of promoting "abstinence from gambling, opium, alcoholic liquors, debauch, slander, lying, theft, and gluttony."

America now has about twenty thousand members.

But the strongest claim that Adyar can make on the gratitude of the world, is its library of palm-leaf manuscripts. Here are shelves and shelves of ancient rolls, written by the monks of Tibetan monasteries and the pundits of the Ganges plains. It contains the garnered wisdom of elder civilizations, this library. There is an atmosphere of perfect peace here—where Pierre Loti studied twenty years ago—something of the quiet heart and level eyes of the Asian mystics. In the work of translating and classifying these manuscripts a group of learned Brahmins are engaged, and although the work progresses slowly from lack of funds, still it does progress. Slowly but surely the knowledge of long ago, which would have been one with the all-consuming dust of India but for the enterprise of Adyar, is being brought in print to Western eyes. Who knows what treasures of vision these pundits may unlock?

Here then in Adyar, and elsewhere, is a society of persons, the Order of the Star in the East, waiting and working for the coming Manu. "The striking of His hour is nigh when He shall come to mankind again as He did so often in the past." And we, who see but as in a glass darkly, can yet give our respect to an earnest band of workers who are preparing for the Kingdom that is to come, as they believe, in the days that are near at hand.

CHAPTER XI

WHERE CRIME IS A RELIGIOUS DUTY

NEARLY everything in India is on so large a scale that other countries seem dwarfed by comparison. Not only has she more races and more languages, more gods and more conjurors, more peripatetic philosophers and strolling poets and degenerates, more saints and more political agitators, but she also has more professional criminals.

Of all the thieves in this world the most cheerful, the most unabashed, and the most successful, is the Crow of Hindustan.

When Mark Twain visited Bombay a quarter of a century ago he wrote a little character-sketch of the Indian Crow and stated that in his various incarnations he had been a gambler, a low comedian, a dissolute priest, a fussy woman, a blackguard, a scoffer, a liar, a thief, a spy, an informer, a trading politician, a swindler, a professional hypocrite, a patriot for cash, a reformer, a lecturer, a lawyer, a conspirator, a rebel, a royalist, a democrat, a practiser, and propagator of irreverence, a meddler, an intruder, a busybody, an infidel, and a wallower in sin for the mere love of it.

But Mark Twain left India without discovering something even more interesting—namely, that there are fourteen million people who worship the Crow, and whose chief ambition is to return to this world in the form of crows in their next incarnation.

These people belong to the criminal tribes and are familiarly referred to by their neighbors as "Crims." They are the most snobbish criminals in the world, for they have their own separate Hindu caste. If you were to ask them if they are Brahmins or British they would be as insulted as you would be if some one called you a thief or a jailbird.

For every European in India there are ten hereditary hall-marked criminals-by-caste. For every official of the Indian Civil Service there are twelve thousand of these born "Crims." These upholders of everything but law and order are born criminals just as you and I are born Catholics, Protestants, or Mormons.

Take the combined populations of Australia, New Zealand, and South Africa—and there are still more criminals in India than that, by one third. In short, there are ten million criminals in India, plus amateurs, dabblers, sneak-thieves, confidence-men, dope-dealers, slave-traders, and the like. If you think the British administrators in Hindustan have nothing to do but play polo and drink "chota pegs," these figures will tell their own tale plainer even than Kipling's "Plain Tales from the Hills."

The fact is, the criminals and the Thugs of two centuries ago had overrun India. Trade between towns was well-nigh stopped. Prosperous merchants were strangled daily by the roadside, sometimes for the money they carried, but often for pure mischief. The Thugs worshiped Kali, goddess of blood, even as the modern criminals do; and they killed for pleasure, the prototypes of those who to-day steal for the sheer joy of it. Life was coming to a standstill when the British intervened and exterminated the robber bands that were making travel a terror throughout Hindustan. But although they could subdue the Thugs they could not abolish the criminal caste. The reformation of a whole race of men is an almost superhuman task. But it no doubt will be accomplished "in God's good time," if the British remain in India.

Every child born among the Crows is a criminal and so recorded in the books of the Indian police. Further, every child goes through many years of preliminary tutoring and then through a post-graduate course in the science of picking pockets and burgling houses, and the gentle art of clipping bangles from the ear-lobes of Indian dowagers, just as the Honourable Reginald Fitzwhat goes to Eton and Balliol.

These people believe that the surest way of going to Paradise when they die is to be killed while engaged in their sacred calling of committing crime. They believe this just as strongly as fanatical Muhammadans believe that they will get a through ticket to Paradise if they die in battle against the unbeliever.

It is almost incredible, but strictly true, that two distinguished rajahs are members of these criminal tribes. In order to keep from breaking caste (the most appalling disgrace that can befall a Hindu) while avoiding the danger and discomfort of a wicked life, they steal from each other. They do this once every year in much the same spirit that we observe Christmas. They exchange visits, and the guest awaits an opportune moment when his host is out of the room and then hides the latter's jeweled betel-nut box in the folds of his gold-embroidered robe. Instead of turning the royal thief over to the police when he discovers his loss, the host retaliates by stealing some object of similar value. For example, in the dead of night, after putting a sleeping potion in his friend's coffee, he may tiptoe into the latter's chamber and pocket his wrist-watch. In this way both rajahs appease the pangs of conscience without unnecessary risk. But if they were not to commit a crime once every year they would feel disgraced and would be unable to sleep in peace—that sweet innocent sleep of the man who has done his duty in that state of life to which it has pleased God to call him.

It is believed that these criminal tribesmen, who are now scattered so far and wide over India, were once

temple-servants. A learned ethnologist informed us
that their history was as follows: During a great famine these temple-servants were crowded out of their
sinecures by Brahmins in search of an easy living.
Never having earned their bread by work, when ejected
from the temples they naturally were too proud to
stoop to vulgar labor and insisted that the public support them. The public, however, was apathetic: the
whilom temple-servants had a grievance: soon they began helping themselves to anything they could lay hands
on, and the respectable although superfluous officials
of one generation became the criminal class of the next.

Their leaders divided India up into districts, much
as some corners of England and Scotland are divided
into game-preserves. Even to this day, each tribe has
its own private hunting-ground. Every tribe also has a
chief, and under him come the head men who boss the
gangs. Although they are proud of their caste and never
attempt to conceal their identity except when in the act
of committing a crime, the identity of the head man is
usually kept secret.

Here is a typical Crim story: Three members of a
certain gang were walking down a highroad one day
when they met a Brahmin coming in the opposite direction.

"Keep to the other side of the road, low-caste ver-
min!" shouted the twice-born. This is a common attitude
for a Brahmin to adopt because he is ceremonially

defiled if a member of the untouchable classes gets 'twixt the wind and his nobility.

"You cock-eyed son of a bow-legged scorpion! What do you mean by calling us low-castes?" retorted the Crims angrily. Whereupon they seized the Brahmin, bound him, and hustled him off to their cave in a near-by forest. When they brought him before their chief, it was commanded that the wearer of the Brahminical thread be stripped of his ornaments and clothes. Then an old outcast sweeper-woman was sent for, who was paid a generous fee to cook for the Brahmin. Not only did the chief force his haughty prisoner to eat this unspeakably defiled food, but he compelled the Brahmin to occupy the same bed as the sweeper-woman, to the delight of the latter and the abject terror of the former, for such contact meant that his caste was well-nigh irretrievably broken. To regain his position in Hindu society after his release he had to make out of silver and gold an image of the sacred cow large enough to enable him to crawl in through its mouth and come out, reborn, through the other end. In this way the twice-born purified himself from the unhallowed night he had been forced to spend with the sweeperess.

When a Crim breaks caste he regains his social position in a somewhat different manner. The most common way in which such a calamity can befall him is to be sent to jail. When released, before his friends or even his family will associate with him he must undergo what is known as the "toddy baptism," which means that he must go on a spree. In fact, the more nights he sleeps in the village street, the more he beats his wife and smashes up the furniture, the more rows he attempts to kick up with his neighbors, and the more snakes and other green crawling things he sees, the purer he becomes. The drunker he gets the more completely is he purged of his sins—especially that most inexcusable of all sins, the sin of getting caught.

When a gang of these hall-marked, high-class, snooty felons plan a little coup, certain evil omens may cause them to postpone the enterprise until a more auspicious moment. If they pass a milkmaid on the road, they are elated, for it is a sign that success awaits them. Like. wise it is considered auspicious if the gang meets some one carrying money, rice, fish, or water, or if they catch a pig. In hunting the Indian hog they indulge in some odd practices. Armed with stout sticks they run after the pig and crack it on the legs in order to cripple it. Then they stick its head in the sand and kill it by suffocation, in order not to lose a drop of its precious blood. To the Crim pork, next to fried snake, is the rarest of all delicacies, although most of the other peoples of India look upon it as unclean.

As to evil omens: If they hear the howl of a jackal just as they are about to break into a house, they will turn back. Or if they see some one spill water from an earthen chetty, or if a white cat crosses their path, or if they hear the screech of a kite wheeling in the air above, or if they happen to pass wailing mourners, they will then abandon their project. But strangest of all, if any one near them happens to sneeze, instead of saying, *"Gesundheit!"* "God bless you!" or *"Salute!"* they regard it as a sign from their patron goddess, Bogiri Mahalakshmi, that the day is unfavorable. It is a common thing, in a criminal-tribe village, to see people turn abruptly about and retrace their steps when some one sneezes.

After encountering any of these evil omens they must model another mud image of their goddess and make additional sacrifices before proceeding with their plans. We visited criminal villages in different parts of India. Although they were most obliging in showing us their methods, they consistently refused to model an image of their goddess for us. After all, they have their standards of "good form," like other people.

Having decided whose house they are going to rob, they do not try to force the door, but invariably make their entrance through the roof. First they remove the tiles or thatch over that part of the bungalow which their women spies have previously ascertained to be the sleeping-quarters. Then they mumble a prayer to Bogiri, and drop a few pebbles to make a slight noise. Experience has proved that if any one in the room is awake he will call out upon hearing the pebbles. But if there is silence the Crims descend stealthily and remove the jewels from the ear-lobes, wrists, and ankles of the sleepers. So adept are they that ninety-nine times out of a hundred they get away without waking their victims, and even if some one is disturbed, and discovers what is going on, in the confusion they escape through a door, which they carefully unlatch as soon as they descend through the roof.

Some years ago an attempt was made to isolate all the criminal tribes and keep them in restricted areas, where they could amuse themselves by swindling each other instead of the world at large. But there were too many of them and the scheme "went phut." Other experiments were tried; all were forlorn failures.

CHAPTER XII
THE MAN WHO STOLE SIX POLICEMEN

As all men know, one of the finest feats ever performed by any police organization of any land was when the British police in India wiped out "Thugee," the fanatical secret religious sect made up of thousands of devout Thugs, who roamed the highroads of Hindustan strangling every man, woman, and child on whom they could lay their hands. When captured, some of the Thug leaders had more than four hundred cold-blooded murders recorded in their game-books. They tallied them in tens just as you would count your points in bridge. That was many years ago, and although the Thug is no more, the professional criminals of India continue to multiply, and the problem of what to do with these fourteen million hereditary law-breakers has only recently been partially solved.

After many vain attempts to find a solution, it was decided to unload them on the missionary societies, and the most of them were turned over to an organization that thrives on so-called "impossible jobs"—the Salvation Army. Some of the criminals, of course, exemplify the adage that Rome was not built in a day.

It is to Stuartpuram, the largest criminal-tribe center in southern India, that we go in order to see something of these curious human beings whose moral code is so exactly opposite to the precepts of Moses.

After an all-night ride north from Madras along the curving shore-line of the Bay of Bengal, we drop off the train at Bapatla just as the "sun comes up like thunder" out of Burma across the Bay. We elbow our way through a throng of Telegu folk as dusky-hued as Zulus. But they all have straight black hair and refined features, and the men are naked except for their mammoth white turbans and microscopic loincloths. The dainty, bronze figures of their wives and daughters are draped in brilliant red saris, while ear-lobe, nostril, wrist, and ankle are hung with gold bangles representing the family profits from the sale of cocoanuts.

A topaz-colored Telegu, with silver ear-rings, salaams to the ground and announces that he has been entrusted with the honor of escorting the sahibs to the bungalow of his "father." By "father" he means, of course, father in spirit—our host, Ensign Robilliard, the ex-Scotland Yard detective and Singapore police official, now of the Salvation Army, who has devoted himself and his family to the task of bringing the message of the Gospels to two thousand people whose principal aim in life is to break all the laws of God and man. His "father's" limousine is waiting outside to take us to our destination. It proves to be a springless bullock-cart, and in it we jolt between rows of giant cactus across a desert as barren as the Sahara until at the fifth mile we come to an oasis of paddy-fields, mango-orchards, melon-patches, flower-gardens, and a village of Palmyra-leaf huts with mysterious white cabalistic signs painted with lime in front of each doorway, as a notice to passing evil spirits that they are not to trespass. This is Stuartpuram.

In the midst of the fertile stretch the sturdy bhials stop at a stone bungalow surrounded by young palms, rubber-trees, and luxuriant tropical flowers. Here we find the ex-Scotland Yard inspector and his family in the midst of a settlement of two thousand highwaymen, jailbirds, and other neighborly folk.

After a curry tiffin Ensign Robilliard takes us to the nearest village to meet the community hero, one Angadi Venkatigadu, "the man who stole six policeman." If any of these people ever do return to this world after death in the form of crows, surely this cunning old brigand will be the first. Few more daring deeds of lawlessness have been recorded than those of this doddering old villain who spends his declining years chaffing and scoffing at the younger generation. To him they seem to have degenerated into mollycoddles and peaceful, weak-kneed, law-abiding citizens. We found him one of the cheeriest murderers unhung. Although his hair is as gray as his skin is black, and his joints creak like a rusty hinge, and his muscles are drawn and stringy, there still is a tricky twinkle in his watery old eye.

"In his prime," said Ensign Robilliard, "Angadi Venkatigadu was the cleverest brigand in southern India. His specialty was bribing and terrorizing officials, and he was the champion wire-puller of the Madras Presidency. So successful was he that no matter what manner of crime he and his friends committed, no one dared to arrest them. So frequent were the robberies in the district where they operated that the attention of the governor of the Province was attracted. The governor correctly surmised that the band was in league with the local officials. So six picked men were sent in from another district with orders to round them up.

"But the local agents of the law, who had been getting their bit of loot from each robbery, warned Venkatigadu, and when the would-be pursuers arrived the Crims ambushed them and carried them off to their jungle retreat. Then Venkatigadu and five of his men put on the uniforms of the six picked policemen, took their rifles and pistols, and boldly went up and down the country-side posing as officers of the law, robbing with greater audacity and more impunity than ever before. Unluckily for the gang, one of the prisoners escaped and gave the alarm at police headquarters in the

town of Gontur. Had Venkatigadu not been careless
and forgotten to cut their throats, all might have been
well.

"This time a European police inspector and a posse
of thirty heavily armed men set out from Gontur to
run the gang to earth. Again the Crims were tipped
off by their police confederates, and when the posse
arrived the gang was safely under cover. However,
that night, just to show their utter contempt for the
minions of the law and the British Raj, Venkatigadu
and his pals crept into the police camp and clipped off
the tails and ears of all their pursuers' horses.

"Months later, when they had grown careless again,
the members of the gang were caught. By then scores
of charges had been lodged against them. But they had
accumulated so much loot that they were able to buy
witnesses to prove alibis for their more serious offenses,
so that the prosecution was only able to obtain a very
light sentence of a few months, which merely supplied
the Crims with a much-needed rest from their arduous
activities—a holiday at Government expense."

Robilliard tells us that a Crim is always ready to
adopt a child—in fact, a score of children, if given the
chance. When they manage to abduct one they always
announce publicly that it is a grandchild. Experience
has taught them that hunger sharpens a child's wits.
So when training them in the rudiments of the profession they let them go hungry, and then start them off with

something petty, like chicken-stealing. Youngsters become particularly adept at this and several demonstrated their skill for us, much to our amusement and to the evident satisfaction of their proud parents, whose pride and pleasure were comparable to the feelings of the average American mother and father when their offspring becomes valedictorian of his class.

This is the way chickens are caught: The young Crim chews a bit of unhusked rice until it forms into a small ball covered over with prickles from the husk. When he sees a chicken approaching he spits out this ball. The fowl seizes it and chokes just long enough to enable the youngster to catch it and run. Another children's sport is catching sheep. The presence of a youngster gamboling about near a flock does not cause the average sleepy shepherd to suspect that there is villainy afoot. But if one of his ewes strays from the flock, the young Crim catches it and shoves a prickly pear down its throat before it has time to bleat. The pear seems to paralyze the sheep and prevents it from either moving or making a sound. Then after nightfall, if the shepherd has failed to note the missing sheep, the child's parent or guardian carries it off.

After a child has become proficient in his kindergarten course in elementary crime he is allowed to attempt more dangerous deeds and eventually receives his degree of M.C. (Master of Crime) before proceeding to his life-work.

It is a common thing to see a juggler with a trained monkey entertaining a crowd of villagers. Frequently this vagrant is a criminal tribesman and his performance a ruse to attract and hold the attention of the village folk. Usually his confederates are two or three naked children. Each child is trained to carry a small pair of sharp scissors concealed in his throat. The nakedness of the children disarms suspicion. But while the man and his monkey amuse the crowd these imps slip in and out amongst the spectators, snipping off money-bags, reaping a harvest of rupees from the turban-ends where the men of southern India carry their small change.

Robilliard tells us of a criminal gang that was discovered in the act of robbing a house. The news quickly spread throughout the village and the people of the community formed a great ring and started to close in slowly in the hope of catching the entire gang. Finally the ring arrived within a few feet of the criminals. Another moment and the capture would have been made. But at the psychological moment the leader of the gang, who was a man of the world, threw down several handfuls of rupees. Immediately there was a scramble and the villagers fell over each other in trying to get them. Taking advantage of this opportunity, the Crims made a rush for freedom, broke through the ring, and disappeared across the fields. At a sacrifice of thirty or forty rupees they escaped with the rest of the loot. We met that Crim leader, who is now past eighty, and we took off our topees to him as a man who would have been a millionaire or a marquis had he had the advantage of our culture.

As another illustration of the keenness and nimbleness of wit of his protégés, Ensign Robilliard tells us of an escapade that concerned an American missionary. This man was in charge of a settlement of a thousand Crims. There appeared to be more dogs than people in the community. This so annoyed the missionary that he sent for the head man and urged him to cut down the dog population. The chief demurred. So by way of encouragement the American offered a bounty of four annas for every dead dog brought in. The chief and his councilors withdrew and met in council. After a hurried conference the chief returned and told the missionary that his associates desired to accept the proposal. Several hours later dead dogs began to pour in by the dozen. The missionary eyed the rapidly growing pile of mangy pariahs with satisfaction. But in the midst of the ceremony up rushed the station-master from the neighboring village, followed by a crowd of his fellow-townsmen. Instead of producing their own pariahs, the canny tribesmen had pushed off to the nearest town and rounded up all their neighbors' pets, for which they were collecting the reward of four annas per head from the gullible missionary.

No record, except a vivid criminal tradition, remains of the missionary's remarks.

CHAPTER XIII

WHERE THE FEMALE OF THE SPECIES IS SUPERIOR TO THE MALE

WITH the criminal tribes of southern India "woman suffrage" has been a dead issue for centuries. To them, the female of the species is superior to the male. They even worship a goddess instead of a god. For this they give two reasons: In the first place, they look upon motherhood as the most sacred and important thing in life with the single exception of the pious act of committing crime; and in the second place, they are open-minded enough and generous enough to admit frankly a fact that they say all men should know, namely, that women are cleverer than men. "They make better criminals."

The Crim intelligence corps is made up entirely of women spies. Disguised as simple gipsies, these adroit Jezebels go about selling baskets. This enables them to get in touch with the garrulous women of the villages without exciting suspicion, and gives them the desired opportunity to extract bits of useful information from witless housewives. And further, if the lord and master of the house seems to have a roving eye and a gallant fancy—so has Jezebel. Soon they have gathered enough knowledge of village affairs, from silly women and fickle men, to enable them to make their plans. Then the spies report to their chief, who calls his councilors together. But before discussing the project an idol of mud, the image of their patron goddess— Bogiri Mahalakshmi—is modeled. Each time they meet a fresh image of the goddess is molded and her eyes are painted with wide circles of lamp-black, and her ears and nose are loaded down with gold and silver ornaments. Then a sacrifice of a pig, or a sheep, or a goat, or a white cock, is made to her. The nature of the sacrifice usually depends upon the balance on hand from the last foray. After leading his devout band of law-breakers in a few words of prayer, the Crim chief and his fellow strategists listen to the reports brought in by the women and decide how many people they must murder and other details.

The women of these tribes do a considerable part of the more dangerous work. In addition to acting as spies they also carry all of the loot. Most men in southern Hindustan wear the merest excuse for a loincloth. This makes it impossible for them to conceal much stolen property about their persons. But with the women it is different, for they are able to carry a great deal under their dresses. To disarm suspicion further a woman often pretends to be *enceinte,* and walks two or three miles behind the rest of the gang when it is on the prowl. Nevertheless, a veteran native police official can recognize a criminal woman as easily as the average European can distinguish a gipsy. But it is only under the most exceptional circumstances that the law justifies a policeman in searching a woman.

However, the Indian constable knows that when he meets a criminal woman on the highway, in all probability her sari covers a multitude of sins and the spoils thereof. So he stops her and attempts to frighten her by peremptorily ordering her to hand over the stolen property. But the women are a match for the police and go about prepared for just this emergency. They carry small bladders two or three inches long, under the folds of their saris. These bladders contain a red fluid. When a policeman stops a woman she falls to the ground in apparent fear and terror, and if she is carrying a child she drops it onto the ground with just enough bump to cause it to howl lustily. Then she throws herself about, gesticulating, or covers up her child from the imaginary fury of the policeman, and in so doing cleverly breaks the bladder. When the policeman sees the fluid trickling under her sari he thinks he has caused a hemorrhage, and fearful lest he should be held responsible, clears off, leaving the woman to continue her journey with a light heart.

If a Crim decides he wants a helpmate to share the joys of his life of wrong-doing, he must, in accordance with the immemorial Oriental rule, pay for her. She may cost him as much as five hundred rupees. But if he cares nothing for beauty he may be able to pick up an old hag, to make his curry, for as little as ten rupees. A special tent is erected for the marriage ceremony. To this tent the bride is taken by relatives who disrobe her and cover her from head to foot with yellow scented powder. Meanwhile the bridegroom stands at the door of the tent with a weapon resembling a big carving-knife, proclaiming to the world that henceforth he is to be reckoned with as her protector. After certain incantations and ceremonies the powder is washed off, the male presents his mate with a new loincloth, and the ceremony ends with a feast and plenty of toddy, which takes the place of champagne.

British law supports the old customs of India when-ever possible. There are a few striking exceptions such as suttee—the old unwritten law that led widows to sacrifice themselves on the funeral pyres of their hus-bands. But here is a less spectacular but almost equally barbaric tradition that has thus far escaped revision at the hands of meddling Puritans from the West:

When a Crim divorces his wife, the money paid to her family on the occasion of the wedding is refunded to him. But he can refuse to accept it, because if he does, then he forever relinquishes all of his conjugal rights. By refusing to accept the return of the mar-riage fee (and at the same time allowing his beard to grow) he retains the right to claim all children to which she may give birth if she marries a second time. For instance, if a girl is born, husband number one can claim her and then dispose of her in the usual way upon the matrimonial auction-block when she comes of age. If a boy is born, husband number one claims him and uses him as his assistant on his unlawful occasions. Meanwhile the marriage fee is held by the Government, and from the day the wife is liberated husband number one receives interest on the money from the Government at the rate of about two per cent per month. So by this arrangement he not only holds the right to claim all of his former wife's future children but he draws interest on his original matrimonial investment as well. One result of this custom is that women are rather discouraged from indulging in the luxury of a second husband.

In southern India all women who can afford it load themselves down with gold and silver bangles, and there are several gangs of criminals who specialize in relieving them of their baubles. These master craftsmen work in broad daylight. Their only tool is a pair of sharp snippers. Usually the Crim cuts through the ornament itself. But if he is obliged to hurry, then he frequently snips through the ladies' ear-lobes as well; and if his victim endeavors to cry out, he simply strangles her.

One of the most cunning criminal organizations in

southern India is known as the "Broody Gang," and
the members of this organization are confidence-men.
They regard themselves as the élite of the whole criminal caste. They devote themselves to *selling stolen
property without ever actually parting with it.*

The object they usually have for sale is a money-belt
containing fifty or sixty genuine English gold sovereigns.
Even if they wanted to they could not sell these
sovereigns to a reputable bank, because no bank would
buy them from criminal tribesmen, even at a discount.
But there are many merchants who do not belong to
the criminal caste, yet who secretly do considerable
business with thieves. "Fences," we would call them.
It is one of these individuals that the Broody Gang
attempts to victimize first. They make an appointment
to meet him secretly. The would-be purchaser goes
to some near-by stream, ostensibly to wash his dhotie
and turban. While he is engaged in this innocent occupation the Broody representative comes up to him
at an opportune moment when there are no other people
about. All unknown to the buyer, the Broody brings a
number of confederates with him. They wear red turbans, which seen from a distance resemble the head-
cloths worn by the police. These men at first remain
in hiding at a distance of a hundred yards or so. At
the moment when the belt of sovereigns is being handed
over and the Crim has the buyer's bag of money in
his hand, he shouts, "Police!" With his hand still on

the sovereign-belt the buyer turns to look in the direction indicated by the Broody. This gives the latter just the moment he requires. Quick as a flash he drops the other's bag of money in his loincloth and takes out a bag of stones and bits of metal that he has brought for the purpose. The buyer, in alarm, drops the sovereign-belt and snatches back what he believes to be his bag of money, and dashes off at top speed to avoid being caught by the red-turbaned men whom he sees approaching. The Broody hurries off in the opposite direction—with both the sovereign-belt and the money.

Next day the members of the Broody Gang walk boldly to their victim's house. They find him wailing and moaning after the fashion of the East. He curses them bitterly and demands his money back. They refuse because they know that he doesn't dare tell the authorities. Every day, to the intense distress of their victim, they call at his house, and remind him that if the story becomes known, he will get a longer sentence of imprisonment as a would-be receiver of stolen goods than they will as thieves. All the neighbors see them, and knowing them to be criminals they ask the merchant why these visitors are coming to his place. The only reply that he can give is: "They want to sell me some gold, but I have refused to buy it." Then (Robilliard declares this occurs invariably) some gullible neighbor who thinks he sees a splendid chance to make some easy money, says to the first victim: "If you are not going to buy it, I will, if you will arrange for me to meet the Broody Gang secretly."

Of course the Broody Gang swindles the second man in the same manner, and they work their game until they have caught four or five in one community before they move on to another locality. Each man swindled is afraid to disclose his secret, because if he did, even though he would have the satisfaction of seeing the Broody gangsters sent to prison for three years, he himself would be sentenced to five.

Many of their schemes involve considerable expense, so each tribe keeps its own banker. This gentleman holds a semi-official post, and his duty is to advance money to his colleagues so that they can carry out their crimes without being inconvenienced by lack of funds and up-to-date equipment. If the robbery is a success the banker receives from fifty to one hundred per cent on his loan. But if the affair proves a failure, he marks it down against the man who played the leading rôle, and either the latter or his descendants are obliged at some future time to repay the banker—or the banker's descendants. With the banker it is a case of "heads I win and tails you lose." But of course there is always the chance that the banker may also be apprehended by the police, in which case he too may spend his days making little rocks out of big ones on the lonely Andaman Islands. If a criminal banker loans, for example, one hundred rupees, the record of that debt is sometimes handed down from generation to generation for a hundred years or more, until it amounts to a lakh of rupees or more. Then if one of the descendants of the man who borrowed the original hundred happens to have a beautiful daughter, the descendant of the banker is entitled to demand the girl in payment or to compel the father to sell her when she reaches maturity and turn the proceeds over to him.

The criminal tribes are the cleverest cattle-rustlers in the Orient. This is their method: They pass through a village with a herd of five or six hundred animals stolen on previous occasions, and as they drive the herds down the streets they cause as much confusion as possible and get tangled up in every side lane and courtyard. The result is that when they emerge on the opposite side of the village they have the animals they entered with, and most of those belonging to the villagers as well.

When one of them dies his friends tie his big toes together, place balls of rice and tobacco at his feet to provide nourishment for his soul during transmigration, and then bury the body in a grave as shallow as possible. The object of this shallow burial is to encourage jackals to dig up and devour the body. If the jackals fail to molest the grave it is considered an evil omen. In fact, it indicates that the deceased was not really a true criminal at heart but a holy, God-fearing hypocrite and a thoroughly moral rotter. So he is sure to be disgraced by reincarnation in a lower caste, or as a tiger, a cat, or a rat—forms of animal life that they particularly detest. But if the jackals do devour the body the relatives are overjoyed, for this ghoulish happening indicates that all is well, and that the deceased will enjoy the coveted honor of reincarnation in the form of a crow.

As Mark Twain said of the crow, the incredible result of their patient accumulation of all the damnable traits is, that they don't know what care is, they don't know what sorrow is, they don't know what remorse is, and their lives are one long thundering ecstasy of happiness, and they go to their death untroubled, knowing that they will soon turn up again as an author or lecturer or something, and be even more intolerably annoying to their fellow-men than before.

But their training in crime has made them far quicker-witted than the average Indian. It is for this reason that Ensign Robilliard and his fellow-workers believe that once these people are persuaded to give up their criminal habits, they will develop into some of India's most useful and capable citizens. We have no doubt of it. Directed along right lines, the talents they employ in pious thieving will find as full a scope in trade. At any rate, a cheerier and more likable crowd of swindlers, cattle-thieves, and murderers we have never met—nor hope to meet.

CHAPTER XIV

GOLDEN GOA OF THE PORTUGUESE—A LAND WHERE TIME STANDS STILL

NORTH from Madras lies Humpi, capital of the Hindu dynasty that was overthrown by the nawabs of the Carnatic, and a little further north we come to Bijapur, where these "soldiers of the Prophet" built their southern capital. At Humpi there is wealth and luxury and power but little we can smile at or sympathize with. The baths, the streets of the dancing-girls, the elephant-stables, the cinematographic bas-reliefs in the Rama-swami Temple, are all interesting enough, especially to the archæologist, but to us, travelers of the "Kali Yuga," they make only a faint appeal.

Bijapur until recently was a city of ruins in a plain of prickly pears, but the energetic British made it the headquarters of a district some years ago, cleared roads, repaired buildings, and generally put the place in order. Some of the works of a bygone dynasty have been turned into houses and offices again, to the horror of æsthetes, but we are not among those who would raise the cry of "Vandal!" as soon as something that is old is put to modern use.

The most notable "site" is the "Gol Gumbaz" or mausoleum of the round dome. It is the second largest dome in the world (St. Peter's claiming a diameter of a few more feet) and has a whispering-gallery that echoes and reëchoes a cough seven times in tones of stentorian thunder. Even a sigh can be distinctly heard sixty yards away across the dome. But the most attractive thing in Bijapur is the old gun called "Malik-i-Maidan," or "Lord of the Field." It is a cannon of colossal thickness and earth-shaking weight, with a dragon's mouth. With immense labor the nawabs of yore used to drag it to battle. Frequently it lay on people and crushed them deep into the red soil of Bijapur. It has a range of two hundred yards, and can fire accurately a whole hundred yards. It was fired, for the last time perhaps, to celebrate the armistice of November 11, 1918.

In the old days the gunners of the Carnatic used to use bags of copper coin when they were short of grape-shot. Having filled the Lord of the Field with gunpowder and coin of the realm right up to the dragon's back teeth, they said a prayer for the prosperity of the king and a malediction on his enemies, and put a torch to the port fire . . . boom! whizz! slosh! went the coppers into the foemens' ranks. Bang! whack! crash! went the

Lord of the Field against its recoil wall, with a thunder of sparks and smoke. Sometimes the enemy fled appalled and the Malik-i-Maidan was crowned with garlands of victory. Sometimes, again, the attackers rallied and, stung to fury by the pennies in their calves and other parts of their person, massacred all the gunners. But on the gun they could not wreak their vengeance. He was unbustable and indestructible. After all these years the dragon's mouth still gapes over the quiet Bijapur of the British just as it did in the heyday of the nawabs of the Carnatic.

Across on the west side of India, at Castle Rock, we again leave the stupid British territory, where trains run to time on round wheels, and dip down the Braganza Valley to Portuguese Goa, where time stands still and train wheels are elliptical, being worn to that shape by the action of the sand necessary to give them a grip on the gradient during the upward journey.

Mormugoa, the port of Goa, consists of a station, a ship, a quay, a fort, and a hotel. There are no inhabitants to speak of. Across the hill there is a delightful little bathing-place, and tired travelers are recommended to rush rapidly into the sea there, like the Gadarene swine. Here the rollers from the high levels of the monsoon come swinging in, green and cool and splendid, bringing with them oblivion from the sordid cares of voyaging, and a new zest for life. Afterwards, at the hotel, there is the excellent wine of Serradayres, at three rupees a bottle, to make the traveler vow to visit Lisbon at the first opportunity.

Next day we take the ferry and bus to Panjim, or New Goa. It takes about an hour to get there, more or less according to the weather and the will of God and the state of the spark-plugs. It is Sunday morning in Goa, this most Christian city in India. Cavalheiros and their senhoras are all in their Sunday best. White clothes and brown faces everywhere. No one seems to be Indian here, save a few gipsy women and coolies. All the others have some of the blood of the West and some of the pride of the West. The pure Portuguese, however, are few, and easily distinguishable. The others range through every color, from *café noir* to *café au lait*.

It is a well-known fact that nothing displeases an Englishman more than to see his ways of dress and speech aped by peoples of other countries. But the French, Portuguese, and other Latin races take the contrary view. In Goa this copying of the West is carried to a quaint extreme—comparable only to the habit of the South Sea Islanders and aborigines of the Gold Coast, who buy shiploads of worn-out Covent Garden stage costumes from the traders.

Derby hats, vintage of 1900, are fashionable in Goa. So this romantic little city looks as though it were popu lated by countless cousins of Potash and Perlmutter.

These particular derbies have crowns that grow perceptibly smaller at the summit, and narrow brims of the sort that turn up quick. Frock-coats are popular too, and watch-chains modeled after those used for snaking logs in British Columbia. The women favor mid-Victorian calico dresses and fussy winter hats that look quaintly grotesque amid the palm and breadfruit trees.

However, only the Christians affect such weird garments. The "heathen" Goanese go about in the miniature loincloths and nose-ornaments worn by their ancestors, who massacred the missionaries when they dared. Nor is it difficult to guess which of these two groups of dwellers in Portuguese India is the most comfortable in this humid tropical climate. It is an amusing spectacle that unreels itself before us as we stand by the statue of Alphonso d'Albuquerque and watch the Goanese trooping past—many nearly naked, but the vast majority decidedly overdressed.

One reason why there are so many Indian Christians in Goa is because the Portuguese dealt whole-heartedly and wholesale in their faith. When the convert-crop failed to come up to their expectations they would baptize a few villages *en bloc,* by sprinkling holy water on the houses. And once the villagers had been thus made Christians by proclamation, they either had to adhere closely to the principles of the faith as laid down by the Jesuits, or risk the tortures of the Inquisition. To become a Christian was an honor, however,

in old Goa. The convert immediately occupied a status
equal to that of his white brother. There was no color-
bar in old Goa, nor are there any notions of racial
superiority now. Either a man is a Christian and a
brother, or a heathen and an outcast, a pariah, a pig.
Naturally the Brahmins don't like the tables turned
on them in this way, and avoid Panjim as they would
a pestilence.

We talked for some time to a theological student, an
agreeable young gentleman whose eyes and teeth were
the only relief in an otherwise unbroken darkness of
face and dress. He was studying for the priesthood
with four hundred of his fellows at the Seminary of
Rachel.

No one in Goa cares what the color of his skin or
your skin may be. Many men have the shrewd bright
eyes of the captains courageous who were their ancestors, although they have lost the physique of their
pirate forbears. Others have the physique, but not the
spirit. But in one way or another the buccaneers left
their mark, and the Goanese are proud, as well they
may be, of the blood that runs in their veins. Goa is
indeed a bit of southern Europe. Occident and Orient
have met here.

At old Goa, while waiting for the leisurely sacristan
to open the Cathedral of the Bom Jesus, we wander
round the deserted cloisters and attics that surround the
main building. Great chests, with lovely old hasps,

processional banners, altar-cloths, chasubles and dalmatics, and all sorts of relics of the great days of the Church are there. There is also a gallery of portraits of former archbishops. "Dr. F. Alexios de Menezes, Arcebispo de Goa 1605," catches our eye, with his somber and quizzical eyes. He stares at us full-face, his fingers in a gold-leaved missal. There is a gold inkpot before him, and a quill pen, also a pair of large gold scissors. What were they for, these very large gold scissors? It is a vaguely disquieting picture, instinct with nameless terrors of the Inquisition.

We enter the Bom Jesus, we see the famous tomb of St. Francis Xavier, and the blessed relics. A crowd of pilgrims accompanies us through the church. A dusky priest, who only throws aside the strong cheroot that is between his lips when he gets inside the door, goes with us as guide. Leading us into one of the side chapels he opens two heavy carved doors in the east wall, disclosing rows and rows of drawers of delicate workmanship that look as though they once might have been for the files of the archbishop, or the delegate apostolic of the Inquisition. With a key taken from beneath his black gown he unlocks one of the drawers near the lower right-hand corner of the maze of compartments, takes out a bunch of keys with which he unlocks another drawer high up in one of the left-hand tiers, and from here takes out yet another bunch of heavy keys. With one of these he opens two small doors. From a black-velvet recess he lifts out a heavy, richly carved silver monstrance. Every one kneels, and the priest permits each in turn to press his lips to the glass in the silver frame before hurriedly relocking the reliquary in its recess.

When the worshipers have left the chapel and gone into the nave of the cathedral to pray before the tomb of the patron saint of Goa, we ask the priest to tell us about the sacred relic. Again unlocking the drawers, he takes it out. There under the glass, imbedded in faded red velvet we see two bones which he tells us are the fourth and fifth toes from the skeleton of St. Francis Xavier. The story of how they came to be separated from the body, which lies in the vault of the cathedral, is one of the most remarkable in the annals of the Church of Rome.

In the year 1554, when the miracle-working body of St. Francis was being exposed to the populace, a fanatical Portuguese lady, Donna Isabel de Carom, under pretence of kissing the sacred foot bit off two of the toes, hoping to be able to carry these most precious relics away with her. But an officiating priest saw the ghoulish deed, and obliged her to disgorge the iniquitous mouthful. Since then the two bones have been kept in this silver frame and thousands of pilgrims come to kiss the glass that protects them from the air.

In 1890 a part of the third toe of the right foot fell off, and at the special request of Pope Leo XIII, was divided into two parts with a miniature saw. One bit

was sent to the Duchess of Villaharmosa in Spain, a relative of the saint. There the relic is enshrined in the
ancient castle of the Xavier family.

Two hundred odd years ago the right arm of St.
Francis was cut off at the request of the pope of that
day and sent to Rome, where it was divided into four
parts, the largest of which is enshrined in the Vatican.

St. Francis Xavier died at Sanchean in China in
1552, but the following year was disinterred by the
Portuguese, taken to Malacca, and buried near where
the Fort of Albuquerque stands to this day. His remains
were again disinterred in 1554 and removed to Goa,
and given a magnificent state burial, during which he
lost his two toes in the way described above.

During the past four centuries the body of the saint
has been frequently exposed to public view. But devotees became too eager to obtain relics, and for years
only a few privileged persons, including the viceroy of
Goa and the leading dignitaries of Church and State,
were allowed to see it. In 1755 the rumor went abroad
that even these dignitaries were taking away souvenirs
of St. Francis, and a royal decree went forth from
Lisbon announcing that it should never more be exposed to public view. But in 1754, owing to allegations
that the remains had been spirited away, the silver
casket was opened and the body proved to be intact,
and in miraculous state of preservation, as it still is.

A decree from the Portuguese republican legislature

in Lisbon is required before the shrine may be un-
locked. Such a decree was promulgated several years
ago and Roman Catholics from all parts of the East
made the pilgrimage to Goa to see the remains of the
great missionary who played such a prominent part in
spreading the Gospel of Christ throughout the world,
and to participate in ceremonies of splendor and magnificence reminiscent of the days of Albuquerque and
Da Gama.

But old Goa is not a place for "sightseeing." We must
be alone, sitting among its ruins in solitude and still-
ness, to be in tune with the spirit of its grandeur. Near
by is a squalid village of six huts, all that is left of
Golden Goa, "Goa dourada," the richest city in India
in the sixteenth century. But we turn our back on that,
and look beyond to the mountains standing against the
white-flecked sky of the monsoon, with the silver streak
of the river below them. We hear the lap of the water
against the jetty of the viceroys, and the plaint of the
wind through the disdainful palms that have lifted their
heads above the courts and the palaces that are no more.

Gradually, to the ears of fancy, the old city comes to
life. The cathedral bell is ringing to summon all true
believers to an *auto da fe*. The spirit of the fierce old
Christians who founded this city and planted the cross
in a foreign land seems to surge back on the notes of the
bell. And its voice strikes through our modern spirit
with an agony of fear. We do not believe as these men

believed. We are heretics beside them. We see the stake
with its pile of fagots, there in the center of the Cathedral Square. The priests of the Holy Inquisition have
come for us. We are bound and take our place in the
procession behind the lifted cross. Then thrice, and
again thrice, in penitence and in terror we march
around the square before the eyes of the people, while
the bell rings slowly, very slowly now, as for souls about
to render their last account. The executioner has seized
us now. Our shoulder-blades are against the stake. In
our nostrils is the savor of the kindled fagots.

Then we start and awaken as from a dream.

CHAPTER XV
THE CAVES OF AJANTA

HAVE you ever heard of the Caves of Ajanta? No? Then perhaps you are lucky. They are on the Deccan plateau of south-central India. We were recommended to visit them by no less an authority than Sir John Marshall. He said that we should see them at all costs.

Now Sir John Marshall is the director-general of the department of archæology for India and Burma. He probably knows more about this country than any other living man. He has been here forty years or more, and during that time has traveled more than 250,000 miles in India. His dominion includes all the ancient wonders of Hindustan, such as the Taj Mahal; the ruins of the seven cities of Delhi; the red-sandstone capital of the Moghul Emperor Akbar the Great at Fatehpur-Sikri; the ruins of Golconda; the Black Pagoda of Puri; and nine hundred other cities, temples, and monuments of the magnificent past. Under him are forty thousand scientists, artists, caretakers, and other workers. When Sir John Marshall tells you to see certain things in India, at all costs, you should see them, because he is the man who knows. Sir John told us that the Caves of Ajanta should be seen because they contained what are believed to be the finest examples of painting produced by artists anywhere in the world prior to Michelangelo. But if you ever contemplate visiting the caves we advise you to make a careful study of the works of Michelangelo, Leonardo da Vinci, Titian, Murillo, and any one else you can think of, before you brave the rigors of the hotel season in the Deccan. That is our advice, as friends; but there is no doubt whatever that Sir John Marshall is right and we are wrong.

To reach these caves it is necessary to journey two hundred and fifty miles northeast of Bombay by rail, and then another twenty unforgettable miles. When we hear that our enemies have visited the Caves of Ajanta by bullock-cart we shall be well content.

We left Victoria Station, Bombay, in the evening of the hottest day in two years. That speaks volumes, for Bombay is too hot for comfort ten months out of twelve. So we may not have been in the proper frame of mind to enjoy high art from the start of our journey. Indian railway carriages are built to accommodate four persons at night. But there were five Europeans in the one we occupied. The three strangers evidently had been trifling with toddy, for they were approaching the last stages of hilarity. Two of them occupied the berths above us and the third uncoiled his bedding-roll on the floor. They sang till two and snored till four. By the latter hour we had fallen off to sleep only to be rousted out by our bearers, and obliged to leave the train in our pyjamas at the little junction of Pahora, where we were to catch a narrow-gage train on toward the caves at 6 o'clock. Pahur was the way-station on the meter-gage line in Hyderabad where we started on the final stage of our trip to Ajanta. The only conveyance available was a springless bullock-cart in which we were doomed to journey twenty miles over an unmetaled road.

There are bullock-carts of forty different types in India and there are at least twice that many varieties of bullocks. This was a two-wheeled cart, iron-tired, with a wooden bed about a yard square resting on the axle and level with the tongue. Over it was a canopy of bamboo matting like the canvas cover of a prairie-schooner. It was held together by hoops with jagged edges and nails that stood out for a half-inch all over the interior, so that they tore our clothes as we bumped along. The chauffeur of this traveling Inquisition sat on the tongue while we climbed in behind. Our heads were against the roof and our knees against our chins and our backs braced against the driver's back. The temperature ranged from 120° to 150°, and our tempers ranged from 150° upwards.

Now life in a trotting bullock-cart, as every shikari

who has ever done a shooting-trip knows full well, is about as comfortable as life aboard a destroyer in the North Sea.

However, we were determined to see "India as she really is," and felt the bullock-cart was a good place to begin. Millions ride in these bhail-gharis: the flivvers of Hindustan. And cattle are sacred. The cow *is* India. She is typical of all her patient people, a creature of love and worship. . . . To kill a cow is an unspeakable crime, punishable, under the rule of Hindu monarchs, with tortures worse than death. Even now, in some native states, the capital penalty is still in force against the slayers of the sacred gai. And the bull Nandi ("the Happy One") is the favorite vehanam or vehicle of the great god Siva.

What, then, could be more suitable than to travel in a conveyance approved by gods and men? What mattered it if we suffered the tortures of the damned in the temperature of the inferno? We were seeing India.

Well, we got to the rock-bottom of the bullock-cart question, and we feel we are not likely to ride in another such perambulating torment until the frescoes of Ajanta start to life from the storied past.

The sun had made long steps across the sky by the time we reached the rest-house of Fardupur, said to be four miles from the caves. The rest-house was certainly restful. The attendant chowkidar had gone for his afternoon siesta; there was nothing to eat and not a soul in sight. Over the landscape brooded a pervasive peace.

After a time of uneasy waiting, during which we despatched a servant to summon the guardian of the rest-house, we again folded ourselves up into the chariot of Siva, and lurched on till we got to a sign-post. One arm pointed "To the Caves," the other "To Ajanta." Unfortunately neither arm pointed along any visible track, so we trusted to our charioteer and continued on our way over a red-hot rocky plain, meeting nothing but a few stunted trees and some sullen wayfarers. From the latter we asked our way and were rather cheered when we learned that it was only a mile on to the caves. We were in the mountains now. We crossed several of them, we rounded contours, we dipped into valleys, we forded streams—still no caves. At six miles, if it is six inches, from the Fardupur rest-house we arrived at our destination.

The great Caves of Ajanta! One of the wonders of the world!

Imagine a semicircular ravine about a hundred yards across, with perpendicular bluffs of black rock. The caves are carved out of this rock. You climb along a mountain path until you get to Cave No. 1. It is labeled "No. 1" in gold, and all the caves bear the same aureate reference to the guide-book, so that you can read all their sizes and ages—so many feet across and so many years B. C. . . . Let us skip sixteen caves, and work our way to the center of the crescent. There is a spring here. While thirstily quaffing it and registering a prayer to the Demon of Cholera, let us look round these works of a by-gone priestcraft with our twentieth-century eyes.

One is reminded of childhood, and the terrors of childhood. These burrows were dug by some super-children of the past. One feels, standing in their shade, a great thankfulness that one is not, as the builders were, in the night of history. And then again, is Ajanta so very old after all? Two thousand five hundred years —old enough in all conscience to inspire respect. Yet the Pyramids and the Parthenon—can these Aryan burrowings compare with those glories of Egypt and Greece, in age, in beauty? No! a thousand times no! Yet they arrest the attention for another reason.

The fear and the faith of men long dead are carved in these caves out of the solid rock. That is their claim to human interest. The chisels of a million workmen, first and last, must have struck on those stubborn stones. With a great patience, with a great docility, the people of those days, under the guidance of their priests, must have fashioned these temples to Gautama Buddha. And the cynical tragedy of it! To think that they should have hewn out these shrines and idols for the king's son who renounced his kingship and the pomps and vanities of the world, and tried by his example to abolish also all priestcraft and superstition. But the priests (who knows by what artifice of the Brahmins?)—the priests of Buddha—made rich temples and carven images to Siddhartha, the prince who gave a pure philosophy of self-forgetfulness to the world. A thousand thousand devotees must have come to worship here in the darkness and mystery of these shrines, and to praise Buddha, the enlightened prince who abhorred all idols. A thousand thousand men and women, boys and girls, have come, through the dark corridors of Time, to these halls of a hundred pillars, and with many bowings laid their heads on the threshold of the altar, and with gold and silver and the widow's mite made oblations at Siddhartha's shrine, while shaven hierophants droned the litanies of Buddha, and saffron-robed acolytes swung aureate censers, whose fumes curled and mounted over the glyphs of the doorways and the brilliant frescoes of the porch.

Most of the caves are dim like the inner shrine of a modern Hindu temple. Some are small and some are vast.

The frescoes! Here we find something that we can unfeignedly admire. There were artists here in Ajanta in those days of long ago. A blue Vishnu embraces his Parvati; a king goes hunting; slaves and deer and cattle are limned to the life. Perhaps these are the most wonderful paintings in the world, considering their age. What fee did the artists get? What bribe induced them to work in these houses of gloom? Their line is perfect, their coloring bold and sure. There were artists in those days, such as the old earth was not again to know until the pope loved Raphael, and Leonardo worked for the king of France. Who were these men? They have vanished, like the priests who paid them; no trace or memory of them exists. Yet their work is the one touch of light and happiness in these crass and fetid caves.

In all the dark veharas where the stupid monks (for they were stupid to live like that) lived two thousand years ago, there broods a spirit of fear—fear that drives men with flails more terrible than any taskmaster; fear that after all these ages is not yet dead in the hearts of men.

The stench, the blackness, the noiseless stir of bats, the looming figure of Buddha, the sense of all the wasted toil of serfs, of all the ruined beauty, of dead hopes, dead creeds, *death* . . . that is the keynote of Ajanta.

Long centuries of decay oppress the soul in these sanctuaries that never see the light of day. And not the soul only; they disgust the nostrils also. Little gray beasts scurry over the stones; one darts out into the sunlight, and holds its head in its hands; indeed the smell is enough to make a squirrel squeamish, let alone a Christian.

For immemorial years these caves have been the breeding-place of bats. They cluster thick, thick on the ceiling, and their dead lie on the floor. A shaft of light from the doorway strikes across the threshold of Buddha's altar. There, on the threshold, in the dusty sunlight, lies a dead bat, with wings outspread and rat-teeth bared. It lies there, decaying, on the place that prehistoric foreheads touched and that was once odorous with the marigold and jasmine laid there by the hands of girls aquiver with awe at the nearness of God. . . .

The Caves of Ajanta, marvels of India—we experience a sense of having been displeased, yet strangely impressed, as indeed we feel so often during our pilgrimage among weird religious pageantries to the Black Pagoda.

CHAPTER XVI

THE MAGNIFICENT MOGHULS

IN the dark night of Indian history the sins and splendors of Akbar, Jahangir, and Shah Jehan flash with the brilliance of a comet's tail. Of all the kings that troop across the printed page of history, killing and scheming, loving and dying, surely the builders of Delhi, Agra, and Fatehpur-Sikri are the most romantic and the most lovable. Our hearts go out to the Great Moghuls.

Yet at Agra, where we find Moghul achievement at its best, we hesitate to type impressions that have been recorded a hundred times before. All that can be said of the Crown Lady's Tomb, the immaculate and immortal Taj, has been said by Sir Edwin Arnold in verse and by Havell in prose, better than we can resay it. The rest lies with the spectator.

And here Mark Twain's warning will not come amiss. Do not allow your imagination to build some glittering figment of fancy, some jewel-house of dreams, so that you will wake up disappointed at the reality of the Taj. For you can be disappointed in anything on earth, if you make up your mind to be disappointed by expecting too much. And although indeed the Taj seems too light and lovely to have been builded of hands, a radiancy of love, a glorious concept of devotion stronger than death made visible in marble against the turquoise of the Indian sky—still, remember that it is human.

Possibly, you will not think it the most beautiful thing you ever saw. Years ago, for instance, the Government of India saw nothing beautiful in it at all, for the Taj was about to be demolished and its marble sold by auction. The only reason it did not share the fate of the Delhi Palace was that there were not enough bidders.

Opposite the Taj, a black Taj was to have been built, and the Jumna was to be spanned by a causeway. Alas, that Shah Jehan's power crumbled before he could complete his grand design! The supreme effort of his genius was spent on the tomb of his beloved. While the empire went to pieces he wrought and planned in precious stone and marble. He gave his life to art. And who shall say, seeing the result, that it was not worth losing an empire to make a Taj?

From the Jasmine Tower, in the fort, you may see a view of surpassing loveliness, the view over which the old imprisoned emperor looked out, with dying eyes, to the tomb that enshrined his love. Probably there is not a more haunted place in the whole of India.

Here the luxury of the Moghuls reached its zenith.

You may still see the sumptuous baths where the almond-eyed and cream-skinned ladies of the Moghuls took their ease, and the jeweled walls against which young lords from Kabul leant, as they quizzed the dancing-girls of the court, and the state rooms where the emperor passed the hot hours of the long, long Indian day, and the delicate cascades of tinkling water that lulled his day-dreams, and the tender fretwork of marble in that room where all the gems of the known world were gathered.

No rulers of earth have left records so human as those of the Great Moghuls. Read Baber's diary, for instance, or the "Institutes" of his great ancestor Tamerlane. Look at the pictures of these jolly Tartars with their slant eyes and wasp waists and lion shoulders. See how kind they are, in spite of their occasional lapses into wolfish cruelties. See Tamerlane, for instance, with the heads of his enemies strewn all around his charger's feet, holding out the hand of friendship to a captured king. They spilt much blood and no little wine in their time, yet loot and lust did not dim their artistic sense. Through all the Moghuls ran a love of beauty, which came to its fullness in the time of Shah Jehan, overshadowing the empire of his fathers, and destroying it. Their empire has vanished, but the monuments and the deeds of the Moghuls remain, to challenge comparison with any of the landmarks of history.

Think for instance of Baber's renunciation at the

sick-bed of his son, Humayun, who lay dying. He said: "O God, if a life may be exchanged for a life, I who am Baber, give my life and my being for Humayun!" His prayer was granted, in three weeks the great spirit was no more and Humayun reigned in his stead. Has history any nobler deed? Has any monarch had a better "curtain" to his career than he who is buried at Kabul, among the roses he loved so well?

After Humayun came Akbar, a contemporary of Queen Elizabeth, who settled the administration and established the revenue system as it still stands to-day.

Akbar is one of the most remarkable men who ever lived. Like Napoleon and Alexander, his ambition was insatiable. Unlike them, he established a kingdom that endured for two hundred years, and might be still in existence to-day if his descendants had been worthy of him. His power over men and beasts was remarkable. He killed tigers on foot, he rode mad elephants that no one dared approach, and he could "back" any horse that was ever foaled. As to men, at that common crisis in an Oriental monarch's life when a relative comes with a gang of armed men to murder him, his action was typical. He was alone, unarmed, in his nightshirt, having just left the harem. Akbar asked the gang what the matter was, but he followed the question instantly by a hook to the leader's jaw that felled him on the spot. At once he was master of the situation. Some of the palace guards came up, and Akbar told them to drop his would-be murderer into the moat. They did so, but the drop was not very far (you can still see the place where all this happened at the south corner of Agra Fort) and the gentleman in the mud of the moat did not seem to be quite dead. So Akbar had him hauled up again, kissed him affectionately (for he was a relative, you see, though business was business) and then after having had him trussed up, pitched him over again, head first, so as to put the poor fellow out of his pain.

Later, Akbar built a new capital not far from Agra, as the British are now doing not far from Delhi. But in Akbar's day no one talked of extravagance. You may still see in the Hall of Public Audience at Fatehpur-Sikri, his new capital (that now lies in ruins less ruin-ous than the British capital) a large and extremely massive ring of stone in one corner of the courtyard. To this ring a mad elephant was tethered. Troublesome demagogues came to a sticky end in the great emperor's time. They were handed to the elephant, and ended their career in one squelch.

When his cook tried to poison him, he forgave her freely. Stupidly, she tried again. This time, the emperor retired to the little bedroom (you can still see it) apart from the rest of the palace of Fatehpur-Sikri and slept over the matter. Next morning, the cook was taken out onto the plain to the north beyond the lake, by a small party of soldiers. You will notice various small thorn-trees dotted about this plain, just as there were in Akbar's time. The soldiers chose a place where two young trees grew close together, and bent their heads down so that they came together. Then they tied a leg of the stupid cook to each tree. At a word from the Commander of the Ten, in charge of the party, the saplings were released and sprang upright. Heigh, presto! the cook was no more.

But with all his summary methods, Akbar was a just and merciful ruler. He conciliated the Hindus, by whom he is still revered. He married Hindu princesses; and he even tried to found a state religion that would weld his empire together. The scene of this experiment, which would have influenced the history of the world if it had succeeded, was the Great Mosque at Fatehpur-Sikri.

One day he came to Friday prayers with his new creed ready to enunciate. When the two-bow prayer was done, he went into the pulpit with the intention of saying the following words:

> "The Lord to me Dominion gave,
> He made me wise and strong and brave:
> He girded me with right and truth:
> No praise of man can sum his state,
> Allahu Akbar, God is Great. . . ."

But some instinct made him falter and hesitate halfway through this creed. He stammered a little, then relinquished his place, to every one's relief, to the accustomed leader of the prayers, and said no more. His credo remained unuttered, and will never be known in its entirety, although we may suspect that the phrase "Allahu Akbar," which may be translated either "God is Great" or "Akbar is God," was not without its place in the project. Doubtless, however, his genius for government warned him that the time was not ripe for tampering with the people's faith. And yet—and yet—had he done so, had this marvelous man succeeded in finding a common denominator to India's religions, who knows what the future of India would have been?

CHAPTER XVII
THE GRAVE OF NATIONS

"IT is a far cry to Delhi." *"Dilli dur ast,"* as the Persian proverb runs. India is far away, in space and time, from the peoples and problems of the West. Yet lately she has come nearer. Britain has fitted her with a tailor-made democratic dress and she has been taking the air on the boulevards of Paris and the avenues of Berlin and Washington. So India with her vast resources in life and treasure is gradually assuming a position of more and more importance in contemporary history.

His Exalted Highness the Nizam's adviser on railways, on a tour of America several years ago, was shown the new State capitol at Madison by a University of Wisconsin professor.

"Say, what do you think of that?" queried the scholarly dean. "I guess it's one of the finest buildings in the world," he added, perhaps slightly ruffled because his visitor failed to rise to the occasion.

"Rawther a creditable edifice, don't you know," ventured the conservative Englishman.

"Where have you seen any finer?" asked the pro-

One of the important shrines in the "Southlands of Siva" is the phallic temple of Nandi. the sacred bull of Tanjore. Most of the worshippers are women.

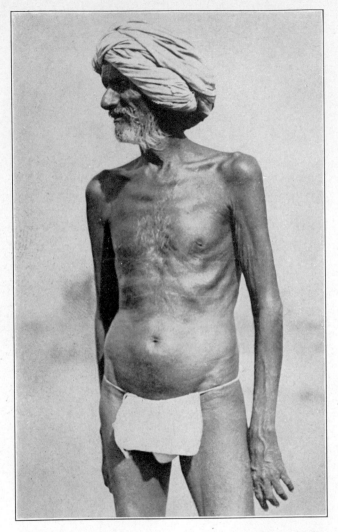

He was known as "the chief who stole six policemen." As Kipling said: "And the uniform 'e wore was nothing much before, and a little less than 'arf o' that be'ind."

fessor, a trifle irritated at the lack of enthusiasm.

"Ah well, I should say the buildings in Delhi are slightly superior," was the railway man's tactful response.

"Delhi?" replied the Wisconsin man. "Where's Delhi?"

"In India."

"Oh, Delhi, Indiana," said the professor brightly, "I've never been there but—"

Well, if you ever see the real Delhi you will see the Indian Empire in epitome.

Indeed you can see old empires at your feet if you care to climb the Kutb Minar in the Delhi plain. You can see the graves of nations and of men, leading way back into the cloudy dawn of time—an object-lesson without a parallel in the world.

From the Kutb Minar, you may see the rise and fall of five civilizations, and contemplating thus the tide of human affairs, the things of to-day come into their historical perspective. How do the present-day movements, you ask yourself, fit into the picture? Where does Mr. Ghandi come in? If he ruled in India to-day would he be a second Asoka? What is the difference between the old king-time and the new dispensation? Are the leaders of the non-coöperation movement of the same stuff as the Great Moghuls? What of the Emperor Baber, the first "Pussyfoot"? How would he have enforced prohibition?

From this Kutb Minar tower of the conquering Turkoman you may see, if you will, across the centuries, to a time eight hundred years before the she-wolf of Rome suckled Romulus and Remus: when the Aryans had descended from the North (a branch of our own family) upon the fertile plains of India, and had founded the first city of Delhi, the city of Indra-prasthna, now represented only by a few mounds, and the name of an up-to-date Hindu girls' high school.

Since that time five cities and five nations have flourished and decayed at Delhi. Each rose by the sword to the Empire of India, and each fell by the sword to the dust of India. The sixth Delhi is the present city, around which the glories of the Great Moghuls live— in fort and mosque and tomb. And the seventh city is even now being completed by Sir Edward Lutyens, the architect who has left his mark on the British Empire from Calcutta to Golder's Green.

In the Chandni Chowk and all the bazaars of Delhi you may hear a rumor current. It is that a prophecy is about to be fulfilled. He who builds a new Delhi, the soothsayer declares, is always fated to perish in its ruins, and therefore the days of the British dominion are numbered! Soon the jackals will yelp with those eerie hunting-cries that the visitor to Delhi knows so well, round the ruins of Raisina, the new English imperial capital, and the little gray squirrels will hunt in the houses of the rulers.

Yet Sir Edward Lutyens goes on building cheerfully, and the Indian legislature (not quite so cheerfully) votes the funds to carry on the good work.

Why? Why is India building a great new city, that will take millions of pounds to complete, as a memorial to the British Raj? There is unrest and discontent, there is poverty and crime. Yet withal there is a comfortable sense of permanency in the British administration. Even the most excited extremists don't really believe that the English are going to leave the country for a long time yet. Mr. Ghandi has warned Young India that it will have to deal with the "most tenacious race on earth, who have been accustomed to self-sacrifice from childhood." And at this writing he is in jail. So are the other leaders. Non-violence and non-coöperation are all right as long as there is a policeman a few blocks away, and a few British soldiers somewhere in cantonments in case the mob gets out of hand, but there isn't an agitator in the country who could tell you what he would do if he were suddenly and violently projected on the throne of Akbar—still less could he do it.

Politics in India, in spite of all the assertions to the contrary, are still based on British bayonets. But it is the babus, not the British, who rely on the bayonets. As to the British, in case of revolution perhaps many of them would take service under one chieftain or another as in days of old: some would be murdered, no doubt: others would be millionaires. But whatever happened, the clerk and the small shopkeeper would have their faces ground in the dust and their daughters enslaved, as in the good old days that the agitators are so fond of talking about. Hence the clerk and the shopkeeper and the merchant, while dallying with sedition as an elegant amusement, are quite certain that the British Raj, whatever the rumors of the bazaar may be, is destined to endure. The British Raj is there to see that their profits are not interfered with. . . .

But from the summit of the Kutb Minar, we see some of the real facts of India lying there in the broad daylight: the skeletons of the civilizations she has created, and then killed with her climate and her creed. Neither the genius of Asoka and his line, nor the power and the glory of the Moghuls, was destined to endure. The fierce sun and the wily Brahmin took their toll. They sapped the energy and the faith of the conquerors. Now their empires lie in dust and ruins. There was something wanting. It was not courage or sound philosophy, certainly. Neither was it bad organization, for what the ancients lacked in typewriters and telephones they gained in speedy and picturesque administration. Their deeds were not hidden away in blue-books, or their acts subject to the delays of counsel and debate. They stood out, with some magnificent gesture, plain for all the world to see. Take the case of Baber, the first of the Great Moghuls, who had learned to drink wine from some jovial cousins of his in Herat,

when he was king in Kabul, and who had rarely been
sober during his invading march from that town to the
conquest of Delhi. This is how he embraced prohibition, on the eve of the battle of March 16, 1527, against
the Lord of Mewar, the battle that was to lay India at
his feet:

He collected all the gold and silver goblets used in
his drinking-parties, and then and there ordered them
to be broken, and the fragments distributed among the
poor. Then he and his courtiers, to the number of three
hundred, vowed never to drink wine again, and poured
out on the ground all that they had brought with them.
Having thus "knocked with all his might at the door
of penitence," Baber summoned all his officers about
him and appealed to the old spirit of Islam. Said he:

"Noblemen and soldiers! Every man that comes into
the world is subject to dissolution. When we are passed
away and gone, God only survives, unchangeable. Whoever comes to the feast of life must before it is over
drink from the cup of death. He who arrives at the inn
of mortality must one day inevitably take his departure
from that house of sorrow, the world. How much better it is to die with honor than to live with infamy. The
most high God has been propitious to us, and has placed
us in such a crisis that if we fall in the field, we die the
death of martyrs: if we survive, we rise victorious, the
avengers of the cause of God. Let us then, with one accord, swear on God's Holy Word that none of us will

even think of turning his face from this warfare, nor desert from the battle and the slaughter that ensues until his soul is separated from his body."

And with one accord the hosts of Baber swore to win that day, or fall as Ghazis. The issue of the day proved them, in the emperor's words, "the avengers of the cause of God."

CHAPTER XVIII

THE WELL-JUMPERS OF DELHI

THERE is a jumping-well at Delhi, near the Kutb Minar, which was built for the sport of the Moghul emperors, who found it an agreeable diversion to make their slaves jump down the narrow shaft. It is especially made for well-jumping, this Moghul well. One side of it has been cut away to water-level, and in its masonry shaft four archways have been made, so that the falling bodies of the jumpers can be seen.

Or, if you prefer, you can stand above the well and see the jumpers fall eighty feet to the green water below, in which there is a circle of reflected sky. It is a long, long way to the water. The shaft is only eight feet wide, therefore if you jumped with the slightest outward impetus you would hit first the far wall and then the other, rebounding violently from side to side. A mess, not a man, would touch rock-bottom. The only way to do it is to step off as if you were stepping down a stair.

The ramp that leads down to water-level has been paved with broad flagstones, making a sloping stair-

way. On this the Moghuls sat, no doubt, with their
ladies, watching the well-jumpers, while peacock fans
waved about them, and slave-boys brought them sweetmeats and green tea in little cups, after the Turki
fashion.

What scenes of tears and laughter this old well must
have witnessed: slaves trembling at the well-mouth in
terror, and pallid courtiers ordered to jump off for a
joke! What scenes of triumph also, and applause from
the royal ladies when some favored slave received a
carelessly flung purse as the guerdon of his courage!
Alas, that some of the vividest scenes that the eye of
mortal man has witnessed, should have passed unre-
corded and unremembered! The Moghuls on the
movies would have enriched the imagination of the
world.

Nowadays all the well-jumpers are very old men.
Government has forbidden the teaching of their art, as
likely to be dangerous and unsuitable to little board-
school boys: hence the present old men, hereditary descendants of the men who amused the magnificent
Moghuls, may possibly be the last exponents of their
art. Already they have passed the allotted span of life.
They are bent and wrinkled and infirm. Allah the
Merciful has numbered the times that they are destined
to jump into that water, before they shall awake one
morning beside the waters of the Blessed in Paradise.

And Allah the Compassionate will see to it that their descendants do not starve. Indeed, their children are well-jumping already, so that there shall be "a remembrance of former things." They practise by night, the nice little board-school boys, when the moon is high and casts a silver circle of light into the bottom of the well. They stand on the cornice of the lowest archway, some fifteen feet above the water, and look down to the green and silver below, where they see their future mirrored. . . . And then, like their fathers before them, they leave their ledge as if stepping off a stair. The moon sees many things in India that the British do not see. This is the least of them.

The doyen of the well-jumpers is over ninety-eight years old. He was therefore in his twenty-fifth year at the time of the Mutiny, and must actually have been in the service of the Emperor Bahadur Shah, the last of the Moghuls. Does he remember the emperor and his court? And what of the Mutiny? Surely he must have some memory of that terrible May morning when the mutineers had arrived from Meerut, and the palace ran red with the blood of white men and women and children? That morning when the old emperor saw and trembled at the slaughter?

But no! . . . During the Mutiny he used to jump down the well for sahibs. And before the Mutiny also he used to jump down the well for sahibs. Sahibs were very liberal in those days. Sahibs used to give good baksheesh then, four or five rupees to each jumper. And a rupee bought twenty pounds of flour then, instead of half a pound as at present. These are hard times, and they are all poor men.

The others are not quite so old, but they are not at all more talkative. They know nothing about the Mutiny, and they do not care.

Or is it that they have seen things of which they cannot speak: murder, reprisals, untellable atrocities? Surely they are keeping something back? Surely they cannot have remained outside the passions, the fears, the intriguing, and the unrest of those exciting days? Can they have been blind to the agonies of empire, not fifteen miles away? Can they have been deaf to the rebel guns and blind to the glitter of the sword of Islam? They can. They were. In India this is so. There is no memory but that of custom. Wars and mutinies, plagues and pestilences, make but a ripple among India's myriad lives, a ripple of death that is soon untraceable among the millions who swarm and breed and die.

Each man to his trade. It is the business of kings to rule, of soldiers to fight, and of well-divers to dive. They dive very cleverly, these graybeards, and their eagerness to show their skill gives the spectator a heartache. They are so frail and bent and wrinkled, the ten old men who survive (there were twenty-five before the

World War) that one feels that they should be telling their beads rather than counting their baksheesh.

Once or perhaps twice a week, during the winter months only, a party of tourists comes to watch them. Men and women from Manchester, Chicago, Tokio: from far horizons and with alien minds they come here to see this old intimate amusement of the Moghuls, which seems to keep some memory still of their whimsical ways. But to the tourists this is just a stunt, an incident in crowded days of jugglers, fakirs, and what not. Glancing at their wrist-watches, and thinking of what tips to give, they see the old men go down, and then hustle for their car to see some other show. Yet nothing wrought in stone or ink or iron is such a tie with the past as these old men, who hold feebly to a life that links our times to the old king-time of the earth, gone never to return. Here, swift and vital, life for the lens of the cinema flashes by us—the whim of a dead emperor. With the divers, unless their sons continue the joke, the emperor's whim will die.

So far there has been no casualty in the jumping. One by one the graybeards have fallen asleep. On their string beds they know their time is short. But when sahibs come to see them jump their slow pulses quicken and their old eyes glitter. Another ten rupees to buy them bread and meat. And beyond money, there is the sport of the thing. They have the pride of artists in their skill.

It is a moment of rapture for them when they jump.

Youth floods back as they fall. They show the world that though ears be deaf and eyes be dim they have physical prowess still.

Each man who jumps expects a rupee, and well he earns it. How many men of eighty in Europe or America would care to dive eighty feet?

They are happy, these graybeards, and their lives are as straight and clean as their descent into the well. It is a hard life, but a gay one, for Allah, who sees into the hearts of men, has found courage there, which men and angels respect, and has rewarded them according to their deserts. May their days be long in the land that the Lord their God has given them, and may they be full of years and honor when they step off the ledge of this mortal life!

CHAPTER XIX

THE LODESTAR OF HINDUSTAN

HINDU RAO'S HOUSE, the Ridge, Delhi: Needless to say, this is not our permanent address, for Hindu Rao's House is a ruin, a ruin known in every English home as the place where two fierce engagements were fought, over seventy years ago, when the dominion of India swayed and hung in the balance on this Ridge at Delhi and five thousand British faced forty thousand well-armed mutineers.

Around us are the graves (and something more—is it memory or imagination?) of the men who died to re-take the town. We look southward toward the walls of Delhi that still stand as they did when "Bobs" (he who became Lord Roberts) was a subaltern in the Ludlow Castle Battery down there, and the immortal John Nicholson got his death-wound by the Kabul Gate, just beyond those trees to our left, on the day when Delhi fell and the last of the Great Moghuls gave up his empire to the British. Those days have left a heritage of history, to be read in humility and in pride wherever the English tongue is spoken.

Seventy years. We sit on the roof of Hindu Rao's House looking over the twilit town and plain. Before us lies modern Delhi. Beyond, five ruined Delhis with the story of a thousand years of empire, and a new Delhi, the seventh, with an unknown future. On our left is a long low building covered with snowy whitewash where soldiers and civilians and babus and bureaucrats have been governing British India during the building of the seventh Delhi. To the right is Viceregal Lodge. Behind us stretches the rocky Ridge, tapering like the bow of a ship, and thrusting out into the infinite plain of Hindustan.

Dark, infinite, unknown, magical, immense . . . adjectives fail to convey the sense of size that the mists of evening give to these vast plains.

How to tell of India, in picture and in story, to those who have never seen her? Every writer on India tries to convey to us, till he wearies us with words, the sense of millions and immensity: but the normal man has long ago waterproofed himself against the flood of statistics. Facts about acreage and population just trickle off his brain. Yet if he could sit with us, on this roof, and look out over imperial Delhi, where the lights are just being lit, and beyond, over the immense twilight of the plains, he would feel the truth, instead of only feeling the triteness, of statements such as these:

"There are two million and two gods in the religion

of the Hindus. It is an encyclopædia of religion, not a
religion." . . .

"Islam is a brotherhood of eighty millions of Indians,
and of one fifth of the human race." . . .

"There are eighty languages in India: and more nations." . . .

"From Peshawar to Madras is as far as from Norway
to Sicily or New York to Salt Lake City. India is not a
country but a living League of Nations, with the British
as international police." . . .

"There are three hundred and twenty millions in
India—the population of all western Europe: and more
than the population of both North and South America
and Africa combined. Of this population, two hundred
and thirty millions are cultivators." (As some one with
a mania for statistics and grotesque comparisons has
said: "They would circle the earth five times if placed
in line." Think of it!)

And so on and so forth. But to say these things is mere
weariness of words. Let us not say them—again, at any
rate—but plunge straightway *in medias res*.

The sun has sunk in molten fire across the Jumna.
Heat radiates from the rocks around us. There is not a
breath of air: no freshness, no scent of spring nor any
of its kindly qualities. Spring doesn't exist in India
proper, as a matter of fact, nor does chivalry (save
among the Rajput nation), nor the custom of saying,

"Thank you." This is a hard saying, but (here is another bromide!) India is a land of contrasts, and although there seems no kindliness on the surface, its people are as well-mannered and as warm-hearted as any on this earth.

But the heat—the stifling heat of this April evening! Here, under our noses, is the first fact about India : her climate. The devastating effect of climate is a factor in all her problems, the common denominator to which every ideal and every effort must be reduced.

Consider the case of "Paget M.P."—immortalized by Kipling—who flips through the peninsula in a month and talks of it for a lifetime. He feels that he must get to know the real India. He meets a distinguished Bengali barrister, a Bombay merchant prince, a politician or two at Delhi, and various English officials. And he gets an invitation to an Indian home, where a garland of marigolds is put over his fat neck, and he eats pilaff, sees a nautch, tries a lime-leaf, and (greatly daring) the dissipation of a betel-nut. India of the intelligentsia has no mysteries for him now. There remains the purdah: Mrs. "Paget M.P." explores, and reports that the ladies behind the veil are interested in Paris fashions. His heart swells with generous impulses for the kindly and cultured Indians. He feels, like many others, that he would like to devote the rest of his life to their cause —from England, of course. Having plumbed the problems of the high-brows, there only remains the study of the masses—those poor inarticulate millions for whom

The Taj Mahal.   Perhaps the most gracious and graceful tribute ever paid by a man to the memory of a woman. Built by a Moghul emperor for his queen, a Persian princess.

The great moghuls of India used to entertain their courts by making people jump into this eighty-foot well. Men became so expert that there grew up a race of hereditary well-jumpers.

he already sees himself writing and speaking, a champion of the oppressed.

He sets out in his car one bright winter morning, with his interpreter. As he skims under an avenue of stately trees he reflects what a fine and bracing climate it is. Sheeted wayfarers salaam to him as he passes. A Kim-like boy is taking some bullocks to water. A picturesque country cart makes way for him. And behind his car rises a cloud of dust, symbol of his incomprehension. But "Paget M.P." never looks back.

To his right there is the pale green of young wheat, to the left the dark boscage of a mango-grove. On the horizon are the magical Himalayas: in the middle distance white-robed figures are at work. . . . It is a brilliant and beautiful country.

He arrives at the village he has been recommended to visit. It is a snug hamlet, nestling under a banyan-tree. A picturesque green pond is near by, which Paget would be horrified to hear was drinking-water. He sees mud houses, with thresholds new-plastered with cow-dung, rows of bright cooking-pots and graceful ladies who giggle and veil their lovely eyes after one bewildering glance at "Paget M.P.," and then run away with a tinkle of silver-belled feet.

He talks to the village elders, he chats with the village schoolmaster, and distributes baksheesh to adorable round-eyed, long-lashed children.

Why isn't there better drainage and primary education in India? Why aren't there nitrogen manures and mechanical ploughs? The villagers were *keenly* interested in these things when he explained their uses in the West. What is Government doing? Half the year it frivols away its time in Simla, instead of sticking to business. What the country needs is *more energy*.

And "Paget M.P." is perfectly right. That is all India wants. Energy. Energy tingling at her finger-tips. But, friend of ours on Hindu Rao's house, who is going to supply this energy? Do you think the British haven't tried?

You know what a temperature of 100° is like? Well then, if you will join us on this April evening, you can imagine something—just a very little—of what the men felt like who fell here in 1857. And you can feel in your own self something at least of the conditions under which one hundred and eighty millions of people on the plains of India are living to-day.

> "The little more, how much it is !
> The little less, what worlds away !"

A little more physical understanding, less abstract sympathy. More heart, fewer files. . . . But if you have Macaulay's or "Paget M.P.'s" views that India only needs the blessings of Western civilization to become Arcadia, and that the peasants must be stirred from their "pathetic contentment" and made to bustle about like Americans or Britons on a frosty morning, in order to achieve prosperity—well, just come out and try to make them bustle. If you do you will be buried beneath the immemorial dust of India before many moons roll by.

There was a wealthy Parsee who saw that the Oriental method of coaling steamers was all wrong and should be scrapped. So he brought out the latest Western machinery to take the place of the thousands of coolies and their thousands of little baskets. But no one would operate his machines. They were erected but they were never used. Every day this Parsee still stands on the Apollo Bunder, at Bombay, looking out through his fieldglasses at his great cranes. They are covered with rust and slowly sinking into the bay. Once this Parsee was a rich man, and fat. Now he is poor, and as thin as your finger.

Delhi has become a galaxy of lights. Alipore Road is a shining streak and Viceregal Lodge is resplendent, like a fixed star around which the lesser luminaries move in their appointed manner. Beyond are the plains, stretching out like the unknown infinities of space.

We are at the center of a little universe, in the midst of the houses of the citizens, and soldiers, and rulers, that have clustered around this ancient Ridge, this lodestar of Hindustan, ever since the world was young.

And to-morrow we go out into the land that lies dark before us, to learn more of this country of splendor and squalor, mud hovels and Taj Mahals, pullulating populations and peopleless wastes: of savage tribes like the

Khonds that still offer human sacrifice, and of thinkers more deep than the mind of the West can apprehend, such as the Brahmins, from whose ancestors of long ago came so much of the thought that blossoms in men's brains to-day.

CHAPTER XX

THE MEN WHO KEEP INDIA GOING

THE Indian soldier, to those who just met him casually in the World War, seemed a gentle, solemn creature, clemmed with cold in winter but cheerful enough in a stately sort of way when the sun was shining. Few of the Allied forces got to know him; he remained to the end an enigma, fulfilling the general idea of the "inscrutable East." The only general exceptions were the Gurkas, hillmen of Nepal, who seemed to assimilate Western mentality in a way impossible to the other soldiers of the vast Indian Empire.

Ninety per cent of the martial races of Hindustan are agriculturalists, pure and simple. Round-eyed, hulking yokels, with a gait acquired from following a plough, and wits about as bright as those of the buffaloes they drive, they came down to the recruiting-centers in northern India to take the bread of the Sirkar, for the following reasons:

1. Because it is their custom to have a soldier in the family.

2. To see life, or to avoid getting mixed up in some village love-affair.

3. To be with their friends or relations.

The last is a strong and common motive. Regiments have territorial connections to an extent rare in any other army. It is quite common to find a whole village enlisting in a certain unit. An Indian officer with landed property has gathered all his friends and retainers into his organization; here he rules as a cheerful autocrat. The men are his men, and he doesn't let them forget it on parade. But in the evening, when the day's work is done, the soldiers of the morning are human again. They squat around him in his house, cough at their cigarettes, tell doubtful stories, fill his hubble-bubble, massage his toes, gobble his rice and drink sweet tea, jabber about water-rates and the autumn harvest and how the sahib damned them on parade, and so-and-so's long dog-bitch, and the price of flour—and generally make themselves at home.

In some irregular corps, troopers and privates have been seen to light a cigarette during a stand-easy, and then hand it to their troop or platoon commander for a puff or two, but this sort of thing naturally doesn't happen under the eye of their British officer. Under British discipline there is strict propriety on parade, but in barracks the "happy family" idea is very prevalent, and the British have never been able to convince the

Indian that officers and N.C.O.'s should keep aloof from the men. It just isn't done.

Stupid and slow and strong the recruit arrives. He is looked over, "vetted," and his name is registered. . . . Then he is given khaki "shorts," which seem skimpy and indecent compared to the ample folds of white in which he has been accustomed to clothe his nether limbs. This fellow is from the North, and not a scantily clad native of Bengal or the South. Later, his protesting feet are crowded into ammunition-boots and for weeks he walks about like a penguin. For long months, also, he marches and counter-marches with his fellows, wields a rifle, learns the mystery of aiming, stares at hieroglyphs on a blackboard and scratches unwillingly on a slate (among the Pathans, for instance, there is still a prevalent belief that any learning, save the learning by rote of the Holy Koran, has a deleterious effect on brain and body), while every now and then a sahib watches him at drill, corrects his aiming-practice, smiles on his slate, weighs him. . . . When first the sahib came near, he used to shiver, and become inarticulate with awe. But gradually the sahib takes form and shape as a human being. One day the recruit goes to the mess on an errand and sees other sahibs, of whose existence he was unaware, sitting about in deep arm-chairs, holding sheets of paper in front of their faces.

There comes an auspicious day at last when he is

passed into the first division of recruits, the senior squad.
Now an ogre of a man—a brother Pathan—makes every
minute of his morning's work a torment. He is roared
at, reviled, and sometimes, when no one's looking,
soundly cuffed. This ogre is the drill-sergeant. In a week
or so the ogre has worked his magic. The recruit is ready
to become a soldier of the king. There comes an inspection by the adjutant. Then one evening he learns that to-
morrow the colonel will see the squad. Far into the night,
by the light of a wick smoking in a bowl of cocoanut oil,
our recruit polishes boots and belt. The auspicious day
dawns; the great gray grizzled man glares and stares;
the horrible hour goes by like a flash. As in a dream
the recruit learns that he is now a soldier tried and
proven. Then come maneuvers, long days in the sun
and dust, and at night the bivouac where he rolls himself up with a friend in several blankets and sleeps the
sleep of the just. . . .

In April the leave-season opens and he returns to his
northern village, where the spring is sweet and the roses
are in bloom, and the merchants pass by with silks and
ivories and the gazelle-eyed girls of Kashmir, on the way
to Kabul.

There is no army in the world with such liberal leave-
rules. Many of the soldiers of the Indian army own their
own land, and unless they were given frequent leaves
of absence to see to their crops they would not serve at
all. Two and a half months' holiday out of twelve is

the average; less than this would mean loss, or even ruin, in byre and homestead.

The pay is not very good (less than a dollar and a half a week, besides food and clothes) but no one, from the gorgeous staff-officer who sits at his desk in Simla to the sweating recruit in the plains, chooses the army as his career with the idea of making money, or if he does he ought to be in the booby-hatch.

Of late, strenuous efforts have been made in the army in the cause of education. All over the world, the potential value of the soldier in civil life has been recognized; in this respect India is in the forefront of the times. About $250,000 a year is budgeted for to educate Jack Sepoy. At the Indian Army School of Education in Belgaum it is hoped to start a model village where the one hundred and sixty student-instructors may learn the soundest ideas in agriculture and sanitation. At Dehra Dun is situated the Royal Military Academy, to prepare the sons of Indian gentlemen for commissions in the army. Both Jhelum and Jullundur have instituted a King George's Indian Military School for six hundred boys, sons of Indian soldiers and non-commissioned officers. The new syllabus for Indian army schools has been drawn up so that every soldier shall learn something, at least, of the function of representative bodies and the value of the vote. A brightly written weekly in the vernacular, with a circulation of twelve thousand, is published for the troops. Officers and men are encouraged to write their views therein. One hundred and twenty projection-lanterns, with forty thousand slides, dealing with every conceivable subject, are being circulated to the various commands. As never before in history, the Indian soldier is being looked upon not as a fighting man only, but as a citizen who by his discipline, physique, and intelligence may be the hope of India's future.

But Jack Sepoy is not the only man who keeps India going. He has a brother who likewise receives a mere five or six shillings or so a week, and who is equally important.

"If we can win over the police, we have won India!" That is the reiterated cry of the agitators throughout the length and breadth of Hindustan. And it is quite true.

The agitators can't understand why the police refuse to be won. Indeed, it *is* something of a miracle when you consider that the pay of a police constable is eighteen rupees ($7.00) a month, out of which he has to feed himself and his family. (An American policeman usually gets at least thirty dollars a week to start on and doesn't consider himself a millionaire on that.) In addition to the poor pay there is another, more subtle, influence at work, which should alienate the loyalty of policemen, but doesn't to any appreciable degree at present. The boycott. Unless you have lived in India you can hardly realize the true terror of the boycott.

You are dependent on the barber to shave you, the village washerman to wash for you, the tinker, the tailor, and a host of others. Suddenly, you are deprived of all the services that only society can render you, and which you lose caste by doing for yourself. It sounds quite simple to get your wife to wash your pocket-handkerchiefs, but it isn't at all simple. Her big brother comes along and wants to know why you are bringing disgrace on the family. You are tied down by caste regulations, and it is just here that the boycott gets you. To their infinite honor, the Indian police have done their duty in the face of moral as well as physical threats.

Brutality, corruption, "Russian methods," are constant charges against the police. Now there is no doubt that at any rate until a few years ago the torture of under-trial prisoners existed. Also bribery was not, and is not, unknown. It would be surprising if it was unknown. And a very little explanation will show why these things should be.

As the shell is to the tortoise, so is the armor of untruth to the Indian witness. Without some form of physical suasion, it is extraordinarily hard to get at the facts of the case. In the old days instant death, or for more trifling cases, summary mutilation, was the punishment awarded to any one who wasted the time of the court with vain words and false witness. But now this is no longer permitted. The mild Hindu can exercise his imagination as much as he wants to.

"Of course, I didn't tell the truth," protested a peasant lately, when taxed with perjury. "What do you
think I went into the witness-box for?" It is with people
like this that the police have to deal. In many districts
armed thieves and rascals of every description are on
the increase. To get evidence against them is next to
impossible. The only way to track down the gang is to
make any of their number apprehended reveal the where-
abouts of the rest.

In the old days a red-hot gun-barrel would have been
applied to the prisoner's person, or starving rats would
have been set to niggle his navel. But the sahibs never
approved of these methods, and have abolished them,
so that now they are things of the past. Some blandish-
ment has to be devised that will not leave a mark. Even
so, it is a risky business, for if the police are caught
putting pressure on a prisoner or a witness, heavy pun-
ishments await them. Still, there is no doubt that many
and ingenious experiments have been made in the privacy of the under-trial cell, experiments in refined and
civilized torture, many of which have been lost to the
world, alas! because the geniuses who invented them
were illiterate and unable to record them for the benefit of posterity.

Some, however, are remembered and known: notably
"trial by trampling beetle," which is supposed never to
have failed to produce the desired effect. The procedure
was simple. An empty cocoanut was placed on the bare

stomach of the victim. In the cocoanut was a large beetle.
The beetle just tramped around and around. That was
all. But the maddening reiteration of its tread, and its
slow and persistent efforts to find a way out, so worked
on the nerve-centers of the tramplee that after an hour
or so of the nervous strain he was ready to tell anything
he knew, and sometimes much that he did not. Here,
of course, is one of the difficulties: you can loosen a
sullen tongue by deprivation of sleep, beating on the
knuckles, or letting water drip for a few hours on the
back of the patient's neck (all these methods are quite
simple, leave no mark, and reduce the most hardened
criminal to a wreck), but how are you to ensure that the
sullen tongue, once wagging, will tell the truth?

Indeed, this difficulty is insurmountable, and therefore torture is seldom resorted to even in privacy. A
good criminal counsel is "briefed" instead, which is
only a still more subtle form of torture than the creeping
cockroach. No constable nowadays would dare to give
evidence by illicit methods if there was the slightest
chance of being found out. If he tried to do so he would
be fired, and lose his one dollar fifty a week in next to
no time.

As to corruption, which undoubtedly exists, it must
be remembered that the Oriental can do nothing without
baksheesh. A thoroughly honest official makes the poor
Indian feel uncomfortable. He suspects that there is a
catch somewhere. It reassures him greatly to be able

to slip a silver coin into somebody's palm. Bribing the
police in India is a sacred custom. As beer is to the
British workman, as popcorn is to the baseball fan, so
is baksheesh to our Aryan brother. He would just hate
to have to get along without it.

There are 193,000 policemen in the 247 million square
miles of British India, excluding the native states. That
is to say, there is one policeman to every 1,250 people,
or to every five and a half square miles. And there is
only one white officer to every thousand native policemen. Each police group covers a territory of the average
size of Rhode Island, often with no railway, and with
perhaps only one improved road in the whole district.
Everywhere else they travel by horseback and are out
of touch with the telegraph. These are a few facts that
people don't realize when they talk of the corruption
of the police. The real fact is, the British have achieved
a miracle of order and integrity. They haven't advertised
their difficulties, that's all, but it *is* a miracle, none the
less, that so few men, so poorly paid, should keep India
"safe for the agitator."

It is the Indian police (and back of them Jack Sepoy
and the latent power of the white troops garrisoning
the country) on whom law and order rest. It is they who
"keep the place going."

But what of the famous Indian Civil Service, you
ask? Are they not the real rulers of India? They get the
press notices, the eulogies of the premier, and most of

the credit when things are going well. But rulers! No, that went with the first post-war reform scheme, a few years ago. They are magnificent men. It is not their fault that they have lost the old control over their districts.

The police get most of the kicks and few of the annas and rupees that fall to the lot of the administrators of a district, but they don't complain. Their work is absorbingly interesting, especially in the Intelligence section, which deals with crime on the grand scale. This year has been a testing period for the Indian constable. The police are having an anxious time weathering the foaming rocks of anarchy, which are always to the lee of a young democracy.

CHAPTER XXI

BABUS, BAKSHEESH, AND BUREAUCRATS

GOOD WILL between white men and brown keeps the Indian Empire together. Its existence is often questioned, but it does exist, none the less, else India would infallibly disrupt. Experiments in a crude democracy, such as those initiated by the British of late, have undoubtedly lessened the sympathy between the two races, but there is still a good deal of common sense on both sides, in spite of the politicians. It is the soldiers and the subalterns and the merchants and the minor officials, then, who ballast the Indian ship of state. In the last resort, the relationship between the two countries is a human one, and would not exist a day if the ordinary Indian didn't really rather like the ordinary Englishman.

There are about fifteen hundred men—Indian civil servants—in whose hands the administration of the country actually rests. Of these, about five hundred are employed on various jobs (revenue, railways, census, industry, political, etc.), while of the remaining thousand, some are judges and the remainder district officers.

The district officer is the most severely tested bureaucrat in the world. His district is often as large as a State of the American Union, while the people in his charge may speak several different languages and belong to twenty or more religions. Their civilizations may range from cannibalism to Calcutta University degrees.

The young "civilian" starts life comfortably. He arrives at the age of twenty-two, full of ideals and English beef, and is made an assistant collector on a salary of about $2,500 per annum. He is known as the "stunt sahib," which is short for assistant, and learns all about the proper people to shake hands with, and who is to be offered a chair, and Oriental circumlocution, and other abominations of the heathen, as well as something of the world in general and of his own province in particular.

At first he is graded as a third-class magistrate, with powers of imprisonment extending to a month, but he soon rises to be a second-class and then a first-class magistrate, with powers of imprisonment up to two years, or a fine of $300, or both. After ten years' service his pay will be $5,000 a year, rising to about $10,000 after twenty years. After twenty-five years he can retire on a pension of $5,000 per annum. He is then under fifty years of age, but generally speaking old for his years, owing to the climate and the nervous strain.

The Indian civilian is a descendant of the picturesque potentates of the Moghul era, and the English nabobs of the East India Company's time, who traded and ruled and fought for half their lives in India, and then came home with big fortunes and bigger livers.

The present-day civilian regulates his life on less romantic lines, but something of the gorgeous past clings to his office as magistrate, collector of revenue, and representative of the king.

"He reigns supreme within his little state,
His smile sheds honour and his frown means fate!"

Around the central star revolve a galaxy of resplendent but poorly paid officials. No Duke of Plaza Toro ever had more sycophantic followers than the Indian district officer!

On the revenue side comes a superintendent ($2,000 per annum) of land records, an inspector ($500), a revenue officer ($60), for every group of villages, and lesser officials, on the principle that "little fleas have lesser fleas upon their backs to bite 'em"—until at last the peasant pays his dues. The lesser revenue officials are not as poor as they might seem with their amazing emoluments of one pound a month, for they are mostly professional letter-writers, recorders, notaries, forgers, or money-lenders.

On the legal side there is a whole yard-full of pleaders, each marshaling his own crowd of bought witnesses, and, inside the court, readers, more pleaders, police ushers, court messengers, punkha-coolies, sweepers, men

to splash water on mat screens during the day-heat, and
men to bring water for the men who splash, and a little
boy to change the pen-nibs and the blotting-paper,
called the "daftri," and last but possibly not least, the
litigants themselves. Then there is the office staff, with
a superintendent on $1,000 per annum, two assistants on
$500 each, an individual called a "wasl-baqui-navis,"
or "writer of arrears of rent," who keeps track of un-
decided revenue litigation, and various minor clerks,
down to the farrash, or inkpot-filler.

Then come four personal and eight public messengers
resplendent in crimson coats, and the official tent-pitchers
dressed in gray. The pay of all these public servants is
fixed at $50 a year. This is all in addition to the private
and particular staff of servants of an English gentleman
in India. A district officer will have at least fifty. No
wonder there is yet another official on his staff, called
the "nazir" ($125 per annum), in charge of petty dis-
bursements.

Besides looking after his servants, administering the
law, collecting the revenue, the district officer is also
the nominal head of the police in his district—

> "The good Magistrate, our Rulers say
>   Decides all night, investigates all day,
>   The crack Collector, man of equal might,
>   Reports all day and corresponds all night.
>   Oh, could I raise my fascinated eyes,
>   From Salt, Stamps, Cesses, Income Tax, Excise,

> Could I with Janus, boast a double face
> Incongruous scenes alternately to grace,
> To twin tribunals twin delights afford,
> Please the High Court and gratify the Board,
> Then all were well and I might touch the goal,
> A round square man within a square round hole!"

When our civilian gets to his club at about seven o'clock on a hot-weather evening, after twelve hours' work with the temperature at 130° Fahrenheit, he has earned the whisky and soda and the rubber of bridge with the sessions judge, policeman, and civil surgeon, who make up the hot-weather population of Dustipore. What a life!

Yet the old civilians liked it. They were doing big work in those days, and they thought that their work was going to endure. Lord Irwin and Sir John Simon were school-boys then, and probably neglecting their history. Now the old order changeth and giveth place to the new democracy, and the Indian Civil Service will remain a magnificent tradition.

"Do you think much bribery goes on among your subordinates?" we asked a collector recently. "I think not," he answered. "I cover a good few miles a week, as you know"—we were at the moment on tour riding along the tow-path of a canal in a remote country district—"and any one who wants to make a petition or complaint is always free to come to me."

"But they have to bribe your servants before they

can see you," we suggested. "Not in my case," said the collector. "I know how common bribery is, but thank goodness I have an old servant—this fellow with my fly-whisk—whom I can absolutely trust. He goes with me always, and I know the dear old boy wouldn't take a penny, even if he was offered it on bended knees." "Wouldn't he?" we said, looking with some interest at the old graybeard who followed the collector's horse.

"Yes, indeed, I'd trust him with—" At that dramatically chosen instant a native flung himself across the collector's path. The collector dismounted and inquired what was the matter.

"At last I can speak to you," faltered the villager. "Long have I been trying to get my case heard."

"What was your difficulty?" asked the collector kindly.

"The difficulty," said the peasant, indicating the aged sub-official, "was that man. He wants more money than I possess to take me to you. I am a poor man, sahib. You are my father and mother, and the threshold to prosperity!"

CHAPTER XXII
WATER-WIZARDS

NOW the British have been blamed for a lot of things since they came to India—from the perfidy of Clive to the failure of the monsoon, but no one up to date has accused them of not building railways and canals. True, even these efforts of theirs have been a cause of murmuring.

Napoleon said that an army marches on its belly. The same may be said of nations. Food is the first factor in national prosperity.

Now in India, as elsewhere, the cry of the intelligentsia is for education. Laudable as this desire may be, man must eat, whatever happens. A rich intellectual pabulum won't keep any one alive. Plenty of food is even more important than plenty of professors. There is no department more important, therefore, at any rate in the desert area of India, than that of irrigation. "You can't fill people's minds until you fill their insides," an irrigation officer told us.

The railway is a vulgar child of this age of steel, prejudicial to caste and the contemplative life. But al-

though it is the work of the Satanic Government, the
public prefer it to the idyllic ox-cart of the Golden
Age. So with canals. At first people liked them. The
great efforts that were so successfully made to bring
barren districts under cultivation, and to produce prosperity and material welfare where formerly had been
a few filthy camelmen in an arid waste of sand and
thorn—these things were perhaps dimly appreciated and
understood. But later the patriot got to work. He saw
Mother Ganges being asked to fertilize fields. Alien
engineers dammed and diverted her sacred waters. Was
such an indignity to be permitted? No! A thousand
times no! Near Hardwar, in deference to popular prejudice, a gap six feet wide has to be left in a certain
weir so as not to cramp the style of Mother Ganges.

Later, the social student came along. He said that
irrigation was bad for the people. Prosperity enervated
them, in fact. They should go back to the ways of their
fathers and lead a fine open-air life in their rag tents
among the camel-thorn. No one paid much attention to
the social reformer, however, until the theorist appeared,
who explained that soon the land would be water-logged
and breed terrible miasmas. His attitude we will dis-
cuss below.

But the irrigation department was undeterred by fad-
dists. Having set its hand to the plough in those days of
forty and fifty years ago when the big canals were
mooted, it has never once looked back.

As a result of this work India has at present 60,000 miles of canals (more than twice as much as would girdle the earth at the equator) and irrigates thirty million acres. This last figure conveys nothing to any one, of course; still, it licks creation so far as irrigated areas go. The next on the list is America, who when she develops and completes her pending projects will have three and one-quarter million acres under irrigation. While on the subject of the biggest things on earth, we may state that the Bandardarah Dam near Bombay holds up two hundred and seventy feet of water, while the Arrowrock Dam in the United States, which is three hundred feet deep, cannot really claim to be bigger because at least a hundred feet of its depth is merely mud. Anyway, India intends building a dam on the Sutlej River to hold up four hundred feet of water. This colossal project will irrigate the desert state of Bikaner and electrify half the Punjaub from Delhi to Lyallpur. The cost may be seven million pounds sterling; the acreage it will serve will be three millions, more than all the land at present irrigated in America.

Then there is the Sukkur Barrage on the Indus. It will cost twelve millions sterling and cultivate five million acres.

Taking it by and large, the Indian irrigation department has on hand as much work as it has already completed—say, another twenty-five million acres, which makes fifty million acres in all. Fifty million pounds

sterling are at present invested in canals yielding the
profitable return of nine per cent, and possibly another
fifty million will be required to complete the good work.
That finishes the figures! . . .

If you will look at a map of the Punjaub you will
see the towns of Lahore and Jhelum about one hundred
and fifty miles apart. Thirty years ago all the country
between these two towns was a waterless desert. Not only
that between the two cities, but the whole tract west-
ward for two hundred miles to the Indus River. Thirty
thousand square miles of country (say, the southern
counties of England) were absolutely barren. They
supported neither man nor beast save an occasional long-
haired camelman and his supercilious thorn-eating
flock. Now this land is a fertile and populous district.
In its center the flourishing town of Lyallpur bids fair
to rival in a decade or two the capital, Lahore. Every
one in India has heard of the canal colonies: how a wilderness was made into a garden, almost overnight, certainly as quickly as ever Moghul of old transplanted a
population to serve a whim. But outside India people
hardly realize the work of the British water-wizards.

Now these Moghuls of modern times who have
worked the miracle are just ordinary men. Just beef-
eating, whisky-drinking Englishmen who smoke pipes
and play tennis and will be retired with their propor-
tionate pension as soon as it is possible to replace them
by Indians.

These are the men who have done so much to lessen famine in India. There hasn't been a serious famine for twenty years. Every year perfects the arrangements to prevent it. Roads, railways, and canals link province with province. They have made India a country. Given time they will make it a nation, in spite of the Indians!

But there is the theorist still to be met—he who finds sermons in stones and books in running brooks and anopheles in aqueducts, and asserts that the Kingdom of Babylon sank into insignificance owing to its mosquito-breeding waters.

Now in the reign of the good King Charles there lived a certain Doctor Brown who wrote a book called "Vulgar Errors." In his day the "vulgar" had erroneous notions about quite a number of things, from the habits of beavers to the olfactory peculiarities of Jews. "All Jewes do stinke" was a maxim in those days that the good Doctor Brown found it very difficult to dislodge from the public mind. He quoted facts and figures and expended much ingenuity and eloquence on behalf of the chosen race, but we doubt whether he convinced any one in King Charles's time.

So with the irrigation-fever myth. It sounds plausible. That it is not in accord with facts is no reason in the public mind why it shouldn't be true. Yet for the last decade and more careful statistics of the survival-rate and general stamina of the population of canal colonies have been kept, and the figures show conclusively that

the population in irrigated districts, being more prosperous, is superior in physique to the people of the ad-
jacent barren lands.

These are the facts. Whether they will convince any
one we don't know, and, to tell the truth, we don't much
care.

CHAPTER XXIII
SERVANTS TO HIS HIGHNESS THE SAHIB

WHEN you hear that you can get a valet or butler at board wages of from two to three dollars a week it certainly sounds cheap, but then no one outside India can realize how little work a human being can do, and how many servants it is necessary to keep, and what a lot of looking after they require.

There used to be a hereditary class of servants in India who took pride in their work, but they are getting rare. They are all old men now. Their sons go to school and wear "khaddar," which is a peculiar sort of cloth made in India that Mr. Ghandi decreed that his followers should wear in order to save India from the blight of the Manchester capitalist.

The old hereditary servants used to serve a race of Englishmen who are becoming as extinct as they: the "burra sahibs" of the days when vast fortunes were made and men of vast ambition came to India. The modern Englishman, with his regular pay and regular leave to England, prefers the deft Portuguese servant, or the merry Mug, to the old whiskered waiters of Lucknow, or the stately Hindu Kahar, both of whom have their pride and their prejudices. The old servant moved with dignity in a large dim house where there were softly swinging punkhas and softly speaking lady sahibs and masters who sat long over their brandy pawnee of an evening. All that is changed. Cars, cocktails, short skirts, short leaves to England. Life is not what it was. As well ask the giant tortoise to travel by subway express as to expect old Rustum Beg to adapt himself to a modern household.

Rustum Beg's day is done, and he knows it. There is a thing called "education," which he does not possess and despises as being bad for the brain and subversive to true religion, and which is his stumbling-block. Without it nothing can be done nowadays. His son cannot even get a little post under Government without passing some absurd examination.

And so Rustum Beg pinches and saves (especially pinches) in order to send his son to school. The Government exists for the people, as the sahibs are never tired of declaring. In other words, it exists for the purpose of finding employment for his relatives. Surely that is logical. Any one whose brain has not been vitiated by the fumes of alcohol and the flesh of swine could see that. . . . He squats in his cool bottle-khana polishing the glasses and breathing at his hubble-bubble, whose bamboo stem is never far from his lips, although as a Muslim he should abjure such things. But the old order

changeth, he says. He can no longer be strict. There
is a race of monkeys abroad in the land, black babus
and white babus, who worship a god called "Democracy," forgetting that there is no God but God.

Old Yusuf Ali, the cook, agrees with Rustum Beg.
He has grown gray in service, and although he hasn't
learnt to cook an omelette decently, he certainly makes
astounding curries and luscious pilaffs. He has a large
packet of testimonials, wrapped in a blue handkerchief and strongly scented with snuff, to show what
a fine fellow he was when Queen Victoria was young.
Since those days sahibs have become hurried and exact-
ing.

The last "chit" he got was worded thus:

"Yusuf Ali has served me as cook for three weeks.
I can cordially recommend him to any one who wants
a man to do him thoroughly well. He leaves owing to
illness (my illness)."

A fine chit, and yet, by Allah who seeth into men's
hearts, there was something in it that caused him to be
turned from door to door until the present lady sahib
(may Allah give her increase!) decided to give him
a trial.

Jaganandranath, the bearer, or personal body-
servant, is a very understanding man, the servant *in
excelsis,* the butler beatified. The English were kindergarten kids at the butling game when India's servants
were announcing: "The soup is served, your High-

ness!" Jaganandranath's ancestors were probably sitting calmly and discreetly and placidly (just as he sits to-day) in the bottle-khana of ancient Aryans, when the present peerage of England was still skipping about in woad, shrouded only in the mists of antiquity.

Jaganandranath wears whiskers and an impenetrable reserve. Something of the splendid past of India is in his bearing. He is as silent as the grave and as slow as the giant sloth. No frailty of man can move him. Centuries of dignified service are in his mental make-up. He can make allowances for everything under the sun except vulgarity. If the sahib fell under the table after dinner Jaganandranath would carry the sahib to bed impassively. If the sahib stood on his head he would hand him his socks with as frigid a respect as he now hands him his hat. Jaganandranath is ready to do anything in reason, except to move with the times. This he respectfully but firmly refuses to do, considering it a claptrap affair of clocks, compared to which the eternal verities of Master and Man, Slave and Sultan, are as a butterfly to the Himalayas. When not brushing his master's clothes he manages a lot of servants who are not, like him, blue-blooded domestics by caste.

There is the chowkidar, for instance. He carries a spear but he has the habits and the heart of a dormouse. If a thief comes the chowkidar runs away, too terrified even to call out, unless indeed the thief is a personal friend, in which case his slumbers are not disturbed.

Then there is the bheestie, or water-man (many are the tales told of the bheestie, the humble youth whose province it is to slip into the bathrooms of princesses), and the sweeper, vilest of the vile, porter of ordure and eater of offal, who ranks mentally just below the water-buffalo; there is the musalchi or pantry-boy, the second khitmutgar who helps the first, the dressing-boy who helps Jaganandranath, and several malis or gardeners. Then each horse has two servants, one to groom it and one to give it grass. Each of these retainers has at least one wife. If she does not bear him children he takes unto himself a handmaiden, or another wife, or both. All told, the establishment of a bachelor is likely to number some fifty souls, and that of a married man double that number.

All these souls sit in the sun and sleep all they can, and scratch and squabble. But chiefly they sleep.

Their children seem born good, and are strangely quiet, and play long, long games with each other in the dust at the back of the house by the stables, and their eyes are full of the mystery of the East, which is not really mystery at all, but just a placid vacuity.

CHAPTER XXIV
ABSALOM ADRIFT

THIS new India of the mills and factories that seems to have sprung into existence overnight at a wave of some magician's wand, the India of the capitalist, is a curious and in some ways a pathetic product of our age of steel, a pathetic compromise between East and West. The clothes, the temperament, and the training of the peasant have not fitted him for a life among machines.

With his flowing robes and his sacred threads, with his long hair and frequently long beard, with a religion which asserts that the oceans were made by Vishnu churning a mountain of butter with a cow's-tail whisk—a religion, moreover, which declares that an American-made motor-truck about to drive into the small of your back is nothing but Maya, illusion—and with a boyhood spent in patching little ploughs with bits of string, it is obvious that the average peasant's aptitude for looking after a thirty-ton derrick or a fifty-spindle loom is very small. But times are changing (perhaps more in Asia than anywhere) and the coolie of this generation will be the chauffeur of the next.

Nations, like individuals, have periods of sleep and periods of activity. There is an alternation of day and night for the mass mind as for the individual consciousness. India, for instance, is at this moment awakening from centuries of slumber and adjusting herself to civilization as she finds it. The British claim that this is due to their rule, and no doubt the claim is just. The British have made it possible for India to open her eyes. And when India has yawned herself wide awake, she will clap her three hundred and twenty million hands and the mosquitoes of Western bureaucracy will disappear. The Nemesis of those who awaken sleeping giants has the Government of Delhi by the short hairs.

The chief figure in all this industrial and mechanical complication is the Indian woman, amidst looms that shuttle and belts that whirr and iron fingers that snatch at those she loves. The Indian coolie woman goes as she has gone since immemorial time, with her child in her arms. Among humming wheels and plying pistons she walks sedately through the machines behind her spouse, as, three thousand years ago, Sita followed Rama through the forests of the Vyndhya. Sedately she squats among the iron voices of Mammon. Her children crouch beside her on the floor, while she cooks her husband's lunch and hands it to him among the looms. In industrial India the unit is still the family.

The Indian looks out of place in a factory—of that there is no doubt. And his family, which he always insists on taking with him, looks even more so. In a jute-factory every inch of the floor-space is occupied by women and children, living among the legs of the workers and between the march of drive-belts. If an efficiency expert were to visit the scene, he would break out in a cold sweat and collapse on a heap of hessians, which is the polite English term for gunny-sacks.

In all the factories we visited, a host of babies squatted, scrabbling on the floor, making messes and mud pies and staring at the foolish grown-up game of Industry with collyrium-ringed eyes.

Occasionally a child puts his finger into a reciprocating part. The mother is philosophical about this. The goddess Kali has claimed the little one. She hopes for better luck with the next. So far, no employer of labor has cared to interfere with the privilege of the mothers, and we hope they never will. Of safety devices there are a plenty, but we doubt whether they do much good, as also whether the "safety first" protagonists of Europe and America have a very practical field of effort in Indian industry. "Safety first!" . . . It is a slogan with little enthusiasm behind it.

Yet the present system in India works. It is the only system for India to-day. If any manufacturer tried to interfere with family life he would get no workmen, and as a matter of fact, accidents are few. The two commonest causes of injury in workshops, haste and over-strain, are both absent from the Indian factory. If a

workman likes to take a day off, or a week off for a
pilgrimage, nothing is said. Labor is not expected to
work more than four or perhaps five days a week, and
is paid accordingly. And if a Sikh mechanic likes to
keep his hair as long as Absalom's, and a few tufts get
tangled with the whirling machinery and are woven
into a jute bag by mistake, no one minds—except the
Sikh!

The Tata Iron and Steel Company is probably the
most up-to-the-minute organization in India, and is certainly the biggest employer of labor. At present there
are 35,000 men at work over an area of twenty-five
square miles. Their pay-roll is nearly $300,000 a month.
Pay of the unskilled laborer ranges from $4\frac{1}{2}$ annas to
12 annas a day (an anna being about two and a half
cents), while the higher grade receives from 30 to 90
rupees a month ($10 to $30). Executives receive from
300 to 3,000 rupees a month ($100 to $1,000), while the
chief general manager gets something like $50,000 a
year.

The city of Jamshedpur, like the "works," has grown
in the last few years, from a barren plain. In 1908 there
was nothing on the site of Jamshedpur but rocks and
trees and an aboriginal village. Mr. Jamshedji Tata
came along with the idea of starting an iron foundry.
He founded it all right, all right, at a cost in the last
fourteen years of over ten million pounds sterling, and
eventually (according to a high civil official who ought

to know) it is going to have the area, wealth, and population of sixteen Sheffields.

Subsidiary companies, to the value of about twenty-five million pounds, have been formed, namely, the Agricultural Implements Company, the Tinplate Company, the Steel Wire Company, the Enfield Cable Company, the Enamelled Ironware Company, the Peninsula Locomotive Company, and the Jute Machinery Company. When all these are working there will be a population of 120,000 in the city, of which more than 50,000 will be actually engaged in industry.

This place, like the new Delhi, was a wilderness in 1908. But see the difference between business and bureaucracy! One remains a ruin, whereas the other is a prosperous town, with a blast-furnace half a mile long, the biggest in the world. Of course, the place looks unfinished; still, you could not expect pleached alleys and old-world lawns, and the mellowness of a cathedral cloister. It is new and bright and tidy, and greatly prosperous.

Three quarters of the laborers are unskilled, and are aboriginal tribesmen and tribes-ladies, who live apart from the more skilful and civilized community, to their mutual benefit. The quarters of the tribal workingmen are no experiment in town-dwelling. It was found that aborigines were not happy except in houses that they had built with their own hands. But sanitation is imperative in a place like Jamshedpur, and the primitive folk didn't bother with things like that. So they were settled in groups of ten thousand, and each group was allotted an area of about one and a half square miles, in which they could build any sort of house they pleased, with the sole restriction that there weren't to be more than twelve houses to the acre. This plan answered excellently and every one was pleased.

There is a lot of nonsense talked about the happy savage whose happiness is turned to misery by civilization and machinery. Now gaging happiness is a difficult and delicate matter. Perhaps it is not to be judged by the "world's coarse thumb and finger" at all. But if we may venture an opinion, we would state that these savages who go singing to their work, and look happy and healthy, prefer the factory to the forest, and find it far more agreeable to shop at the Army and Navy Stores at Jamshedpur than to grub for roots and other provender in the neighboring jungle, as their fathers did, and their relations do. Anyway, they none of them want to go back to the jungle, and they turn a deaf ear to the agitators who tell them that machines are a Satanic device of the West.

A welfare commissioner, on the up-to-date American plan, looks to the benefit of every one at the works. He buys grain in bulk, getting it far cheaper than the poor could buy it. He inspects the primary schools, he trains the Boy Scouts, and inquires into any cause of complaint. Also he keeps up a Beggars' Home, at considerable expense to the company. The reason for the Beggars' Home is that a host of idle rascals come from all over India to sponge on their relations who are earning good money. Now, for the relatives it is a quasi-religious duty to care for their indigent kinsmen, no matter how preposterous their claims may be. To get over the difficulty and avoid having their employees milked dry, the company looks after all their poor relations.

The welfare commissioner is an Englishman. All the doctors, however, are natives of Bengal, and it is interesting to note that half a million persons yearly are treated in their well-kept hospitals. Every one for miles comes to be treated for every infirmity to which flesh is heir, from maternity to ingrowing toe-nails.

On schools the company are spending a lakh ($35,000) a year, and two lakhs ($70,000) on their Technical Institute. For these outgoings they should reap a tenfold reward in increased efficiency. There are two churches and an American Baptist Mission in the town—also a club, a race-course, a golf-course, and a couple of elementary polo-grounds. Outside the twenty-five square miles of town and works the forest begins, and the rivers flow. Jamshedpur is really just a clearing in the heart of a primeval forest. A day's march from the new blast-furnace wild elephants are stamping in the thickets, and tigers stalk the deer who come down to the forest pools.

The works themselves are much like any other iron and steel works. You may see the safety-valves of hell alifting, the molten ingots coming out of the mouth of the pit. And you may see a magnetic crane, strolling overhead, suddenly fascinate one of these ingots so that it leaps into her arms. . . . And you may see the crane carry off her prey to the rolling-bed, where it is stamped and punched and pulled until it becomes a girder or a steel rail. Naked natives slouch about with oil-cans, their offspring mewling on the floor. Here and there a white man, blue-jeans-clad, clean-shaven, tobacco-chewing, stands by titanic levers.

India is opening her eyes and looking out onto the new and wonderful world of the twentieth century. She is studying its inventions and resources in her own quiet, Oriental way. Soon she will mine her own coal, cast her own steel, make all her own clothes. India will become an industrial nation. Already the cotton-mills of Bombay and the jute-factories of Calcutta are an earnest of a new country of loom and shuttles and mine that has arisen among the nations of the earth. Towns are springing up out of the forest scrub to supply the needs of the army of semi-nude aboriginal tribesmen who are the parents of the skilled craftsmen of the future. In Calcutta and Bombay there are great labor settlements. Factories and refining-plants are springing up all over the country, even as far north as

Rawalpindi, where the Attock Oil Company has tapped
an immense accumulation of high-grade fuel.

Meanwhile, the mills and factories are paying dividends of one hundred per cent, and the Scotchmen and
Parsees who own them are worried to death about paying the supertax.

Nor is the industrial awakening of India confined to
any one district: throughout the Punjaub also the inex-
orable laws of economics are driving men from the
plough to the work-bench. Very curious it is to see boys
whose childhood has been spent in twisting buffaloes'
tails and digging their toes into the tenderest parts of
these docile animals, learning to control newer methods
of locomotion, and trying to develop a light hand on the
steering-wheel and a delicate touch on the throttle.

Clumsy, careless, heavy-handed, but earnest, tenacious, and sober, the Indian has made up his mind to
be a mechanic. Not one or two, nor one or two thousands, but about one hundred million Indians (although they may not know it themselves as yet) have
determined to be mechanics.

Industrial India is still very young. No Indian child
(or very few) has had time to grow up in a factory and
be a workman in his turn. He has not yet learnt the hereditary and highly paid craft of the steel-worker or the
tinsmith. But he will. And when once the three hundred
and twenty millions of India, or even one per cent of

them, take to machines, the fabled gold of Ormuz and of Ind will be nothing to the huge material prosperity of the country.

If India really becomes Industrial India, its enormous buying power will affect all the markets of the world. In the next decade this emergence of Industrial India is going to be one of the big things in history.

CHAPTER XXV

A PARLIAMENT IN PYJAMAS

HE would be a bold Bolshevik who would attempt with poison gas or propaganda to run the gauntlet of the gold and crimson "chaprassies" who guard the gates of India's experiment in democracy—the Legislative Assembly at Delhi.

Slow and stately attendants in the gorgeous liveries of Moghul times precede us up the stairway and bow us into the Strangers' Gallery. It is five minutes to the hour. Already the more punctual members are slipping softly into their numbered seats. Here in this austere auditorium are assembling the representatives of a hundred races, sleek babus from Bengal, Parsees in long white coats and black-lacquer hats, Muhammadans in red fezes and golden pugris, bearded Sikhs in towering white turbans, a tall Pathan with the mustachios and swagger of his fighting race, Jains, Mahrattas, Moplahs, and English merchants, all men successful in business, law, or husbandry. An air of Whitehall solidity and ordered repose has been wrought into this chamber by its British architects.

But who is that hairy-looking member who has just taken his seat? He looks for all the world like Pithecanthropus erectus. Possibly he represents one of the aboriginal tribes of Behar and Orissa. His brows are furrowed in thought. In his countenance we seem to see the wisdom of an earlier age as he stares at the Speaker's chair. He is about to rise to some point of order. But no, the Assembly is not yet in session. What a nervous fellow he is! He's reaching for his notes. No! I believe he is scratching himself. Now he has put his paw in the inkpot, and curled his tail up over the back of the seat.

Here comes one of the pompous scarlet chaprassies, moving with more agility and less dignity than usual. The self-appointed member skips over the benches and with a chatter of disgust bounds out of the august assembly. Fortunate it is that the president has not yet taken his seat, for had a stranger been observed during roll-call grave complications might have ensued, since the simian is a sacred creature in the eyes of the majority of the members of this body. On the other hand, if he had not bolted in such a hurry he might have been entertained in the lobby with milk and peanuts.

Enter the president. The members of India's rainbow Assembly rise to greet the commanding figure of an Englishman in his dark robes and white, full-bottomed wig. A Yorkshireman, a journalist, a politician, and a distinguished member of Parliament, as president of this polygot Oriental legislature he seems to the manner born. His stately manner and charming voice contribute largely to the dignity of its deliberations.

In the matter of style and title this legislature is the most prolific on earth. Such mouthfuls as Bhupatiraju Venkatapatiraju Garu and Rai Bahadur Patri Venkata Srinivasa Rao Pantulu Garu, etc., must be constantly on the president's lips. But they do not daunt him in the least. He enunciates them with a mellifluous ease that is the wonder of old officials and the envy of the young ones.

Of the legislators on the floor below us a hundred and three are elected members, chosen by an electorate made up of one and one-half per cent of the people of India. Forty other members are hand-picked by Government. Naturally these latter call for little comment. One of them, the finance member, looks like Lord Curzon and succeeds in preserving the Oxford manner of that great pro-consul, whatever the deficit in his budget may be.

The honorable law member, Dr. Tej Bahadur Sapru, immaculate in his morning-coat, is the sartorial cynosure of the Assembly, rivaled only by the bird-like grace of Mr. Bradley-Birt of Calcutta and the more massive magnificence of Prince Afsar-ul-Mulk Mirza Muhammad Akram Hosain Bahadur, a royal scion of the dynasty of Oudh.

These legislators before us, serious of mien and gay

of costume, have divided themselves into two parties, albeit parties that as yet are not very sharply defined. They call themselves "Nationalists" and "Democrats." The former may be roughly described as adherents of the established order, while the latter provide the fly in the ointment. But in the present flux of Indian political opinions these distinctions are somewhat arbitrary.

The gentleman with the melodious, hypnotic voice now addressing the Speaker is Sir Sivaswamy Aiyer, one of the leaders of the National party. Not only is he a good speaker but my British friends tell me that he is thoroughly sound in his theories and policies, from an Anglo-Saxon point of view. He has a following of about forty members.

There are two leaders in the Democratic party. The first is Rao Bahadur Tiruvenkata Rangachariar, a clever lawyer who looks like the Hindu god Ganesha, the Remover of Obstacles. He himself seems to be more accomplished at creating obstacles than removing them, for he is a radical in politics, although like all good Brahmins he is an ardent conservative in everything connected with social custom. His rival is Dr. H. S. Gour, a serious, nondescript-looking man with a bullet head who lacks something of the adroitness of his high-caste Madrasi fellow-Democrat.

Although the majority of the members take themselves and their new political duties with profound seriousness, one of the Bengali representatives made a remark on the floor of the Assembly one day that did not increase his popularity with his fellow-members. Said this bland babu from Bengal:

"You know my house is just across the road from an insane asylum, and every time I enter this Assembly I feel as though I have simply walked across the road from my home."

Mr. Jamnadas Dwarkadas, who has just risen and is speaking easily and fluently with an extremely self-confident manner, has a white scarf thrown negligently across his throat. He is a Theosophist and a disciple of Mrs. Annie Besant, of whose most moderate and most constructive views he is an able exponent. This erect, electric figure may go far in Indian politics. He seems to have the vision of the East and the energy and capacity of the West. What a pity that the silver voice and silver hair of Mrs. Besant are not here to adorn the Assembly! Perhaps purdah-politics and the admission to the legislature of women like Mrs. Besant, and Miss Sorabji, the distinguished Parsee educator of Poona, will be India's next experiment.

Below us, with mysterious cabalistic scars on his head, sits a gentleman in a light suit with large black checks. The first day he wore that costume it came near being responsible for setting fire to the Assembly auditorium. On his way to the session his braces broke. The keeper of a little stall in the bazaar saw his signals of distress and loaned him a rainbow-colored comforter, which he tied about his waist. But before reaching the Secretariat Buildings, he slipped in a puddle of water and got the comforter soaking wet. Upon his arrival he threw the comforter over a radiator to dry and slipped into his seat holding up his trousers with his hands. Ten minutes later there was an odor of burning cloth, and when the legislators turned they saw their portly fellow-member holding up his trousers with both hands and jumping up and down on a blazing comforter.

Right over there across the auditorium from us, like Humpty and Dumpty, sit the two members from Malabar, one a Muhammadan Moplah whose jungle constituency was responsible for the rebellion in Malabar, while beside him is the gentle Hindu representing constituents whom the Moplah's electors were forcibly converting to Islam by massacre.

Sheikh Abdul Majid, the Delhi sweetmeat-seller whose election was a leg-pull of the Non-coöperators, sits at the back of the Assembly near the door, mumbling in his beard. He wears slippers and a scrubby fez. He doesn't understand a word of English, so his thoughts are centered on his little shop, where the flies buzz around the lolly-pops under the clock-tower in the Chadni Chowk. He wishes he were there now among his sticky sweets. But the watchful eye of the Democratic whip, Mr. Padamji Pestonji Ginwala, will brook no diminution of duty. Hour after hour he is constrained to listen to a language he dislikes and to debates that he doesn't understand. And all for twenty rupees a day! "Isn't life an omelet?" thinks Sheikh Abdul Majid.

This Chadni Chowk purveyor of sweetmeats once nearly caused a chief commissioner of Delhi to have an apoplectic fit. Mr. Claude Barron, C.S.I., C.I.E., F.R.G.S., I.C.S., was a veteran civil official, who carried his titles, honors, responsibilities, and thirty-two years of service with the dignity that was his due. It was the revolutionary resolution that Sheikh Majid placed on the order paper during one session which perturbed him and shocked his brother bureaucrats. The sheikh requested that he, as the representative of the people, should be consulted by and associated with the chief commissioner in all the latter's administrative acts. His proposal caused much consternation and amusement in the Assembly. However, the Honorable Mr. Barron still continued to hold sway over the imperial enclave of Hindustan.

We are listening to the budget debate, that distracting problem of how to have your cake and eat it too, which since time immemorial has disturbed the equipoise and stimulated the eloquence of parliamentarians the world over. And here, as in more experienced bodies, much time is devoted to trifles. For one hour a heated debate rages as to whether the Assembly shall dispense with the services of its chief ceremonial attendant, a pompous Indian officer reminiscent of the glorious days of Akbar, who is retained at a salary of 300 rupees a month to bow the members to their seats. One of the representatives, dressed in European clothes, by the way, proposes that a lowly chowkidar, or night-watchman, at 50 rupees a month, be substituted. The motion is hotly and indignantly contested by members in pyjamas and turbans as well as by an English sahib from Bombay, on the ground that the proposal is an insult to the dignity of India's parliament. The commander-in-chief and other ministers of Govern ment who draw 5,000 pounds sterling a year sit listening to this debate. One can imagine their feelings.

But after an hour of sarcasm, ridicule, and good humored repartee, the Assembly gets down to business. Up to that time we haven't been particularly impressed. In fact, we are in a mood to scoff mildly and perchance to cavil and criticize. However the acumen, skill, temperance, and ability shown during the remainder of the debate are a revelation. The members of this parliament in pyjamas take a half-hitch in their belts, wade into India's financial morass, and slash about with courage and considerable common sense. The debate finally winds up with a flat refusal of the Government's budget as a whole.

But that is neither here nor there. The fact that sticks in one's mind is that during the last century a little island, six thousand miles away, by force and foresight has built up a gigantic empire here in southern Asia, and that in this century before our very eyes, the descendants of Britain's merchant adventurers have brought peace, prosperity, and this parliament to a land whose people have never known what these three things were before.

One wonders what the destiny of this parliament in pyjamas is to be.

CHAPTER XXVI

SMITH AND ISAACS ON THE THRONE OF AKBAR

WHEN the inhabitants of Hindustan refer to the good old days, as they frequently do, they mean the Golden Age of India, and have in mind the time when Akbar, Jahangir, or Shah Jehan sat on the Peacock Throne of the Moghuls in their exquisite Diwan-i-am. But to-day the Indian Empire is bigger and richer than in the days of the Moghuls. Her chief administrator, the viceroy, wields a power that the descendants of Tamerlane could not hope for, with their early and imperfect communications.

On my first visit to India I spent a day with one of the modern successors of the Great Moghuls, his Excellency the Earl of Reading—the noble earl who not many years ago made his first visit to India as Rufus Isaacs, a cabin-boy on a "tramp," polishing brass as his boat steamed up the Hughli to Calcutta. Disraeli, as prime minister of Great Britain, occupied the highest political eminence to which a Jew has ever risen in Great Britain—in all the world, for that matter, during modern times. Isaacs comes next, a Jew bearing the

half-regal title of Viceroy of India. You may be sure
there was much scathing comment over whisky and
soda among the bureaucrats out East, but it did them
no good.

I found at least one similarity in the reigns of Akbar
and Rufus Isaacs. Both were periods when there was
an epidemic of building imperial cities in impossible
places. To-day glorious Fatehpur-Sikri is in ruins and
has never been rebuilt, and Raisina, the new Delhi of
the British Raj, is nearing completion.

The Viceroy's day is heralded by his English valet,
bearing a cup of tea, pulling the blinds, and saying,
"Six o'clock, my lord!"

How different from the Moghul habit of being
roused from slumber by slave-girls massaging your toes
or holding a goblet of sherbet to your sullen lips! While
Jahangir reclined on his divan a barber curled and perfumed his beard, and anointed his head with sweet-
smelling oils: but the ruler of to-day shaves himself
with a safety-razor.

Attended by an A.D.C., the viceroy spends an hour
in the saddle each morning, and then follows his ride
with a cold shower and a simple breakfast of eggs and
bacon, fruit and cream. The Moghuls, on the other
hand, began the day by exhibiting their imperial faces
at a window of the palace in order to reassure their
adoring subjects that they had not passed in their majority during the night, and after this repaired to their

marble bath to dally in the steaming-room and the cooling-chamber.

There is an even more striking contrast between the way in which Akbar performed the duties of state and the methods of the British viceroy who now rules in his stead. The Great Moghul usually spent the forenoon dispensing justice from a balcony, where he looked down upon the multitude assembled in the court below. On the left in the courtyard was tethered an elephant, under whose ponderous feet condemned men were crushed at a word of command from the emperor. In the days of Akbar judgment and execution followed in swift succession.

The viceroy, on the other hand, goes to his office punctually at 9:45 every morning and follows a routine as rigid as that of a London or New York captain of industry. But before he takes up work he is obliged to endure a five-minute inspection by his surgeon, who tests his pulse and no doubt makes him put out his tongue and say, "Ah!" This has long been a custom in the Indian viceregal household and is a necessary precaution, because the average British viceroy is prone to put work before health and never admit it when he is feeling ill. The next officials to report are the military secretary and the comptroller of the household. Then comes that all-powerful individual who in Moghul times was called the grand vizier, but who in the prosaic days of the Earl of Reading and his successors rejoices in the humble designation of private secretary, though his name—Sir Geoffrey de Montmorency—has still a pleasant flavor of romance.

The viceroy's day is largely taken up with interviews with members of his council, other prominent Government officials, heads of industries, and rulers of native states. He often works right on through the day and well into the night. As deputy for the king-emperor he outranks every native ruler in India, and receives an even greater salute of guns than his Exalted Highness Asaf Jan Muzaffar-ul-Mulk Rustam-i-Dauran Arastu-i-Zaman, the Nizam of Hyderabad, which translated means "Seer with the Wisdom of the Prime Minister of Solomon, Conqueror of Kingdoms, Most Powerful Hero of His Day, the Aristotle of His Time, Nizam of Hyderabad." Among the Indian rulers who came to interview the viceroy while we were in Delhi, were potentates such as the Nawab of Tonk, the Rani of Gondal, the Mir of Khairpur, the Jagidar of Alipura, the Deshmukh of Phaltan, the Rajah of Puddukkottai, the Khan of Kalat, the Jam of Las Bela, and hosts of others, all of whom look to him for protection.

Luncheon-hour at Viceregal Lodge is generally utilized as a time for entertaining people whom his lordship wishes to meet in a semi-formal way. His lady plays a prominent part in this portion of the day's schedule, for the rôle of a vicereine calls for unusual tact and a charming personality. These qualities she possesses in a very marked degree.

Perhaps no woman in the history of India ever wielded greater influence than Jahangir's queen, Nur Jehan, who stood behind the purdah at his councils and gave him sound advice during the most critical days of his reign. In modern Indian history there have been striking parallels, for many a vicereine has been credited with assisting the viceroy in much the same way.

What a contrast between the gorgeous costumes worn by the Moghul emperors and the garments of a British viceroy! One of the earliest European travelers to visit India, in describing the physical appearance of the Great Moghul, recorded that his Imperial Majesty wore a red turban, on one side of which was a ruby as big as a walnut, on the other a diamond of equal size, and in front an enormous emerald shaped like a heart. The turban was crowned with waving plumes. Around the Moghul's waist was a sash wreathed with a chain of pearls, rubies, and diamonds. About his neck hung a heavy chain of gold. On his elbows and wrists were bands set with diamonds. On every finger were priceless rings. On his feet were gold-embroidered buskins studded with pearls, with sharp toes that turned up. On either side of the emperor were eunuchs equipped with gold maces and white horse-hair whisks with which to drive the flies from the imperial face. While before the Moghul "went drums, trumpets, and loud music and many canopies of cloth of gold set in many places with great rubies."

The British viceroy, on the other hand, wears the same Jodhpur breeches when he rides as are worn by his staff, and by every other white man in India. Instead of the eunuchs of the Moghuls, a young A.D.C. attends him. In the forenoon he is usually attired in an ordinary lounge-suit, and rarely puts on a morning-coat excepting when there is to be a council meeting. At dinner he wears an ordinary tail-coat unless the occasion is a special one, in which event he wears the ribbon and jewel of the Grand Master of the Order of the Star of India, sometimes the insignia of the Grand Master of the Order of the Indian Empire, and of a Grand Commander of the Bath.

One traveler who visited the court of the Moghuls stated that the business of state was transacted when the emperor was in a fit condition to deal with it (this was Jahangir, not the hard-headed Akbar), adding that he was often prevented by "drowsiness from the fumes of Bacchus" and that "often in extreme drunkenness he fell to weeping and to divers passions."

Fortunately there is no parallel here! Recent viceroys have been abstemious men, rarely touching anything stronger than soda-water.

CHAPTER XXVII
THE GENTLE ART OF MASSACRE

THE city of the Sikhs and of sunlight, where pigeons and pilgrims flock to the Golden Temple and lave in its turquoise lake. It is a place to see but not to linger in, unless you are immune to flea-bites and dyspepsia.

Go to the Khalsa College first, where the youthful Sikh is being led along the primrose paths of Wisdom, Truth, and Beauty. See the young Sikh at work and at play and at prayer. Get acquainted, and you will find that he has been taught the grand old lesson that "manners maketh man." Some of the boys will offer to show you around the city. Go with a student if you can, but avoid guides, of course. There are no guides in India: "guide" is a euphemism for a harsher word.

You will want to see the Jallianwala Bagh, where General Dyer fired on the mob during the disturbances in 1919. It is just a vacant "building-lot" in the middle of the city, about five hundred yards square, with a tree and a well near the center, and the rubbish-heaps and the air of desolation one associates with building-lots that haven't been built over.

Jallianwala Bagh has been bought by the municipality to be turned into a place like the Memorial Gardens at Cawnpore: this, at any rate, was the intention of the extremists, but so far nothing has been done. A movie-show has placarded the narrow entrance (through which General Dyer couldn't get his machine guns) with posters featuring Eddie Polo.

The story of the shooting has often been told. It happened in April, 1919. A crowd of about 30,000 people ran amuck, killed three European bank-managers, soaked them in kerosene oil, burnt their bodies, and looted their banks. An electrical engineer was murdered, and a lady missionary who happened to bicycle past the crowd, not knowing her danger, was brutally assaulted and left for dead. Some Hindus picked her up later, however, carried her to their house, and saved her life. The cause of all this was, roughly, hatred of the British. The mob idea was, "Down with the British, and let's get the loot!"

General Dyer arrived two days after the murders to take charge of the situation. He refused to palaver with the extremists and roundly declared that he was the sole authority, and that any one who disobeyed him would be dealt with according to martial law. But the Indians, unfortunately, were drunken with words. They didn't believe General Dyer meant what he said.

On April 13th, hearing that there was to be a meeting of agitators, General Dyer paraded through the city at the head of his troops, and proclaimed by beat of drum at the principal points of the bazaar that any gathering of four or more persons would be considered an unlawful assembly, and might be fired on. He also distributed printed notices.

On returning to his camp at 12: 40 P. M., General Dyer heard that the meeting in Jallianwala Bagh was to take place in spite of his efforts to prevent it. At four o'clock that afternoon he left his camp again, with fifty men, fully armed. Having reached the Jallianwala Bagh, he drew his men up and opened fire without further warning. He fired 1650 rounds, and according to official accounts he killed 379 and wounded 1200, but the numbers may have been larger. Having accomplished what he described as "his terrible duty," he marched away, leaving the dead and dying where they were.

Now if General Dyer's critics (and they were legion) had had to march for four hours through the dust and heat and stench and flies of Amritsar bazaar on a May morning, they would have been prostrated by the sheer physical exertion, and probably would have spent the afternoon panting peaceably on their beds; meanwhile the meeting would have been held, Amritsar might have been looted and burned, the Punjaub might have risen, and no one knows how much blood would have been spilt. That is the simple truth. Every one knows it in India. Again, although it does seem deplorable that the wounded should have been left with no attention, it is not generally recognized that there was nothing in the world to stop the relatives of the wounded from going to their aid. What actually happened was that the relatives were afraid of getting into trouble with the police if they identified themselves with the unfortunates in Jallianwala Bagh. Hence the city people looked on, from the walls surrounding the Bagh, at the death-agony of their own kith and kin, without daring to help them. Surely this can have few parallels in history? . . . Thus is the Amritsar massacre defended. But it was horrible, bloody business, whatever extenuation may be advanced.

From the Jallianwala Bagh you may stroll through the city, among the people to whom these things happened a few years ago. The types are more mixed than you would expect to see: the hefty and hirsute Sikh is hardly in the majority, although this is his capital city and contains the chief shrine of his faith. The Punjaubi predominates, a Grecian-profiled, big-boned, solemn follower of the Arabian Prophet, who tends to grossness of habit with middle age. Then you will see the lean Afghan, hawk-eyed and hawk-nosed, wandering with his camels and his carpets over Hindustan, a son of Reuben if ever there was one. The Bombay money-lenders are there also, and the sleek-headed and effeminate Bengalis, and the northern Hindus, Kashmiris, Pathans, Jats, Rajputs, and pariahs.

A hundred years ago these races were at bitter enmity. The grandfathers of at least nine tenths of the lads you may see in the street to-day carried swords or muskets as a matter of course, and lived in a state of war, when Ranjit Singh was ruler in Amritsar. So that a little bloodshed is nothing unusual in the traditions of the citizens—or indeed more than a little all in the day's work.

For instance, a little affair concerning the Sikhs occurred not long after I first arrived in India. There is a rich temple, not far from Amritsar, known as the Janamasthan Shrine. The mahant, or incumbent, of this shrine drew tithes to the value of $50,000 a year from fees, church lands, usufruct of orchards, and other sources. The Akali, or Reforming Sikhs, thought $50,000 a year too much, and thought also that the mahant was too fond of dope and dancing-girls. Accordingly they planned to take forcible possession of the shrine. The mahant objected, naturally, and appealed to Government for protection. The representative of Government said that he couldn't interfere in religious disputes. The mahant said that in that case he intended to engage a body of armed watchmen on his own account if Government had no objection, in order to defend his property. Then Government rubbed its hands together and bowed the mahant to the door, without committing itself in any way to anything except that it did not want to commit itself to anything in any way.

The mahant was a practical man. He hired a hundred Pathans, armed them with blunderbuses and knives, and laid in a stock of kerosene.

Along came the Reformers, swaggered up to the shrine, and demanded admittance. They entered, one hundred of them, and squatted down in prayer in the courtyard of the shrine. Now all around the court there is a broad wall. On this wall climbed the Pathans who had blunderbuses, while the remainder whetted their knives. When the Akalis were in the middle of their prayers, forehead on the ground, and backside up, the Pathans opened fire. When they had fired off all their ammunition the others finished the job with knives. Then they collected the bodies. Some they put into a lime-kiln, others they burnt. By evening all the Reforming Sikhs had *entirely disappeared*.

Probably the mahant created a record in the murder line, both as regards callousness and actual numbers disposed of, but like all men who plan things on a big scale he wasn't as badly hit as the small investor. The Pathans who only slit one or two throats got it in the neck with a six-foot drop, whereas the mahant, on the plea that his Pathans were out of control, escaped the death-penalty, and went to visit the Andamans for a decade—less time off for good conduct. Meanwhile the Reform party are keeping a few tins of kerosene ready against the time he gets out. . . .

But let us change this ensanguined ribbon of our

portable typewriter, and finish our view of Amritsar with the glories of the Golden Temple. It is certainly like nothing else in all the world, that gold dome reflected in that jewel lake, gorgeous and unreal, in spite of the blinding sunlight, with the unreality of a restless day-dream. Or rather, it is what a monk would have dreamed in the Middle Ages of Jerusalem the Golden. It *is* with milk and honey blessed, its halls are jubilant with song, its bulwarks glow with jasper, and there are (not angels certainly, but—) pilgrims casting down their golden crowns of marigold around the glassy sea.

We have said that it is a place to see but not to linger in. In order to learn to like the Golden Temple day by day in every way better and better and better, we should have to spend our time paddling round it in bare feet (for shoes are prohibited) among pigeon-droppings and cow-dung, and some of the hungriest fleas in Hindustan. After all, there are better things to do in this world, so it beseemeth us. And we had best admit frankly that we liked the Golden Temple less and less the longer we saw it.

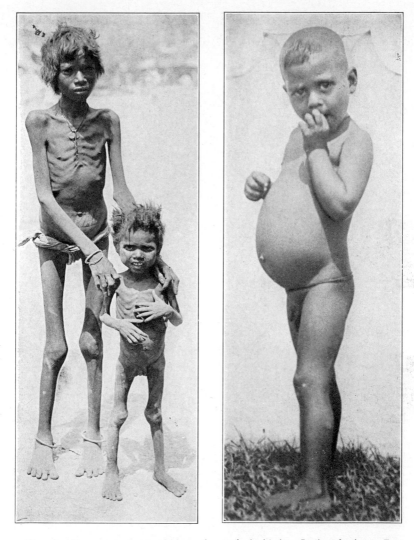

Occasionally we encounter victims of a typical old-time Indian famine. But today, when famine threatens in one region, the British rush grain quickly by rail from another. So now we usually see children with little tummies like that of the youngster on the right.

The shrine of Janamasthan at Nankhana-Sahib in the Punjab, and the high priest who burned one hundred of his enemies in oil.

CHAPTER XXVIII

A SAVAGE TALE—WILL IT HAPPEN AGAIN?

ᏟᎯᏟᎯ

ALONE among the Union Jacks that fly from sea to sea there is a flag in Lucknow that is never lowered at night but remains always at the masthead, from sunrise unto sunrise.

The reason for this all men know, for the crosses of St. George, St. Andrew, and St. Patrick that float over the riddled Residency looked down in 1857 on a feat of arms unsurpassed in the history of the world, and unsurpassed in the history of England both as to the greatness of its courage and as to the greatness of its consequences. Here it was that a thousand half-starved men kept the flag flying against more than thirty thousand enemies, from June 30th to November 18th. It is a story as undying as that of Thermopylæ, one that will live until the human race perishes from the earth.

There is much to see in Lucknow, but we will go only to the Residency, to that spot which is holy ground to so many of the Anglo-Saxon race now scattered over all the world. And having come, we feel that the Residency is too sacred to write about as we have written of the palaces and temples that we have seen. And we feel the same as to Mr. Hilton, the last survivor of the Mutiny in Lucknow. We talked with him by the grave of Sir Henry Lawrence, the splendid living with the glorious dead, and we feel we cannot make a "human interest story" round the figure of this magnificent old gentleman who served at the Martiniere Post as a boy.

Rather we will glean from old diaries some intimate details of the struggle—for to do more is impossible— details of the struggle written hot from one of the hottest fights in history, in words it were impertinent to think to better.

On May 18, 1857, when the East India Company still ruled over Hindustan, Mrs. Harris, wife of the Reverend James Harris, wrote home:

"There are rumours of risings all over the country. . . . There is no doubt that this is a most fearful crisis and that the life of every European is in great jeopardy. . . . Oh, mother, mother darling, these are fearful times. Pray for us, dearest!"

On Sunday, the tenth of May, 1857, the Great Indian Mutiny broke out at Meerut, when the bells of the Church of England were tolling and calling the soldiers to worship. The mutineers swept on to Delhi and killed every white person left in it, including women and babies, and proclaimed the restoration of the Moghul Empire. Near the Kashmir Gate in Delhi stood the principal powder-magazine in India. The

Englishmen in charge of it, at the last moment, when no longer able to defend it, lighted a fuse and blew themselves up with the magazine to keep the ammunition from falling into the hands of the mutineers. Whereupon a few thousand British scattered here and there throughout the country were swallowed up in an ocean of hostile populations, but with characteristic resolution and courage they fought the most unpromising fight that one may read of in fiction or out of it, and won it—thoroughly. Next came the siege of Cawnpore and one of the most revolting and treacherous massacres of women and children in the annals of savage warfare. Then the flames of mutiny swept on to Lucknow.

More than half a million retainers and followers of the late king of Oude lived at Lucknow, the capital of a kingdom recently annexed by the British. They hated the new-comers. The African eunuchs who guarded the royal treasure ($5,000,000 worth) feared them; corrupt comptrollers of the court revenues (the revenue on prostitution in the city amounted to fifty thousand rupees per annum) abominated the system that deprived them of their plunder; the royal soldiers of the king of Oude, no longer free to loot the country folk, detested them; the four wives, twenty-nine concubines, and four hundred slave-girls of the late king, together with their friends and relations, called down maledictions on the monogamous, meddling British.

Sir Henry Lawrence, the chief commissioner, worked

day and night to delay the coming storm, in order to provision and equip the Residency for the siege he knew was inevitable. By his wisdom and foresight he saved the lives of five hundred women and children.

On the 30th of June, 1857, there were one thousand Europeans (three fourths of them soldiers), 500 loyal Sepoys (chiefly Sikhs), 500 women and children, and 1,000 native servants of various sorts, all within the Residency compound. Three thousand, all told, against a city of three quarters of a million, and the whole country seemed to rise up around them like a dark cloud.

Round the Residency were 15,000 armed rebels, mostly trained soldiers, in positions from eight to eighty yards (nowhere more) from the hastily constructed defences—eager to loot and rape. For eighty days the garrison withstood a constant hail of shot and shell, losing about ten men a day from wounds or disease. Meanwhile the enemy increased from 15,000 to more than double that number. The British had a thirty-to-one chance of coming out alive. The East India Company's paper was selling in the city at a discount of seventy per cent.

This letter of Mr. Harris's, written from Allahabad in December, after the siege was over, explains things better than any words of ours:

"Aunt G. says, 'It was a comfort to know that although closely beset we were in an impregnable fort.' We were in no fort at all. We occupied a few houses in a big garden, with a low wall on one side, and only an earthen parapet on the others, in the middle of a large city, the buildings of which commanded us, and were swarming with thousands of our deadly foes, thirsting for our blood. God gave us protection and pluck, the former to a wonderful degree or not one of us would be here to tell about it. . . . The brutes never dared to come to fight us hand to hand. They tried hard a few times but were killed in hundreds round our earthworks, so they took to shooting us down by degrees, and this they would have done, humanly speaking, if those brave fellows under Havelock had not come in. Even then, after losing 1,000 out of 2,800 in doing it, the rest were shut up with us for six weeks fighting with us day and night, until old Sir Colin came with 10,000 more. Well, thank God we are all right now."

Again in another letter: "As our garrison daily diminished and help seemed ever further off, the last resource of blowing up the magazine was talked of and tacitly resolved on, in case we could no longer defend our women and children. They would never have boasted of another Cawnpore."

From Mrs. Harris's diary: "June 30th. No sooner was the first gun fired than all the ladies and children were hurried down into the Tye Khana, damp, dark, gloomy as a vault, and excessively dirty. Here we sat all day, feeling too miserable, anxious and terrified to speak. . . ."

Here, in a large cellar, they remained not for one day, but for eighty. Children were born in that vault, a sheet being stretched across a corner for privacy. Children and adults died here of dysentery, cholera, and smallpox. It was so dark that they had to light a candle to see to eat. Their food was chiefly gun-bullock beef, whose toughness was mitigated as far as possible by being stewed, and chapatties of unleavened bread. They had no milk, bread, or butter, except a quite insufficient supply of goat's milk for the children, half of whom died and all of whom suffered from boils and dysentery. Little Bobby Fayrer was a year old in June: ". . . a cherub of a baby boy, the image of Murillo's John the Baptist in the National Gallery." On August the 2nd he was ". . . a skeleton, like a little old man. So were the others. Five babies were buried in one night.

"August 19th. Dear little Herbert D. died at half-past three this morning. . . . We closed his pretty blue eyes, and crossed his little hands on his breast, and there he lay by his mother's side till daylight; then she washed the little body herself and put on him a nightgown and I tied a lace handkerchief round his face as she had no caps. Charlie D. came to see her and we left her quiet with him and the dead baby till eleven, when I was obliged to go in and ask her to part with it. She let me take it away and I sewed the little sweet one up myself in a clean white cloth and James carried it over to the hospital to await the evening burials."

In spite of rapid decomposition it was impossible to bury by day owing to the enemy's fire. Even at night only a shallow pit could be dug for the day's deaths, and after a few weeks the stench became so intolerable, because the bodies were continually routed out by jackals, that on one occasion Mr. Harris vomited for two hours after the night's service.

On July 2nd, at about 8 A. M., Sir Henry Lawrence was killed. He was lying on his bed, hearing some papers read to him by his A.D.C. when he was hit by an enormous piece of shell, and his left leg nearly taken off at the thigh. He was brought over to Dr. Fayrer's house immediately. Mrs. Harris continued: "James prayed with him and administered the Holy Communion. He was quite sensible, though his agony was extreme. He spoke for nearly an hour, quite calmly. . . ."

The directions he gave about the siege, and other matters, are a model of lucidity and forethought. We can only notice here two matters, namely, (1) that all his servants were to receive a year's pay, and (2), "Put on my grave only this: 'Here lies Henry Lawrence, who tried to do his duty. May God have mercy on him!' " There was not a dry eye nor a steady voice at this death-bed scene, save the voice and eyes of the dying Lawrence, who stifled his agony to do his duty to the last.

From Mrs. Harris's diary: "July 3rd. I was upstairs

all day nursing Sir Henry. . . . The firing never ceased a second the whole day. . . . July 4th. Sir Henry L. died at a quarter past eight this morning. . . . His expression was so happy one could not but rejoice his pain was over. . . . James called some soldiers to help carry the bed into the verandah. When they came in, one of the men lifted the sheet off from Sir Henry's face and kissed him."

He was buried at 9:45 that night, between two private soldiers, according to his orders. All may see his grave, and his deathless epitaph. Lucknow is known throughout the world, by the luster of his name.

"July 25th . . . what with the frequent night attacks of the enemy, the crying and the illness of the poor children, the rats and mice which run over us, the heat. . . ." It was a living death for the women and children in the Tye Khana.

Day after day passed without relief. For months the mutineers unceasingly, night and day, fired on the Residency. The strain was terrific, there were two suicides and a murder among the garrison, cholera and the rebels took their toll of ten lives a day: the diaries are catalogues of horror, disease, death, and hope deferred.

Hundreds of times the mutineers stormed the walls, always to be driven back. Month after month the dwindling body of men, women, and children fought smallpox, cholera, and a force from thirty to fifty times their own in numbers. But they kept up the defense with stubborn courage, determined to die rather than surrender.

The first relieving force under Havelock and Outram fought its way across the scorching plains to their relief in the devastating heat of an Indian summer, cutting through an enemy that outnumbered them a hundred to one, losing a third of their men and reaching the Residency with ranks so depleted that they were able only to help the defenders hold out for another six weeks while a larger force under Sir Colin Campbell day by day fought and bayoneted its way to their final relief.

What of the men who lived and died in the trenches? They sleep in the green churchyard. And what of Colonel Inglis, in whose hands were a million sterling, two thousand lives, and England's flag? Ten times was that flag shot down, and ten times he had it raised again. While that banner blows his name shall be remembered.

In the Residency there is peace now, peace and beauty and hallowed associations: green lawns, creepers, hares scuttling from bush to bush. Imagination can hardly recall the tents and blood and filth, the litter of dismembered limbs in the crowded hospital, the squalid Tye Khana, the dead and dying children, the faithful Sepoys, the gallant women, the lean and sleepless leopards of England who manned the ramparts.

CHAPTER XXIX
THE WATCHER OF THE CLOUDS

"THESE things ease the heart of man from sorrow," says an Indian sage, "water, green grass, and the beauty of woman."

Heartsease from the burden of existence—that is the refrain that runs through all the literature of Hindustan. This is as true of ancient times as of the present. When the forefathers of the Pilgrim Fathers were still painting themselves a deep blue, Indian culture was known in Babylon, and when the chariot of Boadicea was scything a lane through the Roman ranks, the Romans of Rome were studying Aryan culture. Literary India at the dawn of the Christian era was acting and reacting in a wider world than the West was to know for fifteen centuries. But release, absorption of the self in the cosmic whole, Nirvana, has ever been the keynote. Hindu art-consciousness rests on the sacramental view of life.

The Vedas, believed by the Hindus to be the very Word of God, are among the oldest books in the world,

and reveal in beautiful simplicity the life of a pastoral
people, the Aryans, who migrated from central Asia to
the Indian plains. The Vedas and their glosses and
commentaries, forming the vast and as yet only partly
translated library of ancient Sanskrit writings, deal
with every phase and aspect of human emotion with a
particularity and a minuteness that have hardly been
equaled.

Coué's formula of getting better and better was long
ago anticipated by the mantra of the Ganges-side;
Freud is an ignoramus beside the psychoanalysis of the
Upanishads; while as regards marital relations the
Tantras make Dr. Marie Stopes of England seem a girl
of seventeen. But although the early Aryans must have
possessed the scientific spirit, as well as a sense of humor and a noble diction, it is an unfortunate fact that
as the struggle for existence became easier the original
material became overlaid and altered, so that now pro-
digious research is necessary to get the gold from the
superimposed dross of centuries of easy living and tor-
pid thinking in a land where 100° Fahrenheit is an
everyday affair.

The later Sanskrit poems of men like Tulsi Das—
the sweet singer of the Ramayana—Kalidasa, and
Bhartihari, who delivered himself of the apothegm
quoted above, are characterized by copiousness, ingenuity, and a remarkable and very modern interest

in the function of thinking. Hardly any intellectual process has been left unaccounted for.

Later in time, and very different in quality, was the Muslim literature of the Great Moghuls, whose era corresponds with the Renaissance in Europe. But Muhammadan literature, of course, is overshadowed by the gorgeous periods of the Koran, whose sonorous magnificence discourages other attempts at eloquence. Besides, the Afghans were too busy fighting to devote much attention to belles-lettres. The "Memoirs" of Baber, however, make very entertaining reading. Some of his speeches should be as famous as the bulletins of Napoleon.

To-day, among the Afghan and Pathan tribesmen, the gift of eloquence is not rare, and the Pathan of Peshawar may be stated, without fear of contradiction from those who know his language, to be the world's best story-teller. Most of the stories, however, are unfit to print. Not so the songs of the wandering minstrels who go from village to village throughout India singing of love and other topics of the day. They should certainly be transcribed into English.

Rabindranath Tagore, the Dante of India, the worshiped poet of Bengal, the English knight, the winner of the Nobel prize, the sweet singer of the Gitanjali! . . . We were on a visit to the poet at his home and school, Shantiniketan (the Abode of Peace), which is about four hours by rail from Calcutta. We came upon the poet looking at the clouds, those scurrying clouds of the monsoon that inspire so much of his liquid, musical verse. From head to foot he was dressed in pontifical white. He wears a shock of gray ringlets and his white beard with its two dark streaks on either side, like veins in Parian marble, adds to his patriarchal appearance.

It was a small thatched house, this home of India's most illustrious son, with nothing of artistry about it except an exquisitely graceful bronze lantern on one of the gate-posts. He obviously doesn't care for the material things of this world, and even the completion of the house and other near-by buildings of his famous would-be-World-University of Shantiniketan goes on in a casual way.

The poet sits on his verandah looking at the changing glory of the sky.

The poetry of Rabindranath Tagore is full of the beauty of the monsoon. Every morning in the rainy season the philosopher-poet of Bengal rises at dawn and sits on the verandah of his little house at Shantiniketan, looking out across the wide sweep of sky towards the massing battalions of the monsoon—sits there until Indra's chariot, the sun, has driven half across heaven to the zenith . . . The rain, too, is in Tagore's verse, and the tenderness of rain-washed distances, while the night sky, in its Indian aspect of a vast vault sprinkled

with the star-dust of worlds beyond our ken, finds in
him a great interpreter. And always and ever present,
in infinite solicitude and eternal power, stands the Im-
manent Almighty. "The steps that I heard in my play-
room," writes Tagore, "are echoing from star to star."

He is a tall man with the dignity of an ancient lin-
eage. Unmistakably, but quite unconsciously, and with
the most perfect natural grace, he bears the blazon of
his poetic and philosophic forebears. No one would
mistake him for a self-made man. He is the product of
a century of mental aristocracy. That is the first thing
we noticed about Rabindranath Tagore. His is a mind
that is not concerned with little things. It is a mind
that ranges over continents and centuries, and is quite
unconcerned with the politics of the parish pump. Yet,
paradoxically, he is the poet of the intimate in Indian
life, for nothing absorbs him so completely as his beloved Shantiniketan, where he teaches young Bengal
the wisdom not to be found in schools.

His eyes are lyrical rather than mystical, and they
change, like the monsoon skies of which he loves to
sing, from thunder-dark to violet. His hands, too, are
those of a poet, plump-phalanged and with pointed
finger-tips.

He greets us softly, in a gentle, rather tired voice.
The peace of the Abode of Peace descends on us.

We have come to talk to him about the present-day
problems of India. But suddenly we have become timid.

We forget our questions. We feel that it would be a jarring note in this atmosphere of peace if we were to drag in the affairs of that workaday world of Calcutta and Bombay that seems petty and diminutive viewed from the intellectual eminence of Bolpur. There is but one theme we feel free to refer to, and that is art. Over Shantiniketan the Muse of Poetry looks down with kindly eyes.

Simplicity and depth of feeling are the keynotes of Rabindranath Tagore's taste in English verse, and Keats and Shelley his favorite poets. Of his contemporaries he speaks with diffidence. Some he praises enthusiastically, as he does Walter de la Mare, but he confesses that many of the poets of the West, like Siegfried Sassoon, use an English so different from that of Keats and Shelley that their diction is beyond him. Then he apologizes with a smile, saying that as a foreigner it is unfair for him to criticize.

Every evening his pupils sit at his feet on the verandah of his thatched bungalow, listening to him as he translates to them the poetry and the mind of the West.

When we asked him if he ever intended to revisit Europe and America, he told us what a shock his last trip to America had given him. That was in 1917. He found the country concentrating on war, and without the patience to listen to philosophers, poets, and dreamers. The whole atmosphere was so foreign and strange to him that he came away a disappointed man.

"I am afraid many of the things I had to say were unpopular," he added, in his soft, world-weary voice, "because an intense spirit of nationalism was sweeping America, and I am opposed to nationalism in every form. For to me every question is an international one. The press and public men were clamoring for what they called 'hundred per cent Americanism.' Ah, but that is a dangerous creed! If America tries to make her citizens conform to a standard pattern she will blot out individuality. She will be unable to contribute her best to the world."

When he returned from his first visit to America, long before the war, the poet seemed to feel as a result of what he had seen that so powerful had America grown, and so advanced had her civilization become, that she would surely be able to avoid war herself, and by economic pressure even be able to prevent long conflicts between other nations.

"But, alas, I don't believe that now," he said. "Here in India, for instance, we shall have more bitter wars than any that have swept our plains in all our thousands of years of invasions.

"It is just possible," he added, "that Hinduism might be a religion of the past before many years, and the inhabitants of India converted to Islam by force."

This, coming from a Hindu, and from one of the leaders of the progressive Brahma Samaj sect at that, dazed us. Then to cap our bewilderment he added:

Some of the monks are so old and weatherbeaten that they look a bit like Bill Fagan. When they do their devil dances they wear grotesque masks and aprons made of babies' bones.

A native ruler of long ago confined 140 Europeans in a room the exact size of this enclosure—the Black Hole of Calcutta. The next day 120 were dead.

"And who knows but what it might be a good thing for India if the Muhammadans were to overrun it again?

"My criticism of British rule in India," continued the poet, "is that it is too perfect. Even the British jurists who preside over our courts distribute too perfect and abstract a form of justice. The Government is so mechanically perfect that it isn't human. I doubt if a more perfectly organized government has been seen before in the history of the world. In fact it is so mechanically complete that it stifles Indian ambition. Under it there hasn't been half the real human happiness, or half the incentive for individual effort, that there was in the days of the autocratic old Moghul emperors. We Indians have been made to feel that we are inferior beings, and we have known only too keenly how few were the important posts open to us. Such a government not only stifles ambition but it smothers the inspiration to do great things in art, science, and letters."

"But what about the new reform plan which is to turn your government over to the Indian people?" we asked.

"Ah, yes," replied Tagore, "it does seem that the thing we have long hoped for is about to happen. But my quarrel with Britain is that she has made no attempt during the past one hundred years to prepare us for this. They are really giving us these reforms because they have been made inevitable by popular opinion. So now they say to us: 'If you do not like the way we run your country, take it yourselves and show us what a mess you can make.' Obviously, the result will be chaos.

"Hinduism is a religion of pacifism, while the teachings of Muhammad transform even our peaceful Hindus into fanatics with a lust to fight. Even now Muhammadanism is spreading rapidly in India. You may not believe it, but the latest figures show that there are more Muhammadans here in Bengal to-day than there are Hindus. So if the Government falls into the hands of the Indian people it probably will mean Muhammadan rule again. But even that would be preferable to the present government, because it would be government by our own kindred."

The final words of Rabindranath Tagore, before we left to catch our train, embodied a passionate appeal against racial hatred. His most cherished dream is of a day when the peoples of the East and of the West will mingle freely, on terms of absolute equality, without social or economic barriers, each people retaining its own individuality.

CHAPTER XXX

THE CITY OF CEASELESS PRAYER

JOURNEYING east from Lucknow we came to a city that was old and sacred hundreds of years before the birth of Christ. There is an unending stream of pilgrims pouring into it night and day all of the time. And they have been coming like that ever since the dawn of history. This city, as you no doubt have guessed, is Benares, where more than a million Hindu pilgrims come every year to bathe in the River Ganges. If the Black Pagoda may be said to symbolize the mystery of India, Benares is the mystery of India.

To the two hundred million Hindus in India the Ganges is a sacred river. The more enlightened regard it as symbolic of the one deity that rules over the universe, while the more primitive believe that it flows from the feet of one of their gods. They think that its waters are so pure that they purify anything they touch. Even the murderer can come here and bathe and have his sins washed away.

It is the ambition of wealthy Hindus to build temples here. But after a man dies there is usually no one to take care of his temple, so it crumbles and decays and slips into the river. Long ago it was the custom for Hindu mothers to bring their girl babies to the Ganges and then toss them to the crocodiles. But that was one of the first things abolished by one of the first British governor-generals of India.

Twenty-five centuries ago Gautama Buddha came here and founded a faith that swept over Asia and still has more adherents than any other religion, although strange to say it is almost forgotten by the multitudes of India. Indeed, it was here on the outskirts of Benares that Buddha preached the first of those sermons which transformed the Eastern world.

The streets of the great city, just beyond the river-front, are dark, narrow labyrinths swarming with pilgrims and holy men and holy cows. One eighth of its population are Brahmin priests who live as parasites on the pilgrims. But all so-called sacred cities, Jerusalem and Mecca for instance, have a similar population.

The Hindus, as we know, have long believed in reincarnation and the transmigration of souls. They think that after death you and I will be coming back into this world in succeeding lives until we finally attain perfection and are taken on to Paradise. And they think that if they come and bathe in the Ganges they will be almost certain to return in the next life in some higher form and not in the form of an untouchable, or of an animal or a snake or a fish. They also have a tradition that if a man is unfortunate enough to die on the opposite bank of the river, across from the two or three miles of temples and steps, on the *left bank* of the Ganges, he is sure to return in the next life in the form of an ass. When Mark Twain came here and heard of this superstition he facetiously remarked that he had frequently met people whom he suspected of having died on the left bank of the Ganges.

Mark Twain was rather bitter about Benares and went on to say that "the Hindu has a childish aversion to being changed into an ass. One could properly expect an ass to have an aversion to being turned into a Hindu. He would lose dignity by it, also self-respect, and nine-tenths of his intelligence."

Many modern Hindus agree with Mark Twain, so far as external practices are concerned. Outwardly, Benares seems a crumbling city of a crumbling faith. But when we know it better we realize that from its ruins, unknown, unguessed-at beauties may arise. For it is instinct with a strange vitality—a vitality that makes it one of the most interesting places in all the world.

Among the more primitive Hindus there persists a tradition that if a man is fortunate enough to die in the sacred city he will go straight to Paradise without returning to this world of torture to pass through any more lives. So thousands of Hindus come here in their old age, to spend their declining years sitting on the bank of the river awaiting their final hour.

When the pilgrims arrive in Benares the first thing they do is to walk thirty-five miles around the city, repeating prayers and incantations in front of weird shrines, some of which do not admit of description. Then they come down to the river and bathe, and as they bathe nearly every movement has some peculiar religious significance.

Every traveler who comes to India comes to Benares, and every traveler who comes to Benares writes about the place. So instead of describing this "religious Vesuvius" we will offer a little advice to other travelers who pass this way:

If you want to see the burning-ghats, and human curiosity is such that you won't be happy till you do, the best way is to see them through field-glasses from a boat in mid-river. You will see best that way, and you will also offend the fewest people. Suppose a few hundred Hindus made a practice of going regularly to one of the cemeteries on the outskirts of New York to kodak the bereaved. Well, if they got away with nothing more than having their cameras smashed over their heads they would be fortunate.

Owing to the fact that they believe in the transmigration of souls, the Hindus think that after death the soul immediately leaves the body. So they see no reason for preserving the dead, and instead of burying them as we do, or allowing them to be devoured by vultures as the Parsees do, they burn them. And the bank of the Ganges

near Benares is lined with funeral pyres. If you die here
you are carried down to the sacred river on a litter,
dipped into the holy water, and then taken back to your
funeral pyre and burned. Do you see that man over there
on our right, the one with the long pole in his hands?
Well, he is stoking the fire that is consuming the remains
of his wife. In the old days if a husband died first, his
wife was considered responsible for his death. So she
would go to the funeral pyre and sit on the logs and be
consumed alive in the flames, in order that her soul
might accompany her husband's into the next life. But
that practice, called suttee, was another of the first things
abolished by one of the first British governor-generals.

To-day, whichever member of a family dies first the
next of kin comes and lights the funeral pyre. He takes
an earthen jar filled with sacred water from the Ganges
and walks round and round the bier, repeating the last
funeral rites of the Hindus. Finally he smashes the jar
and spills the water, to indicate the evanescence of all
human life. Then he takes the sacrificial lathi and bursts
the skull of the deceased while the officiating Brahmin
repeats the fine old Aryan formula telling the soul to
"go forth and follow the ancient path our fathers trod."

A little reflection convinces us that there is nothing
horrible about it at all. In any country, but particularly
in one so densely populated as India, it is an excellent
way of disposing of those who pass on into the next life.
Moreover, cremation seems to have been part of the

tradition of the great northern race of which the ancient Aryans were, and we ourselves are, a part. The heroes of the Iliad were burned on funeral pyres. The peoples of Neolithic Europe seem in general to have consumed their dead with fire.

Everywhere we go in India, and doubly so in sacred cities like Benares, Madura, and Puri, our curiosity is aroused by finding cattle wandering about the streets. Coming from a bank or a post-office, or even your hotel, you often find a cow enjoying a siesta on the sidewalk in front of you. But no one pays any particular attention to it. Instead of molesting a cow, the passing Hindu reverently touches it with his forefinger and then places the finger upon his own brow. For the cow and the bull are sacred animals in India.

In fact, if you are a Hindu and you want to take a particularly solemn oath, instead of putting your hand on a Bible, you pour Ganges water on a cow's tail! More than half the inhabitants of the British Empire consider it as great a crime to kill a cow as to kill a human being. If you kill one, the best way to purge yourself of the awful sin is to make a pilgrimage to a sacred city like Benares. You journey on foot and you carry a long pole with the cow's tail suspended from the top, in order that all who pass may know that you are unclean. During the last ten miles of your pilgrimage you measure your length in the dust. That is, you throw yourself forward, extend your arms as far as you can, measure your length,

stand up and repeat a prayer, and then fall forward
again, until you reach the sacred city. When you arrive
in Benares you eat and drink the five sacrificial products
of the cow—which are not only milk and butter.

All travelers who visit Benares are eager to witness
the washing ceremonies along the river-bank. There
are few sights more beautiful in all the world than the
crescent sweep of the Ganges of an early morning. But
do not spoil it by going too near the bank. If you want
to photograph the ablutions of a Brahmin, do it with
a telephoto lens. These people are at prayer. It is a
beautiful, lustral rite they are engaged in, and you are
not wanted. You are peering into the faces of the people
in the pews.

"Of Savitar the Holy that long ever glory may we win,
   And may Himself inspire our prayers!"

That is the Gayatri—the oldest prayer in all the
world, that has come down to the Brahmins in Sanskrit,
the mother-language of East and West, from the twilight time of history.

Lastly, do not walk too fast in Benares. If you do you
will never understand it the least little bit, and presum-
ably that is what you came to do. Hurry is a mark of
inferiority in the East. Therefore, do not openly pro-
claim your shame.

Let us stroll, very slowly, past the bathing-place of
the Sacrifice of the Ten Horses. You will feel, if you

are at all sensitive, that there is a great subconscious brooding over Benares. A subconscious air of peace and power.

The whole city of Benares is a standing proclamation of the triumph of spirit over matter. It is not material images, like sacred idols or temples, that you will remember as distinctive of Benares, but only moods. You cannot see Benares with the eyes of the flesh, or, if you do, you will want to shut them. Every morning, for the mornings of three thousand years and more, the people of Brahma have come down to the river to worship. They stoop down and sprinkle the holy water of the Ganges on eyes and head. "O Ganga," they say, "Holy Mother Ganga," they repeat, "I salute thy two feet, thy two feet which are beautiful and which are worshiped by good and evil deities. O Ganga, according to our faith thou givest present happiness and final release to all." Taking up the holy water, they let it trickle through their hands in sunlit drops, an oblation to the Giver of Light. Then they sink down into Mother Ganges and are purified in her. Each is utterly absorbed in his devotions. No man looks at his neighbor nor at his neighbor's wife. In this morning-land there is no room for worldly thoughts.

See the Brahmins sitting under the mat umbrellas by the river-bank, looking out across the sunlit river into infinities of space! What knowledge is theirs, which

now the West also is slowly reaching? Knowledge that
they have kept secret for a thousand years and more.
If Messieurs Bergson and Coué came to Benares, would
they not find that their philosophy and their clinic had
been anticipated? What is Bergson's life-force but the
jivatma of the Brahmins? What is Coué's formula but
a mantra of the Brahmins?

The East, a thousand years ago, had reached a certain
point in philosophy and medicine to which the West has
now come. But having reached this point the East locked
up its secrets and went to sleep. Now the West has
shaken the world from slumber. But Benares is still the
center of the ancient wisdom as it is of the ancient
worship.

We wander on among palaces and pilgrims and
shrines and strewn flowers, ash-smeared saddhus sitting
in the slime, sacred bulls, five-legged cows, and holy
men more terrible than skeletons alive. If you look at
these things as we have asked you not to look at them,
you will see filth, depravity, and degradation.

But to the "seeing eye" a different picture is presented.
We see a slice of lemon laid by a child upon Krishna's
altar in case the god is thirsty. We see the widow's mite
of marigold and jasmine laid down in awe before the
shrine of the god. We see the merchant bring a garland
of rosebuds to wreathe the neck of Ganesha—the god
of good luck. We see a yogi, impassive, restrained, with

legs folded in the ancient posture, his eyes drunken with ecstasy, summoning within him the serpent-power of the subconscious.

And to the hearing ear comes a whisper of the ageless worship that has always ascended, and will ascend to uncounted time, from this city of ceaseless prayer.

CHAPTER XXXI
WHERE THE SAHIB GOES TO FORGET

WE have visited all of the hill stations in India—with the exception of thirty-three. We do not know where the remaining thirty-three are, nor what they are called, but we are confident that they are somewhere in the peninsula, for this is a land that boasts of more hill stations than can be visited in a single spin of the wheel of life. To the Hindu mind the reason is simple; there is a hill for every reincarnation. And when one sees what some of the hill stations are like one no longer wonders why so many people seem to patronize an entirely different one in each succeeding journey from the cradle to the grave.

There is as much of the caste system evident in the classification of Indian hill stations as there is in the classification of the pilgrims who visit Benares.

For instance, Simla, Ootacamund, Maymyo, and Mahableshwar are for British officials; Darjeeling for Calcutta's merchant princes and tourists; Mussooree, Kalaw, and Thandaung for those who do not wear social strait-jackets; Poona for the Parsees, Mount

257

Abu for the Jains; Kodai Kanal for the missionaries; and so on.

As evidence of our right to speak with authority on the subject of India's hill stations, we would have it known that we have been to Sheikh Budin. This charming summer resort is built on a barren rock that overlooks the waterless desert of Sind and the parched mountains of Waziristan. It consists of five bungalows and a bar. For those hardy spirits who go there it is a case of a bar, a loaf of bread, and thou, singing beside me in the wilderness. Sheikh Budin is as dry all the year round as Darjeeling is wet during the monsoon. Before going there you are obliged to order a supply of water sent up from the nearest railway station, for no water is available at the bar. After three days at Sheikh Budin we returned to Dera Ismael Khan because we had run out of water and had a choice of dying either of thirst or of delirium tremens.

Quetta, the hill station for Baluchistan, is chiefly famous for its admirable club. The most interesting pastime in Quetta is joining the regular evening rendezvous in the club billiard-room to listen to Colonel B, the retired police commissioner, spinning yarns. Colonel B possesses a niche in the Hall of Fame because he is one of Rudyard Kipling's heroes. But his yarns are even stranger than Kipling's.

The leading indoor sport of Quetta is worshiping Bokhara rugs. When you are invited out to tea, as soon as the chaprassi relieves you of your solar topee, spine-pad, and swagger-stick, you and your host and hostess fall upon your knees on a Jhan Bagy or a Turkoman or a Kiva or a Baluchi prayer-rug, turn your faces reverently toward Bokhara, kiss the rug nine times, quote Chapter Nine from Jenkin's "Handbook on Oriental Carpets," and then tell the threads of the warp over one by one as though it were a rosary instead of a rug.

Visiting Quetta in the middle of the winter after spending a year or two in Madras, Bombay, or Calcutta, is much the same as accompanying Admiral Byrd on one of his polar flights. But in springtime the air of the Quetta plateau is fragrant with the intoxicating perfume of apple-blossoms and the bazaar is crowded with all the strange types of central Asia. You may also see the Indian Army Staff College officers, whose crest is a wise old owl.

We remember Quetta chiefly for the delicious curry puffs served by the Goanese chef at Stanyon's Hotel, and for the "Baluchistan Royal Opera House," as the Tommies call their new theater. It is second only in size to the Empire at Calcutta, and we saw as many as nine people seated in the stalls at the same time. Each hardy customer brings his own blankets and ear-muffs. This magnificent theater, devoted to the advancement of the histrionic art in Baluchistan, boasts of everything but stage-hands, so the actors of visiting companies are obliged to shift their scenery in full view of the audience.

Bangalore is interesting chiefly because of its mammoth Government Building of bright-red sandstone, which from a distance looks as though it would be large enough to accommodate the League of Nations delegates. Perhaps it will one day—when the post of president is offered to Mr. Ghandi. . . .

In the museum at Bangalore are two stuffed monstrosities that the visitor is always shown. One is a baby buffalo with one head, two bodies, and eight legs. The other is a baby zebu with two heads, and only one body. But there is plenty of human interest outside the museum.

The population of this hill station consists largely of retired Indian civil service and army veterans, who live here in a state of blissful boredom. Two distinguished pensioners sat at the table adjoining us in the hotel dining-room. Each evening they split a quart bottle of champagne in silence. They grew very grave over their wine and then went slowly and portentously to bed.

In that land of mystery which is India, and especially in the tropics near Bangalore and Octacamund, there is a mystery fruit—the mango. What is its flavor? Why do you eat it? How should you eat it?

But especially, *why?* A madness seizes the devotees of the mango. The pungent, tarry smell of the fruit is distinguishable from all the other odors of the Indian bazaar: as soon as a mango-maniac smells it his nostrils dilate, his eyes goggle, and his tongue cleaves to his palate, until he is assuaged by the object of his heart's desire. And once he has it, still the mango cannot be eaten. You cannot eat a mango casually, just like that. You must take it to your bathroom, reverently disrobe, get into your tub, and then fall to. Only thus, in the twilight of an Indian ghusalkhana can you woo this mystic fruit as it should be wooed.

There are as many varieties of them as there are varieties of grapes in France and of dates in Arabia. But the one that causes the mango-madness is about the size of an Oregon apple, and shaped like a cache-nut. It is as yellow as saffron. Its skin has the thickness of a cucumber rind. Within this is the succulent sap, and the seed half the size of the fruit. The skin clings to the edible part, which in turn clings tenaciously to the stone. To eat a mango without smearing it all over oneself and everything in the vicinity is as much of a lost art as dyeing with Tyrian purple. For a hundred and fifty years the brightest intellects of Britain have been considering the problem without achieving a solution.

Churlish and impatient lovers of the mango there are, of course, who cannot wait for the supreme moment of solitude when the mango can be wrestled with and enjoyed. To watch these vandal mango-tasters is a pitiable sight. They fly at the fruit, gash it with a knife, or dig with their nails into its velvety skin. The result is always the same. Salmon-pink rivulets of mango juice stream out between their fingers onto the wrist-watches or bracelets of men and maidens, while the seed—the luscious seed that is the mango's chiefest glory—bounces to bosom and floor.

At dinner-time, something has to be devised with knife and fork, but to dissect a mango thus at a dinner-table is to lose all its true inwardness. One of these days some gastronomic genius in Hindustan will invent a pair of curved tongs with which to hold the fruit, and a spoon with a sharp edge to it wherewith to scoop. . . . But India is a conservative country, and perhaps after all the time-honored methods of our ancestors are the best.

Naked and alone, you seize the mango firmly between the toes and stooping swiftly over it, drain its quintessence in one exhilarating draught. Another way, even more satisfying, is to put the whole thing in your mouth at once; after a little practice the lips should be sufficiently flexible. But even Solomon felt that there was something baffling about the fruit, for tradition relates that mango fool [stewed or crushed fruit] was always served at the great king's table—a proof that even that monarch had met more than his match.

As far as the British Empire is concerned, mangoes have existed about as long as Manchester. All the long hierarchy of resplendent personages who have enriched the history of England's dealings with the great depend-

ency, have bent their lips to the mango, from Lord Clive
to Lord Curzon and Lord Irwin. None of these great
men solved the problem, and neither the present Government nor the Legislative Assembly has considered
the question, realizing that it is beyond their powers.

In appearance, the mango is green or gold or red. In
size it varies from a pear to a pumpkin. In taste, it can
only be characterized as quite indescribable.

During the season at least ten million mangoes a day
must be eaten in India, one hundred million flies must
be buzzing around them during the daylight hours, at
least a million cur dogs lick the discarded skins, several
thousand individuals slip on them, and several hundreds a day, at least, die of colic from eating the fruit un-
ripe. The mango, in short, is of national importance.

Yet there is no epic of the mango, no lyric of the
mango, indeed no mention of it in Aryan literature.
There is a conspiracy of silence about the mango. Men
tremble before its possibilities, shrink before the unknown potentialities for good and for evil that lie in its
luscious heart. Alluring yet baffling, with its problems
all unsolved, it remains the mystery fruit of the East.

The afternoon we left Bangalore for Octacamund a
mob of gentle Muhammadans tore a Hindu to bits in the
bazaar, which gave the place the local color it had been
lacking before.

Mussoorie and Murree are both banal to a degree, but
the former is probably the pleasanter of the two, being

less official. There is a hotel in Mussoorie where they ring a bell just before dawn so that the pious may say their prayers and the impious get back to their beds.

"Ooty" is known as the "Queen of Hill Stations," although who calls it that we don't quite know. Perhaps the judges and generals who go there on leave. On "Ooty's" delightful downs all the rank and fashion of the presidency may be seen on horseback in pink coats and top-hats hunting jackal with English foxhounds. The hunting is good, the motor roads superlative. There is no more delightful spot—for millionaires and for polo.

Passing any central Asian village to-day, you may see the ancient game of polo being played in the village street, just exactly as it has been played in central Asia for these last three thousand years. China, of course, which claims the beginnings of polo as it does of chess, spillikins, the dope-habit, and most other diversions of the modern or ancient world, undoubtedly has drawings of polo-matches in progress at a time when the other nations of antiquity were still too busy settling their blood-feuds to devote much attention to play.

But nearer our own day are the Great Moghuls of India, those rollicking bandits who swept down on the fair fat land of Hindustan with their lean hordes of Turkomans, and gobbled everything up. These Moghuls were great polo-players. It is on record that the Emperor Akbar reproved a courtier for slackness in his play, and this Emperor's court and household had to be diligent in their attendance at the polo-ground. Akbar's polo-pony stables are still in existence at Fatehpur-Sikri, his ruined city near Agra, with their great red-sandstone mangers. To any polo-lover they speak elo-quently of the great emperor's practical interest in the game and his grip of details. Akbar was just the build for a first-class player, and if what we are told of his eye be true, that he never missed anything he aimed at—then, mounted as he must have been on the very best animal that money could buy or power acquire, he must have been up to international form. He was strong, stocky, with an exceptionally powerful seat, and a nerve that nothing could daunt.

It is a thousand pities that no more accurate records exist of the game in those days. As far as can be judged, it differed but little from the game as played to-day, ex-cept that the players were not limited as at present to four a side. Ponies were rather smaller, and sticks fol-lowed suit; otherwise the rules were to all intents and purposes identical.

Nowadays, polo in India is becoming a rich man's game, as it has long been in England and America. Gone are the days when the subaltern played his pony three chukkers every polo day and then harnessed it up to the buggy and trotted it to the club, where it waited between the shafts while its master refreshed himself after the exertions of the afternoon.

Par excellence, polo is the sport of kings in India. A big tournament, such as is held at Calcutta or Delhi, where all the "flower of Rajput chivalry" (in fact as well as in name) and all the premier princes of India congregate to play, is for sheer spectacular effect better worth watching than even the fastest of international polo. For speed, brilliance, diversity of strokers, and fine horsemanship there is nothing to compare with a first-class India team, such as those of Jodhpur or Patiala at the present day.

A cheap game polo can never be again in India. Indeed, it would lose half its fascination but for the perfect horseflesh to be seen on the polo-ground to-day. But although polo is not for paupers, neither is it yet the sole prerogative of millionaires. It is a game in which almost every one of the official classes in India can take part, if they have the will to do so, and it is a great pity that the will is not more universal, for there is no finer game in the world, nor one better suited to fit the Englishman for the problems he must face in that country.

Long may the rajah, the soldier, and the civilian meet in friendly rivalry on the polo ground! Here at any rate there is no truth in the saying that "East is East and West is West, and never the twain shall meet"—because they do meet, in terrific encounters in which every nerve of men and horses is strained to beat the opponent. East and West bump and barge and swear at each other and fight a grim battle until the close of play. Then East and

West go off arm in arm, and the best men have won, and everybody is pleased.

What shall we say of "Naughty Naini"? There is a lovely lake there. When the moon is at its full you can row across the radiant waters to the willows by the farther bank. The moonlight falls in patches through the trellis of these willows—ah, what whispered vows this friendly spot has heard! Fortunate it is that the willows of Naini Tal will not tell.

There is also a Royal Naini Tal Yacht Club whose members may be seen wearing their nautical caps and shivering their timbers every evening from six to eight.

As to Simla, the Mecca of the mediocre man, you may voyage from Perim to Pekin during the hot season without finding such pleasant companionship and such superlative port as you may get at the United Services Club. Simla is an interesting place for the student of the human comedy, provided he climbs Jakko Hill once a week and contemplates the sacred monkeys with eyes of understanding.

The only other golf-course as good as "Ooty's" is that of Gul Marg in Kashmir. Gul Marg is eight thousand five hundred feet high and the altitude sometimes causes palpitation among the newly arrived, which can, however, be corrected by asking the advice of the popular chief steward of the club. The gaiety of Gul Marg during its short season, July to September, is something staggering. You dance till dawn, consume a plate of eggs and bacon and play a round of golf—by that time the sun is up; you change out of your evening things, which will be the worse for wear by then, have your bath, breakfast, take a nap; another round of golf; and one o'clock finds you back among the throng who are fortifying themselves with gin and bitters to face their wives at lunch. In the afternoon there is polo, tennis, more golf, or a picnic. Picnics are popular in Gul Marg; you climb up mountainsides with short-skirted enchantresses, munch snow at the Frozen Lakes, pick flowers and ferns, and probably fall in love or over a precipice. In the evening, of course you dance. Finally, when you have compromised yourself, or when you can't distinguish a golf-ball from a liver-spot, you motor down hill to Srinagar and study the lotuses there.

CHAPTER XXXII
THE VALE OF KASHMIR

⧼⧽

As you stand upon the Throne of Solomon—the mountain overlooking Srinagar and its lakes in the far-famed Vale of Kashmir—you may see one of the most remarkable and romantic views on earth: not a view indeed, but a vision of surpassing loveliness.

At your feet lies the painted city of Srinagar, among groves of green, seamed by sapphire waterways. Beyond is the great Dal Lake with its famous floating gardens, past which the Moghul emperors were rowed in stately procession to their lakeside pleasaunces, and past which to-day go the house-boats of the holiday-makers who are spending their well-earned leave among the embowered glades of the Happy Valley. These floating gardens, renowned in story and song, are made in a very simple fashion and for a very utilitarian purpose. They are vegetable gardens, made by cutting aquatic plants a foot or two below the surface of the water, and then entangling sedges and rushes in their stems, to form a woof in which detritus collects: in a year or two an excellent vegetable garden has grown out of the limpid waters of the lake, and golden watermelons begin to sprout where the water-lily has lately been, and cucumbers and tomatoes, greatly to the pleasure and profit of the Kashmiri floating-gardener, whose eye for beauty is not as acute as his desire for cash.

In the distance you may see the gardens of Shalimar: terrace upon terrace of green lawn with gorgeous banks of flowers sloping down to the Dal. These are the gardens where the fierce central Asiatics of the seed of Tamerlane—men of the same breed and the same mold of countenance as many of the chief Bolsheviki to-day— took their queens from the dust of the sweltering empire they had conquered, to live and to love among the fountains of a veritable Elysium. It is small wonder that the Great Moghuls spent their honeymoons here. It is a land of love, as well as a land to love.

Circling all the valley, over the wreaths and pennons of cloud that hang over the margin of the waters, stand the Himalayas, sweeping up and up, and stretching back and back, to the white and eternal solitudes of Karakoram, Kinchinjunga, and Everest. A noble frame to a noble picture, enchanting in its color and unsurpassed in its grandeur.

All over the Eastern world the City of Waters and its surroundings are held in veneration. As men from northern Europe come down for their holidays and their honeymoons to the shores of the Mediterranean, as the New Yorker goes to Florida and California, or the

Montrealer to the lakes of the Canadian Rockies, or the
Spaniard to the Balearic Islands, or the Japanese to
Nikko, or the Cockney to Clacton-on-Sea, so from all
over the sweep of the Ganges plains, from the Brahmaputra Valley, and from the land of the Five Rivers—
from end to end of India as far south as the Vyndhyas—
come profiteers and poets, bureaucrats and babus, saints
to worship at the shrine of Amarnath and sinners to
carouse with the milk-faced maidens of Kashmir. . . .

> "If on Earth there be a Heaven of bliss,
>   It is this, it is this, it is this!"

Dawn on the Arabian Desert has been described as
waking in the heart of an opal; the snow-capped vol-
canoes and glaciers breaking off into Resurrection Bay
on the Alaskan coast are among the most awe-inspiring
works of Nature; and for dramatic suddenness the terrific Grand Canyon of the Colorado is unsurpassed on
earth; but the high Himalayas stand alone, above all the
wonders of the world, above all the things of beauty
and of terror on this planet.

Although the magic of the great mountains is indescribable, yet every man who sees the Himalayas from
the Vale of Kashmir or from Tiger Hill in northern
Bengal, feels that he must bear witness to this white
wonder that has been unveiled before him and that has
taken him, perhaps for a moment only, above the cares
and crampings of his normal world.

For an hour we have been sitting on a moss-covered

rock on the northwest slope of Tiger Hill facing mighty Kinchinjunga and the great white giants of ice and rock that bar the way to central Asia, the home of sages, the cradle of the human race. Although we are nine thousand feet above the plain behind us, we are nearly twenty thousand feet below the mightiest mountains in the world that tower in mid-heaven before us. Across the valley, which drops four thousand feet, rise the guardians of Tibet, with Kinchinjunga, their monarch, standing before that land of mystery, the realm of the Dalai Llama. Below us, to the left and just out of sight, is the road to Lhasa, the road we one day hope to travel. And there also lie the mountains of Nepal and Kat-mandu, the forbidden capital of the maharajah of Nepal. Directly in front of us is the flowery land of Sikkim, paradise of botanists. At the farthest end of Sikkim we can just see, like a dent in the frosting of a wedding cake, the Jelap-la, the ice-covered pass into Tibet. Behind us stretch Bengal, the valley of the Ganges, and the torrid and teeming plains of India.

For days we have been living in soft white clouds, and for hours on end we have been swept by rains that seemed to threaten to remove our bungalow from Senchal Hill to the colossal chasm below Darjeeling. But this afternoon a wind from the direction of Mount Everest blew the monsoon mist out of our eyes and cleared the sky so that instead of seeing a few yards our sight suddenly extended for a hundred miles and more.

Below it is still raining and clouds are tumbling in the valley between us and Tibet, but here the horizon sweeps an arc of a thousand miles from the great hills to the great plains.

Kinchinjunga is just across the valley only forty miles away. It piles up in the sky to twenty-eight thousand feet, only a thousand feet less than Everest, and it is perhaps the grandest mountain of the earth. On either side are Kabru and Jannu, rising to twenty-four thousand and twenty-five thousand feet respectively.

As we sit here on our rock on Tiger Hill watching the clouds go trouping past Kinchinjunga, it reminds us of a military review with Kinchinjunga the king, and the billowy white masses a mighty cosmic army parading before our eyes. See how that big cloud rolls up and completely shuts off Kinchinjunga, just as Foch once overshadowed Poincaré when he marched along the Élysées at the head of his *poilus*.

As the sun drops over the ice-rim of Tibet, the snowy summits of the Himalayas are tipped with gold like the "tyi" of a Burmese pagoda. And behind us the sky is brilliant with color over the plains of Bengal. Here is a high horizon of the vividest ultramarine that looks as if the seas had surged over India as they did over Atlantis of old. The mountains against the sunset seem as though some Titan's furnace had opened behind them.

Far to the northward the "Alpine glow" lights three far-distant peaks. The middle one, inconspicuous owing to the distance, and looking like an ice-cream cone, is Everest. Somewhere on that slope in imagination we see a camp, a handful of plucky Englishmen smoking their pipes and around them coolies cooking dinner, yaks chewing the cud. May the god of the Holy Mountain look with favor on their next attempt!

An hour ago it was dark in this valley at the foot of Tiger Hill, and now that the sunset above has faded, the blue haze rising out of the forest becomes deeper and deeper. It is a dim, indistinct world down there. Far down in the valley below us the little toy houses of the tea-planters become vaguer and vaguer, and the dwellings of Darjeeling clinging to the mountainside melt into the wreaths of azure that creep over the layers of the landscape.

In the high heaven there is a riot of color—alizarine, turquoise, violet, crimson—where the setting sun touches the rain-clouds with his glory. A giant with fist outstretched has passed across the west. And now a gigantic dragon has stretched his length across a hundred miles of Himalayas. A mass of vapor, like thick-flocked wool, rises out of the valley, a white wall through which nothing can be seen. Then slowly, with twisting laminæ, like the iris of a lens, an aperture forms in the white wall and Kinchinjunga is framed in the oval.

The sun is still shining there on that high and haughty crest where the winds of the world are sweeping. A flamboyant flame burns about the crest like a streak of fire, like a comet's tail. It is the banner cloud, the radiance of driven snow caught by the last rays of a sun that has left the world of men but still lingers among the great white brethren of Tibet.

But how futile we stand before the Himalayas, with our cameras and our stylographs and our stammered words of praise! What are our adjectives and ideas? The Himalayas are utterly above the contriving of our language. Only the soul of man may know them. Our puny minds can make some guess of the time when they began, may see some glimmering of the day that will come when they shall vanish in the ruin of the world; yet we know nothing, can imagine nothing, so wonderful is their present glory with the sunset on their stainless snows. They stand, for us creatures of a day, from eternity to eternity. They began before our race began, and before they crumble in cataclysmic night the eyes of our posterity will have closed. Nor tongue nor pen may tell their wonder. We can only look. We have reached a borderland, a zero, an infinity—something that exists but that we cannot express. Throned above all the world and crowned with the glory of the sunset, the Himalayas are indeed the kings of earth.

It is bitter cold on Tiger Hill, and it is dark now, and it will soon be dinner-time. A bath, a dinner, a fire, await us at Senchal Bungalow. And so we take our leave of the Himalayas to-night, going down without turning our backs on his seraphic majesty, Kinchinjunga.

CHAPTER XXXIII
THE LONDON OF JOHN BULL'S TROPIC REALM

OF course, Calcutta and the Indian Empire might have happened even in spite of Dr. Gabriel Boughton and the little Moghul princess whose dress caught fire. For old Job Charnock was a very determined man and behind him were very determined men.

Old Job Charnock founded Calcutta one August day in the year 1690—he just stood there in his breeches on the banks of the river Hughli, and he said, "We'll build a city here!" And he did. In 1700 there were 10,000 people in Calcutta. In 1800 there were 200,000. In 1930 there are more than a million. It is the most important city in the East, richer even than Shanghai.

At half after one o'clock on Thursday, November 17, 1759, Lord Clive was playing cards in this same city of Job Charnock's, when a sweating messenger arrived from Colonel Forde, at Bidera, up-river, asking for an order in council authorizing him to attack the Dutch. Clive didn't interrupt his rubber: having played his hand, he scribbled while the cards were being cut and shuffled:

"Dear Forde, Fight them immediately and I will send you an order in council tomorrow."

That was the spirit! They defeated the Dutch, they drove out the French, and settled down. There were men in those days in Calcutta who

"Now took a fleet, now sold a pound of tea,
Weighed soap, stormed forts, held princes *in terrorem*,
Drank, fought, smoked, lied, went home, and good papas
Gave diamonds to their little boys for taws."

And their descendants are worthy of them. The times are less spacious, perhaps, but they make all the money they can, and that is a lot. If you ask one of the Scotch burra sahibs how business is, a pained look comes into his face. He hates talking of his hundred and fifty percent dividends. So we won't either.

The maidan is the greatest feature of Calcutta. In fact it *is* Calcutta. The place couldn't exist without it. Where else could the non-coöperators hold their meetings? Where could the British ride and play golf? Where could the races and the football matches be held?

At the far end is the Victoria Memorial, a wedding-cake-like affair, not actually ugly, but hardly worth $5,000,000, and at the other end, the Eden Gardens, where twenty years ago the wit and beauty of the capital used to drive of an evening to listen to the band. Now it is the haunt of the babu and the antelope-eyed Eurasian girls, and of sand-baggers waiting for drunken

sailors. Bang in the center of the maidan is the Ochterlony monument, of which Mark Twain says: "Every
day from the battlements of Heaven, Clive and Hastings
look down and wonder which of the two the monument
is for; they fret and worry because they cannot find out,
and the peace of Heaven is spoiled for them and lost.
But not so Ochterlony. Ochterlony is not troubled. He
doesn't suspect that it is his monument. Heaven is sweet
and peaceful for him. There is a sort of unfairness about
it all."

The botanical gardens of Calcutta are practically
without a rival. Sir Joseph Hooker, who is an eminent
authority, says that they have contributed more useful
and ornamental tropical plants to the public and private
gardens of the world than any other establishment,
either before or since. Here is the biggest banyan-tree
in the world, one hundred years old, and with two hundred aërial roots, if you care for that sort of thing.

As to the Zoo, there are some fine specimens (as is
only right) of the Bengal tiger, and an attractive hip-
popotamus with a dentrifice smile. The museum contains the finest existing specimens of the fossil verte-
brates of the Siwalik age—to be explicit, it contains
things like a cross between a dog and a polar bear, and
an eagle and a poached egg. A day in this museum will
teach you more of India than a week of reading.

The place of the Black Hole has been restored by
Lord Curzon (all over India we come across marks of

his reverence for the past) and you may see the actual size of that historic chamber where the British suffered and died—"the seed from which sprang the Battle of Plassy, that laid deep and strong the foundation of England's colossal Indian sovereignty."

To-day the site is marked by an engraved plate and an iron fence. On this spot there once was a room hardly eighteen feet square where one hundred and forty-six British prisoners were packed by the victorious nabob of Bengal. They had space neither to stand nor to breathe. The weather was sweltering hot. The prisoners were confined in the evening. Before dawn all were dead but twenty-three.

Three generations or so ago the story was familiar to every one in the world. To-day no one seems to know anything about it, but as long as men walk this earth the echo of that episode will remain. Those who survived did so by sucking the perspiration from their own clothing, and from that of those nearest them. The details of what occurred in that hole of horrors leave one dumb. It was the ghastly tragedy of the Black Hole that brought young Clive, one of the greatest military geniuses in history, storming up from southern India. It was the Black Hole that brought on that extraordinary battle, whose like was not seen on earth from Agincourt down to Allenby's sweeping victory over the Turks at Armageddon.

The fort, the High Court (a dreadful building, which

the guide-book says is copied after the Halle des Dra-
piers at Ypres, which we can hardly credit, as it is nothing like the Halle), the cathedral, the university, Thack-
eray's house, and Duelling Lane can be neglected.

But every one should wander, for an hour or so, down
Park Street and in old Calcutta, to the cemetery where
Rose Aylmer lies:

> "Rose Aylmer whom these wakeful eyes
> May weep but never see!
> A night of memories and sighs
> I dedicate to thee!"

Leaving the cemetery, he should wander through
the streets and squares built by the English during the
last two hundred years. No other city in the East is built
so solidly, or has such a "London look."

Calcutta is reputed to be one of the most "cliquey"
places in India. Yet the Scotch, who form the bulk of
its society, are the kindliest people in the world—within
strictly defined limits. They dislike the society of foreigners, adventurers, upstarts, and natives. You must
convince Calcutta that you don't belong to any of these
undesirable classes (unless very eminent in them, of
course) before you can cross the threshold of the Bengal
Club, even as a guest. Incidentally (and without exag-
geration, in this chapter that is gradually filling with
superlatives, as a duckpond doth with weeds), the Bengal Club is one of the best in the world. No one who
knows it will gainsay this.

As to the Turf Club, that holy of holies of the racing elect, few even among the Calcuttaites belong, it is so confoundedly select. Here is drawn the world-famous Calcutta Sweep, worth $500,000 or more each year.

Then there is the Tollygunge Club, a delightful sylvan retreat, where paper-chases are held every Sunday. There are young men in top-boots, and girls just out from the British Isles, with the roses of York and Lancaster and the Highlands still in their cheeks, and old burra sahibs and their wives, with complexions of parchment, and ponies squealing, and horns tooting, and khitmutgars bustling around with trays. Every one is talking and laughing and discussing the dance the night before at the Saturday Club, and taking a little cherry brandy as jumping-powder. At last they all make a move to their horses.

They're off! After a few minutes of cracking pace all save the peerless few are out of the race. The remainder jog back to the starting-point, and wait around for breakfast.

Breakfast is a hearty meal of the curries for which Bengal is famous, eggs, meats, fruit salad, and draughts of iced beer, topped off with a little more cherry brandy. Then with Coronas between their lips, Calcutta's sportsmen are ready to motor home, feeling that after all this exercise their livers can stand the wear and tear of Calcutta for another week. And with it all they keep "vera weel" and live to a ripe and revered old age.

It is a rainy Saturday afternoon. The maidan looks as green as green can be. Five games of football are going on. The players are chiefly Bengalis, and they play in their bare feet. One game, railed off from the others, is a first-league match, a Bengali team against British soldiers. A roar goes up as the Bengali outside right makes a good run—a roar such as you may hear at the Yankee Stadium when Babe Ruth knocks a homer into the center-field bleachers, a little shriller perhaps, but still from the heart of the crowd.

Beyond smokes the shipping of the "Satanic English," who invented this football game, and a few things like the new councils, as well as Calcutta, this London of Britain's "tropic realm."

CHAPTER XXXIV
ON THE ROAD TO ELEUSIS

MYSTERIES and signs have an attraction that is as old as it is irresistible. The rites of Orpheus, the cult of Eleusis, the secret words of Solomon, weave a spell about our common intelligence. So also with regard to the mysteries of the East and the magic of Indian holy men: we are ready to believe anything (in reason) about them, and we feel distinctly hurt when a yogi, living in Chicago, spoils the spell by writing a book on yoga, showing how it is done, giving the whole show away, and wrecking another of our illusions. The objection to learning yoga out of a book is, of course, that it is just about as easy as learning golf out of a book.

To know about yoga, you must *be* a yogi. There is no other way. And more, if you practise the breathing, posture, and meditation in the seclusion of your room, without the help of a living teacher, you are just about as likely to get them right as you would be to get the pronunciation of Russian words right by studying a dictionary. This is simple sense.

Go to India, therefore, or forever hold your peace

on yoga. And, having gone, you will realize how difficult it is *not* to hold your peace. How impossible it is, in other words, to reconcile the ancient wisdom with the printed word. Ink and pulp-paper are not proper vehicles for the syllables of the sages.

Without, however, going into a disquisition of the "kingly wisdom" and the "kingly mystery," we may find much that is of absorbing interest in the various sects and denominations of those who study occult things in the land of the occult. And first of all, there are no dabblers in mysticism in India, no "sissies," high-brow widows, or emotional æsthetes. Or if there are, they soon give up to get down to business. The man or woman who sets out to study the hidden powers of Nature in India does so with all the definiteness of a man training for a boat-race. He knows it is a whole-time job, something to be worked for, not talked about.

And secondly, the yogi undergoes real privation. To this extent at least he is entitled to our respect. Abandoning house and home, and all food eaten in towns, he seeks refuge in a lonely wood. Here he shaves off the tuft of hair that every orthodox Hindu keeps in the center of his head, and seeks out a guru, just as the keen golfer seeks out the expert professional. The guru whispers into the ears of the neophyte various instructions as to stance and swing, much like the golf professional, and also gives him some sacred formula, such as *"Namah sivayah"* or *"Aum namah sivayah."* He is then renamed, and goes through a course of exercises in breathing, sitting, and meditation, which frequently terminate his earthly career. Here, for instance, is the experience of one would-be mystic, who decided he would live to be a holy man another day, and has developed into a prosperous merchant instead:

"I spent the greater part of the night awake, with my mind a blank, fixedly repeating the mystic syllable OM. I stared at the sky until I saw a moon which was not there, then gradually the whole heaven filled with moons. I held my breath till I fainted."

If the yogi survives this routine and certain exercises connected with the control of involuntary muscular action, he is given some testing penances—such as standing stark naked in the sun, surrounded by fires; sitting immersed in water for days on end; standing on one leg for a month at a time; or taking a vow of silence for several years. Also he is sent on one or two pilgrimages, begging his way. If he has committed any venial offense, such as adultery or killing a low-caste man, he will also probably have to fee the priests, or if he has done more deadly deeds, such as preventing a cow from drinking, or annoying a Brahmin, he may have to make the pilgrimage to the temple of Jagannath and expiate his offense by measuring his length in the dust all the way to that holy shrine.

When the apprenticeship is complete, the sannyasi (for so he is now called) prepares his own funeral rites, indicating the death of the flesh and rebirth to spiritual life. He then assumes the saffron robe, and is accounted a holy man before all his people.

Soon, probably, he starts smoking hemp—for it is a curious fact that a large proportion of Indian mystics are addicted to this form of intoxication. Later, he becomes a paramahansa, which means a "great goose," and is the highest order of holy man. He goes on many pilgrimages to the great and popular shrines at Benares, at Madura, at Puri, and if he be of an especial piety and recondite holiness he may journey for occult meditation at the Black Pagoda.

Some time ago a "great goose" came to the house of a learned Calcutta Brahmin, with a number of his followers. The paramahansa declared that he was entirely above cold or hunger and required nothing of any kind to sustain life. His followers, however, were not so other-worldly, and ate quite a lot, as the learned Brahmin found to his cost. They also thieved a good deal, and gave other trouble. In fact, they were a very dissolute lot, but the learned Brahmin put up with them for the sake of the one righteous man among them, the great-goose saint who wanted no mortal sustenance. No doubt he was a most remarkable man, endowed with powers above the common lot of mortals, for he kept fat and well on a simple diet of air. Most carefully the Brahmin watched him, and to make quite certain took precautions so that no food could possibly get to the holy man, who never left the room he occupied in the Brahmin's house. So impressed was the Brahmin, after months of observation, with the miraculous power of the paramahansa, that he presented him and his followers with a purse amounting to several thousands of rupees. Years later, however, he was disillusioned. In the course of a journey he saw one of the companions of the holy man tilling a field. He went up to the ploughman and questioned him as to the paramahansa's welfare. The man shrugged his shoulders and smiled, then he said:

"He is not a holy man at all, and as to keeping himself alive without food, that is easily explained!"

"Please tell me," said the Brahmin.

"I will tell you for two gold pieces," said the ploughman.

"Here they are!" answered the Brahmin, quickly. The secret was cheap at the price. After biting the mohurs, to see that they were soft gold, the laborer replied:

"The truth is, he kept himself alive on food I vomited for him."

So it was the Brahmin who was the "great goose," after all!

"Of him who gives natural birth, and him who gives knowledge of the whole Veda, the giver of sacred knowledge is the more venerable father." This is the opinion of Manu, the lawgiver of the ancient Aryans and the earliest sage in history. In short, to be the father of a baby is easier than to beget a new idea. Few will dispute this, but as a matter of fact the saddhus of India are responsible for more of the former than the latter, because one of their chief functions, after they have passed their novitiate and have become full-fledged holy men, is to weave spells for the consolation of the childless.

One of the most interesting of all the classes of saddhus is the tantrick. His is the "serpent-power" known to Egyptian Isis and golden-haired Dionysus. The rites are accomplished by the meeting of eight, nine, or eleven couples, with the fivefold ceremony of union, gesticulation, flesh, fish, and wine. Some among their number practise a horrible form of meditation called "siva sadhana," performed seated on the body of a corpse.

That other acts, more ghastly still, form part of this living religion is shown by the fact that on December 29, 1884, Mr. Krishna Dass Babaji, a respectable clerk, was fined fifteen rupees by Mr. Sen, then the district magistrate of Berhampur, for committing a public nuisance, in that he ate part of the dead body of a woman at Khagra Ghat. . . .

This leaves us dumb. No doubt Mr. Babaji only did this in order to fulfill some rite of his Aghorpanthi sect —still, a fine of fifteen rupees seems unsuitable. It is either too much, or too little, according to the point of view you take.

CHAPTER XXXV
THE MAN WHO RAISES THE DEAD

INSTEAD of going to the Everglades of Florida in search of the Fountain of Youth, Ponce de Leon should have turned the prow of his galleon toward Hindustan. There is a yogi in India who claims to have discovered the principle of life in the sun's rays. He claims to be able with this power to resurrect both men and animals, and to have discovered the Spring of Perpetual Life for which De Leon sought in vain.

We heard of him almost by chance. It was while we were at Puri, the holiest city of the Hindus. We had gone to call on the manager of the Temple of Jagannath, Rai Bahadur Sakki Chand, a distinguished and scholarly gentleman who has retired from an inspectorship in the Indian police to take up his present appointment. His claim to a knowledge of the world and a robust common sense no one can dispute.

We asked him whether he knew of any *genuine* yogis. We said that we had heard that there were still men living in India who were the guardians of the unwritten wisdom of the ages, which is passed from master to disciple by signs and secret words, but which is never committed to writing or divulged to strangers. We said we had heard this, but doubted whether there was any "wisdom" which could not be uttered and enunciated in the usual way.

"I have no doubt at all that there is a secret knowledge," he replied, "and that there are seers to whom it is revealed. But such men are few and far between. You must not confuse them with ash-covered ascetics and juggling fakirs. Here in Puri there is a saddhu who will interest you. I will not express any opinion on his powers myself. But go and see him. His name is Saddhu Bisudhanan Dhan. Any one will tell you where he lives, close to the police lines."

"And has he really got supernatural powers?" we enquired.

"Supernatural? That depends. . . . Go and see him if you are interested in occult things."

We went. But first we made some inquiries about his history and antecedents. He was being watched by the police, of course. He would be watched by the police in any country. A man like him would have been hung as a sorcerer in New England, not so long ago.

Briefly, his history is this: He was born at Hoogli in Bengal, fifty years ago. When a lad of thirteen, he was bitten by a mad dog, and his mother brought him to the Ganges to die. The sight of water terrified him; none the less he was plunged into the sacred river, like all Hindus about to die. Then a curious thing happened. His mother, and the mourners who had assembled for the funeral obsequies, noticed that when the boy was immersed in the Ganges the water sank round his body, and that when he was raised again the water rose also, in a column above his head. An old saddhu who happened to be on the spot declared that the lad was destined for great things. He gave him a root to rub on the dog-bite and prophesied that Bisudhanan would recover and be a great yogi. In a week he would return to see how the lad was getting on.

When the saddhu came back the boy was cured. Naturally, he determined to follow the old saddhu to the ends of the earth, and every one, including his mother, thought this was only reasonable.

Having adopted the sage as his guru or spiritual father, he was levitated with him to Tibet, and there studied the science of solar energy for thirty years or so, among the ageless masters of mankind, who are known to the wise as the "Great White Brethren" and live in the remote fastnesses of the Himalayas, where tiresome travelers can't take snapshots.

After his studies, he traveled for seven years, and then settled down at Benares to help the world. His disciples have given him a house at Benares, a modern bungalow and garden near the beach at Puri, and a flat in Calcutta. They are also building a laboratory for him on the banks of the Ganges. Some of his disciples are men of wealth. One is a rajah. He is on the threshold of the secret of life. In a few years—or a few lives, perhaps—he thinks he will have conquered death. . . . *Chi vivrá verrá!*

Sparrows and small animals that have been dead for some time, he has already succeeded in resurrecting. A disciple who holds a post of considerable importance in the Calcutta government told us about these apocalyptic sparrows. Two birds were carefully and completely strangled by a low-caste man, and after strangulation were left for four hours, to make sure that life was extinct. Then the saddhu came along with his magnifying glass, concentrated a little sunlight on their glazed eyes, and lo! the rumpled feathers stirred, their beaks opened, and with a shake and a hop and a chirrup and a flutter, the sparrows flew away, praising the Lord of birds and men.

Not once, but twenty times, has the saddhu demonstrated this miracle to his disciples. Soon, in the laboratory that is being fitted up for him in Benares, he hopes to begin experiments on a human body.

"All energy on this planet comes from Our Lord the Sun. All power over things terrene is to be found in His rays—if you know how to find the right rays." That, roughly, is the saddhu's theory.

Having found the right rays of the spectrum, he gains control over molecular energy, that vast untapped force hidden in the heart of matter that Western science can reason about, but cannot use. Having reached this latent force, not only will he be able to make dead things live, but he will also have command over the whole energy of the cosmos. So Saddhu Bisudhanan Dhan is looking forward to a busy life.

Meanwhile he disclaims divinity, and explains that he is only a student of the science of "survabigan," "light-power."

We went, then, one Sunday afternoon, armed with a Graflex camera. We were two matter-of-fact, worldly-minded, and, we dare say, extremely circumspect inquirers. What follows we saw with our four eyes.

We found the saddhu giving a lecture to his disciples, about twenty in number, in the verandah of his house. They were chiefly Bengalis, well-to-do, intelligent merchants and officials. The saddhu squatted in a "long chair," with his disciples on the floor. He is a man of full habit of body, with a thinnish gray-brown beard. For attire he wears a single saffron sheet about his loins and the Brahminical thread. His hands were plump and comely. He has a quick, quizzical expression, and exceptionally large eyes, full of humor and with that quality of looking beyond you into infinities of space that is common among people of this class. You would say that he was a magnetic personality, even if you hadn't been expecting to find him a magician.

The mahatma (for so he is called) shook hands and asked us to be seated. Disciples brought chairs. There ensued a painful silence. The disciples stared. At last the mahatma inquired whether we had any questions to ask.

We replied that we had no particular question, but that we had heard of his fame and felt we couldn't leave Puri without seeing him. Would he mind having his photograph taken? Not at all. The mahatma was delighted.

"Ask him any question, and he will answer it," said one of the disciples, after the Graflex had done its duty.

"Well, then, will the mahatma kindly tell us what our object was in coming here?" We didn't know ourselves, as a matter of fact.

Immediately, the saddhu answered that his revered guru had particularly urged him never to answer questions like that. Silence again. Finally we said:

"Will the mahatma show us any evidence of his supernatural powers?"—It was no good beating about the bush.

The mahatma nodded pleasantly, but did not move. He just squatted there in his long chair, motionless, apparently amused.

"What would you like to see?" asked a disciple. "He can make fruit or sweetmeats for you out of the air, or turn cotton-wool into camphor, or he can command any scent you like to come to you from the circumambient ether."

We looked at each other. On consideration, we plumped for the last miracle, as being the hardest to fake.

A disciple was sent to get the mahatma's magnifying glass and a piece of cotton-wool. The disciple showed us the cotton-wool. It was odorless, and the magnifying glass was a double convex lens with a tiny wire handle. We watched the mahatma's every movement. We were within four or five feet of him. He took the cotton in the forefinger and thumb of his left hand and the lens in his right. He focused the lens so that a spot of light shone on the wool. After one second, or less, he handed us the wool. We sniffed. It smelt of violets. Then he tore off another bit of the same wool, focused the light on it as before, and handed it to us. It smelt of attar of roses. Once again, he produced a peculiar native scent.

Then he put the magnifying glass down and sat impassive, smiling slightly, satisfied that he had amused children with childish things. There was nothing near him that could have held the various scents. He himself was nude to the waist. The experiment most certainly was unpremeditated. He did not know that we were going to call.

"Has the mahatma powers of hypnotism also?" we asked of the disciples.

The mahatma and his disciples laughed.

"In the wink of an eye," explained one of the neophytes, "the mahatma could mesmerize you and all of

us here. That is one of the very first things he learned in
Tibet, nearly forty years ago."

Now, true or not, every one present (except ourselves) believed this. And there is contagion in belief.

Among these simple kindly people and in ordinary
surroundings, and with no prayers, incantations, or accessories of magic, and in broad daylight, we felt that
Mystery had been brought close to us, and that we had
touched her garment's hem.

Of the reality of what we saw we cannot doubt. However, we can offer no explanation of it, without a much
longer study of the mahatma's methods than is possible
to us now. Only one thing is sure: that there are more
things in Heaven and earth than are dreamed of in
travelers' philosophy!

CHAPTER XXXVI
THE VOICE OF THE BLUE STONE

WE have come to Puri to pay our respects to the most idolized idol in India, Jagannath, "Lord of the World," the stodgy, grinning god with the face of an Alaskan totem-pole. Along with us have come a hundred thousand other human beings, and billions of inhuman insects. To all of them, excepting members of the Benares Boosters' Club, Puri is the most sacred Hindu city. Even old Barnum would have to admit that the Car Festival of Jagannath at Puri is the "greatest show on earth."

To-morrow is the day of the main event when Jagannath, and his sister Subhadra, and his brother Balabhadra, make their annual vacation-trip to the Garden Temple, a mile and a half away, in the mammoth cars that crunched and squashed so many fanatical worshipers in the good old days before the meddlesome British put a stop to that feature of the holiday journey.

There are more of us here than the number of the followers of the Prophet who make the pilgrimage to Mecca. We have come from every corner of India, from

the hills of Assam to the backwaters of Travancore—
farmers, money-lenders, metal-workers, toddy-tappers,
mendicants, criminals, non-coöperators, babus, lepers,
jugglers, and two women for every man.

Any man who has been guilty of killing a cow, the
most horrible of all crimes in the eyes of the Hindu,
must make the last ten miles of the journey by measuring
his length in the dust, throwing himself flat in the road,
getting up and falling forward again, and so on until he
reaches the center of all things in Puri—the white fluted
temple with the wheel-like top where dwells the Lord of
the World.

If Britain's statesmen could visit Puri with us and see
the Festival of Jagannath they would get a cross-section
of three fourths of the population of India: and the experience might make it easier for them to decide whether
the people of this land are ready to take over the democratic institutions of the West, and whether the "Home
Rule within the Empire" scheme that the new reforms
plan is to give them, will actually fit the needs of these
strange races of Hindustan.

In Calcutta the other night, when we went to Howrah
station to catch the Puri express, we were unable to get
within fifty yards of the main gateway to the train and
had to slip out to the train-shed through a side entrance
used by railway employees. For days thousands and
thousands of pilgrims had been camping in the main
hall at Howrah, eating their rice and fruit there, amid

an incredible stench and mess. Whenever a train was announced the vast throng would jump up, and the men would pile the family bedding, brass jars, babies, and bundles of food on the heads of their docile wives, and then all would surge toward the train. Hundreds squeezed through until the guards slammed the gate. Whereupon the disappointed thousands, condemned to wait over another night, would "turn to sleep again" after the ancient fashion of the East.

There is one unwelcome pilgrim who never fails to visit Jagannath Car Festival. Although the agents of the Government of India stand guard along every high-road and watch every incoming train, this grim visitor not only sneaks stealthily into Puri but he likewise puts in an appearance at every other festival in India. His name is "cholera bacillus" and as a "garnerer of grave-yards" he has no peer. Upon our arrival at the station Indian doctors, wearing red arm-bands, scrutinize us carefully as we pass out with the stream of pilgrims. Later we learn that cholera has broken out a few days before our arrival. Not far from the temple we find temporary hospitals, and there are stretcher-bearers standing in readiness wherever a crowd assembles to attend a ceremony.

In 1920, cholera carried off victims at the rate of over one hundred a day, so the Brahmin manager of the Temple of Jagannath informs us. But fortunately the toll was much lighter this year.

Medical men believe that this pestilence is due to the eating of the fermented temple rice, which has been rejected by Jagannath and hence is highly prized by the pilgrims. Every day a large quantity of food is served to the wooden deity of Puri by the Brahmin priests. But Jagannath has lost his appetite for rice and sweetmeats, so this temple food, after being offered to the god, is sold to the pilgrims, who believe it to contain wondrous powers for driving away all bodily ills. They disregard, alas, the advice of their scientifically trained fellow-countrymen from the medical department of the University of Calcutta, who warn them that the crumbs from the table of their god carry the fatal germs that annually oblige so many hundreds to stay in Puri until nought remains of them but a handful of ash at the burning-ghat for their relatives to cast into the sea. Such is faith!

Puri is situated on a sandy seashore a night's run by train down the coast of the Bay of Bengal from Calcutta. Not a rock nor promontory interrupts the sweep of the beach for miles, and white-capped rollers come tumbling in as they do along the coast near Honolulu.

The waters of the bay at this point are particularly holy, and in searching for the explanation we uncover the story of the origin of the Temple of Jagannath.

As the legend runs, during the Golden Age of Hinduism a certain devout king of Malwa ruled over this section of India, who commissioned one of his Brahmin sages to go in search of Vishnu, the only member of the Hindu trinity who makes a practice of appearing before men in various worldly forms. In the course of his wanderings the Brahmin penetrated a forest, where he met a fowler who worshiped a blue stone, which he said was the abode of a spirit. Up to this point the Brahmin's quest had been in vain, and it was with a feeling rather of curiosity than of hope that he accompanied the fowler to his blue stone. But to the amazement of the Brahmin a voice came from the stone in response to the fowler, saying: "O faithful servant, I am wearied of these jungle flowers and fruits, and crave cooked rice and sweetmeats. No longer shalt thou see me in the form of thy blue god. Hereafter I shall be known as Jagannath, the Lord of the World."

The Brahmin hurriedly returned to his king and reported what had occurred. Calling for his state elephants, the monarch proceeded to the dwelling of the fowler. But when they went into the forest the blue stone had disappeared. The king was bewailing his misfortune when a voice came from a cloud, saying: "I am the spirit of the blue stone. And if unto me thou wilt sacrifice a thousand horses, I will reappear in the form of a log on the waves of yonder sea." The king complied, and sure enough, the log appeared on the waves. It was brought to the king, who ordered his workmen to shape it into an image. But it turned the edge of every tool. After all had failed, an old man, a carpenter suffering from elephantiasis, which made his legs look as large as the log itself, petitioned the king for permission to undertake the task. In spite of the derision of his courtiers, the monarch agreed.

Then the aged carpenter insisted that he be permitted to do his work behind locked doors, undisturbed, for fifteen days. But with the curiosity for which women are celebrated in all countries, the queen began to pester her lord after a few days, urging him to disregard his promise and go and see how the old man was getting on. The unhappy king yielded. But as soon as he unbolted the door, the carpenter vanished, for he was none other than Vishnu in disguise. However, he left behind three images, all with the lower part of the torso and the arms unfinished. One was a representation of himself in the form of Jagannath, Lord of the World; one was of his brother Balabhadra; and the other of his sister Subhadra.

Unhappy King Indradyumna did his best to make amends by erecting a great temple in Puri for the three idols. No doubt he has had his reward in the thousands who prostrate themselves before the shrine he built with the age-old cry of *"Jai, jai, Jagannath, ka jai!"*

So the beach at Puri is regarded as a sacred spot because it was here that the log came ashore: and the temple is looked upon as one of the holiest, if not the holiest, place in India because it contains the unfinished image of the great deity Vishnu, in the form of Jagannath, fashioned by his own hands.

Near the sea-front are the bungalows and palaces of rajahs, native merchant kings from Calcutta, the famous Tagore family, and a cluster of thatched huts shaped like Eskimo igloos, which are used by the pilgrims who come to bathe. The native city centers around the white, fluted, phallic temple, and all the principal streets radiate from it, including the eighty-yard-wide boulevard Bara Danda down which Jagannath rides in his gargantuan wooden car once every year when he goes to spend his summer holiday, a mile and a half away, in the "Garden of Pleasure." In the old days, when the ponderous wheels crushed the life out of the bodies of so many of the pilgrims, this highway was indeed an avenue of death. Even now old women who are tired of life sometimes try to throw themselves under the wheels.

For a reason that no one seemed able to explain, Jagannath leaves his wife behind in the great temple when he goes on his ten-day summer vacation. Of the three cars that make the journey, one is for the Lord of the World, one for Balabhadra, and one for Subhadra. Nor are these mammoth vehicles permanent structures. Like a wealthy American nabob, Jagannath must have a new limousine each year. Three months it takes the workmen of Puri to build the cars. Six weeks prior to the festival we passed through on our way from Madras to Calcutta, and then only the wheels were completed. There are sixteen of these on Jagannath's chariot, and fourteen on each of the others. Each wheel is about eight feet high. They support the tower-like superstructures, which are of the same style as the temple itself. All the lumber is cut by hand.

When we returned to attend the festival we discovered that the cars were not completed, although the ceremony was to take place on the morrow. The explanation for this is that the workmen are paid by the hour, not by the job. But they will be finished late to-night, at the last minute. The Urias of Puri have nothing to learn from our western labor-unionists in this respect. When completed the three land-leviathans will be drawn to the Lion Gate, and to-night tens of thousands of pilgrims will sleep around them in order to be sure of seeing the Lord of the World when he comes out of his incense-fogged holy of holies to-morrow morning.

CHAPTER XXXVII

AT THE SHRINE OF THE LORD OF THE WORLD

BEFORE we finish our chota hazri a khitmutgar announces that our tika ghari is waiting to take us to pay our respects to Jagannath. Not only is the sacred city of Puri celebrated for its barbaric car of Jagannath, but it is notorious for its disreputable tika gharis. Some of them resemble the "Deadwood coaches" that transported the mails and the tenderfoot across the badlands of Dakota in the days of Buffalo Bill. But most of them are of the springless variety, with a board on either side for passengers to sit upon, and a canopy of patched gunny bags to protect them from the sun. They are drawn by ponies so skinny and underfed that they look like the skeletons of saber-tooth tigers in the Calcutta Museum. Their harness consists of odd bits of string. Each of these derelict Hindu hacks has a crew of at least four ragged low-castes—Father Untouchable and his three little untouchables. So it wasn't surprising that our decrepit conveyance, and the poor scraggly ponies who had to pull three of us as well as the driver and his family, got stuck in the sand so often on the way to see the Lord of the World.

A hundred yards from the temple we are obliged to abandon our tika ghari and fight our way through the stream of humanity pouring toward the central square in front of the temple and the Avenue Bara Danda. A sub-inspector of police who has been assigned to come along and make holes in the crowd for us whenever we desire to move about, leads us through a doorway and out onto the roof of a native house, whence we can see the whole ceremony. There must be a thousand others on the same roof. And on every other roof in Puri as far as we can see, thousands of others are awaiting the arrival of Jagannath.

Special places have been reserved for us on the roof by order of the British superintendent of police, who is down there in the square acting as master of ceremonies, and entering into everything as enthusiastically as any of the Brahmin priests.

From our roof we look down on a welter of white turbans and perspiring brown faces. All along Jagannath's private boulevard they are packed. For color and confusion we have never seen a show like this, not even the big festival at Madura for the Fish-Eyed Bride.

Between us and the Lion Gate of the fluted phallic temple are the three gaudy chariots of the gods, each the size of a small cottage. A runway of planks reaches from the ground to each platform, and it is up these that

Jagannath, Subhadra, and Balabhadra are to be carried in state.

Three huge yellow wooden images, with their arms extended in regular coaching fashion, squat on the ground grinning at the frantic brass band that rends the air with its discords. These are the coachmen of the gods.

Each chariot is covered with brilliantly colored strips of cloth and images of fairies and celestial animals. The predominant colors in the decoration of Jagannath's chariot are red and yellow, of Subhadra's red and green, and of Balabhadra's red and black. After the festival the cars are always broken up and sold as souvenirs to the pilgrims. All portions not disposed of in this manner are sold at high prices for fuel at the burning-ghats, a dead person having a far better chance of going direct to Brahma, without returning to this world reincarnated as a crow or a Bengali politician, if his body is burned with the wood from the Car of Jagannath.

While awaiting Jagannath we watch the strange scene below and around us. Here on the roof at our very elbows are more high-caste Hindu women than we have ever come in such close contact with before. The purdah system of shielding women extends to the Hindus of the upper classes, just as it does to the Muhammadans, and one rarely has such an opportunity as this to observe their faces. Although not veiled like the ladies of the harems, when they detect us looking their way they draw their white silk saris across their faces, hiding the heavy gold and jeweled bangles that hang from the lobes of their ears and their nostrils. Their eyes are sleepy and sensuous, the whites of them of a pale horizon-blue.

So densely packed are the pilgrims that the heat generated by their bodies is noticeable away up here on our roof. The air is full of portent . . . distant thunder . . . human expectation . . . the voices of the crowd . . . the bugling of the conches of Jagannath. Dotted here and there among each score of squatting pilgrims, are the pandars or spiritual guides, the men who lead devout Hindu women to beatitude and bankruptcy, and sometimes something worse. These men are notorious throughout Hindustan, and have given a verb—"to pander"—to the English language. They wave small punkhas over their protégées with vigor.

Occasionally when sections of the mob become panicky and start crying and fighting, the whole concourse sways back and forth in waves. At times it looks as though there might be a stampede. Such a tragedy might happen, and hundreds might be trampled on, just as actually occurred some years ago at a festival in Trichinopoly. Small panics there are, but the river of humanity is so vast that the force of each spends itself like ripples in the Ganges, before spreading more than twenty or thirty yards.

Nevertheless scores in the concourse below us faint and have to be carried out over the heads of the crowd,

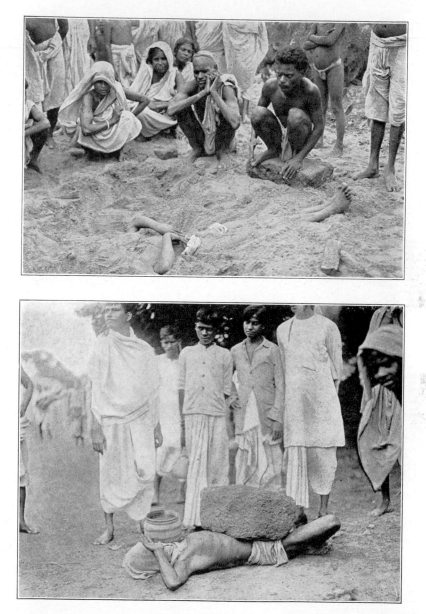

Some holy men half-bury themselves with earth and remain this way for hours, and others lie with enormous stones on their stomachs; all done to impress passing pilgrims with their piety.

The car of Jagannath (Juggernaut) has sixteen ponderous wheels and occasionally crashes into a building.

and hundreds more are bruised. Were it a Western crowd, stiff hats would be smashed, boots ruined, and ladies' dresses torn to shreds. But these pilgrims have no worry on that score.

Temple priests busy themselves passing out palm-leaf fans to their brother pandars, so they can fan their respective flocks. There is one frantic fellow trying to keep the crowd from breaking through the ropes around the cars. His hair is disheveled, his eyes wild, and his agility astounding. He clambers about on the shoulders of the throng, and when he misses his footing and slips he straddles a neck—sometimes a woman's, sometimes a man's—but goes right on slashing wildly with his fan.

The heat and crush cause many to faint. Then priests rush out of the temple with buckets of water and squirt-guns, with which they proceed to give the fringe of the crowd a shower-bath.

When we call the police subinspector's attention to the fact that it is long after eight o'clock, he explains that on a great occasion like this it is a common thing for the gods to linger longer than usual over their toilet. Then he describes to us how in the early morning the priests sing hymns before the doors of the holy of holies, to inform Jagannath and his companions of the rising of the sun, how the priests then remove the divans on which the gods are supposed to have slept, burn camphor in silver vessels, light torches, and serve the idols their chota hazri, consisting of the same rice chapattis and sweetmeats that are later sold to the pilgrims, bathe and dress them, and then clean their teeth vicariously by rubbing their dental reflections in a polished brass bowl. On ordinary days they again breakfast at ten o'clock and at the same time are entertained by some of the temple dancing-girls. During midday the gods, like the Brahmin priests who attend them, enjoy a siesta on the sacred cots, then at night after the evening meal they are anointed with essence of sandalwood, garlanded with flowers amid music, dancing, and singing, and then placed on their cots for the night.

The foremost citizens of Puri are these Brahmin priests of the Temple of Jagannath. The supervision of the establishment is placed in the hands of a Brahmin, appointed by the Rajah of Puri, who holds the title of "temple manager." Jagannath and his companions possess many wonderful jewels, and treasure that is literally untold, for in addition to the ten lakhs' worth known to exist, there is a treasure-room that has not been opened for the last thousand years. It is supposed to be knee-deep in uncut emeralds of the size of eggs. This, and much else, is administered by the temple manager, who is a person of great importance and responsibility.

When pilgrims first enter the Lion Gate they are met by a Brahmin who strikes them with a small cane. The object of this ceremony is to drive away sin from the pilgrim's body. If he gives the priest a substantial present he merely receives a light tap. But if he can afford

to give the Brahmin only a few annas by way of baksheesh, he receives a sound beating. Following this flag-
ellation, the pilgrim proceeds up the stairs towards the
Joya Bejoya doors of the inner shrine. If he is a wise
man he puts on blinkers to prevent his eyes' resting on
the gallery of lewd carvings he will be obliged to tra-
verse. If he shows no signs of passion when he reaches
the head of the stairs, the priests admit him to the inner
shrine. But if he shows evidence of having succumbed
to thoughts unworthy of one who has come to worship
his god, he is sent to another part of the temple, where
the comely Devadasis assist him to a better state. Nor
is he allowed to return and enter the holy of holies until
his worldly passions have been pacified.

All this, and more that we cannot print, the sub-
inspector tells us—but he is interrupted by a shout from
the Lion Gate. This means that the doors of the inner
shrine have been thrown open, so that the multitude
nearest the gate has obtained its first glimpse of the
Lord of the World. For a moment the band ceases and
a hush comes over the crowd. Then a murmur starts
from the Lion Gate and ripples with increasing volume
down the Bara Danda until it breaks against the walls of
the Garden Temple a mile and a half distant. With their
hands high above their heads the pilgrims murmur the
prayer they have come so far to repeat: "O Jagannath,
Lord of the World, have pity on me and release me from
my woe!"

CHAPTER XXXVIII

THE JOURNEY OF THE CAR OF JUGGERNAUT

"JAGANNATH KA JAI! JAGANNATH KA JAI!" Two hundred thousand throats take up the cry and the shout rumbles like a tidal wave down the Avenue Bara Danda. From within the high white walls of the temple where dwells the Lord of the World there comes the answering boom of a great gong. As the police club the frenzied pilgrims in a vain attempt to keep them behind the ropes, a procession of Brahmin priests with peacock fans and yaks' tails comes slowly through the Joya Bejoya doors of the inner shrine and down the temple steps. A ruffle of drums and a blare of conches announce to the assembled concourse that Jagannath, Lord of the World, is about to enter the car beneath whose chariot-wheels in ages past so many Hindus have been "less than the dust."

Men sweeping, not lowly Sudras, but twice-born Brahmins, come ahead of the procession to dust the path over which the gods are to pass. After them come ranks of temple boys swathed in saffron and carrying pikes with pennons bearing the monogram of their master.

These acolytes form lines on either side of the swept path.

"Jai! Jai! Subhadra ka jai!" roars the crowd. The priests are carrying a throne through the Lion Gate. Our Uria companion announces in awed tones that it is the sister of the Lord of the World and that it is the custom for her to precede Jagannath.

In Subhadra's image we expect to see the ideal Hindu beauty, for on the walls of the temples and dwellings in Puri are many excellent paintings of Sri Krishna, India's cerulean Apollo, and of attractive dancing-girls, which indicate that art still lives among these people and that they know a pretty girl when they see one. As the nodding peacock-plumes and jewels of her enormous fan-shaped head-dress come nearer, we look down on the features of the goddess, framed by the black bodies of the priests, with expectant interest.

But we are sadly disappointed. She is just a lump of wood, and about as good-looking as a Polynesian devil-devil god.

Covering the lower part of the image is a saffron-colored sari, the only suggestion of the eternal feminine about the goddess. A week before the festival thousands of handbills were circulated by followers of Mr. Ghandi, demanding that the gods be dressed in khaddar instead of in costumes made from cloth sent out from England. The heading of these leaflets read: "Jagannath wants khaddar." But the temple management refused to be coerced, and as in previous years, the material for Subhadra's gown was a product of Manchester.

"All hail, Balabhadra!" shouts the multitude as Jagannath's brother, another little abortion, is borne in state to the middle car.

But when the Lord of the World comes through the Lion Gate the cheers double in volume, and the thousands seated on the roofs rise to their feet and clasp their hands in adoration such as no monarch of flesh and blood ever received from his subjects. Even the elephants hulking above the concourse in the street below kneel in humble obeisance before this inanimate wood, an idol in which we see the features of an image even more grotesque than the hideous Subhadra and Balabhadra.

As soon as the gods are in the cars the pilgrims break through the ropes and swarm around them, some prostrating themselves on the ground in front of the wheels, some touching their lips to the wood, and some clambering up the sides of the structures and onto the platforms in order to rub noses with the idols.

The scene reminds us of a wood-cut depicting the army of Cyrus storming the walls of Babylon and the defenders hurling them from the ramparts. However, the police and the Brahmin priests, instead of using boiling tar and stones, attempt to keep the frenzied devotees down from the platforms by striking them with thin bamboo canes.

We see a pilgrim hand a coin to a fat Brahmin defending one of the corners of the platform of Jagannath's car. With a look of disgust the Brahmin shows it to a policeman standing near by, then carefully tucks it in the folds of his dhotie, and strikes the pilgrim in the face, knocking him sprawling.

An hour before noon the six huge ropes attached to the axles of each car are stretched out to their full lengths and all persons except the priests and musicians and dancers are driven from the chariots. The great moment of the day has come and the pilgrims fight for the coveted privilege of pulling on the great ropes, which stretch out and out, like elastics, under ten thousand eager hands.

Subhadra's is the first car to move. Balabhadra follows her, then Jagannath.

The priests on the car make obscene gestures to the crowd. The crowd roars with laughter and makes redoubled efforts on the ropes. Suddenly the glittering tinseled cottage lurches forward. Subhadra is on her way to the Garden Temple.

And lo! an Englishman is in charge of the car! It is indeed a fact. Since the days of John Company an Englishman has directed the driving of at least one of the three cars. The first district magistrate of Puri established this strange tradition.

Captain H. R. C. Guise, the superintendent of police in Puri, has officiated at six Car Festivals, and it is worth the trip from Calcutta merely to see him with his barbaric chariot, urging the devotees to greater efforts and ordering them to pull first one way and then another to avoid crashing into some building. Occasionally one of the cars is allowed to get off the center of the avenue, and runs into a house. Then there is trouble, for the house has to come down, Jagannath and his relations being too holy to be moved even one inch backward once they have started on their ride to the Garden Temple. This happens once every two or three years, because the cars are so enormous and unmanageable. For the same reason pilgrims get crushed.

After the three cars proceed about a third of the distance down the avenue a tragedy is narrowly averted by the superintendent of police. The shouting, surging throng presses so close around the chariot he is driving that a group of women and children are pushed directly in front of the wheels. Captain Guise signals for the emergency-brake to be dropped—the brake consisting of a heavy log suspended on ropes just under the front of the platform. It is impossible to let the thousands of pilgrims pulling on the ropes know of the danger in time, but the emergency-brake brings the car to a standstill within a few feet of the women. When the superintendent of police and his assistants pull the women and children out of the way of the wheels they seem not the least bit thankful, or even frightened, and no doubt they would have welcomed the opportunity of sacrificing themselves to Jagannath.

The other two cars are directed by the district magistrate and his deputy. In 1912 the district magistrate (who was an Indian then, as he was also this year) became so worked up during the progress of the cars down the avenue, a trip which usually lasts for three hours, that he threw off his European clothes, covered his body with sandalwood ash, rubbed noses with Jagannath, and became a simple pilgrim.

Every single one of those hundreds of thousands of pilgrims try either to find room on one of the ropes or to get near enough to touch one, during the course of the journey. Those who fail in this content themselves with touching their foreheads to the ropes as they lie in the dust when the cars reach the Garden Temple. Others unravel tiny strands, which they place in their betel-boxes and take back to their homes to ward off evil spirits.

It is nearly three o'clock in the afternoon when the gods reach the end of their ride. From then on until nightfall the pilgrims come and prostrate themselves before them, many lying on their stomachs with their faces in the dust for ten or fifteen minutes. Others burn incense in tiny earthen dishes under the cars: thousands clamber onto the platforms to touch the deities: tens of thousands make obeisance: mendicants dance beside the wheels: and mothers bring their newly born to be blessed in the splendor of the Presence.

Shortly before sunset the Brahmins are horrified to see the shadow of a low-caste man on Jagannath's face. After giving the intruder a sound flogging they go through a long purification ceremony lasting until midnight, before permitting their deity to enter the temple.

The three gods remain at the Garden Temple for ten days each year. Then on the tenth day they are hauled back to their permanent home in the same cars, with the same ceremony. But on the return journey thousands of coolies are hired to do the pulling, because most of the pilgrims have left Puri by that time. On the return ride the three images are decorated with the temple jewels and Jagannath wears a great diamond half the size of a pomegranate in the center of his forehead.

There are several smaller idols at the main Puri temple. One of these is Madan Mohan, a small silver deity only eight inches high. The priests speak of him as Jagannath's "viceroy," because he attends all of the minor festivals of the year as the representative of the Lord of the World.

Jagannath, Subhadra, and Balabhadra are renewed every thirty-six years. This is arranged so that one is built every twelve years and twice as many pilgrims roll up at Puri on these occasions. Each time an entirely new image is made, except for a block of wood imbedded in the body, supposed to be all that remains of the original log carved by Vishnu. The idols are fashioned from a hard wood that resists the attacks of insects, and each is six feet or seven feet high and very heavy.

Before the cars reach the great temple on the homeward trip, Jagannath's wife, another tiny idol, is brought out to meet him in front of the office of the temple manager a hundred yards down the Bara Danda from the Lion Gate. There the following conversation takes place between them:

Mrs. Jagannath: "Where have you been for the last ten days, my dear?"

Jagannath: "I caught a severe cold on the day of the Bathing Festival and went to the Garden Temple to recuperate."

Mrs. Jagannath: (thoughtfully) "Yes, but I've heard that story before, and I'm getting a bit fed up with you and your excuses. But I'll sleep over it. Meanwhile, Mr. J., you may stop out here in the street for the night. Then to-morrow morning if you see the little door above the Lion Gate standing ajar you may come in. But if it's still closed it will mean that you have lost your happy home!"

That is the exact translation of the conversation as given to us by one who has listened to it many times. But the reader will be relieved to hear that Mrs. Jagannath's remarks are pure bluff, because she never fails to welcome her hubby to his chota hazri the following morning.

CHAPTER XXXIX

EASTERN LOVE

IT was a princess at the court of Shah Jehan the Magnificent—Jehanara Begum, the lady near whose tomb live the well-jumpers of Old Delhi—who all unwittingly gave the British their first footing in India. Jehanara was going upstairs to bed, preceded by her serving-wench, when the latter's dress caught fire. In quenching the flames both Jahanara and her maid were severely burned. Being a very modest and very well-behaved young princess, she did not cry out, for fear some of the young nobles who were then rollicking in the Marble Hall next door might come and see her unveiled. To a devout Musulmanee death were preferable to the shame of showing her face unveiled to one who was not her lord or her kith. So the pious princess just rolled on the floor and bore it, and got terribly burned for her pains.

The palace remedies proved useless. Native doctors were called in, but had to conduct their diagnosis in the usual Eastern way when dealing with the "pearls of the palace," through a curtain of padded brocade. They failed to cure her. The poor girl was dying of her burns, and the distracted emperor had a brain-wave and sent down to the British merchant adventurers at one of the East India Company's settlements on the lower Ganges to ask if Western balsam and unguents could perchance alleviate the princess's pain.

Dr. Gabriel Boughton, the doctor at Surat, rode up to Agra post-haste, interviewed the Great Moghul, felt Jehanara's pulse through her padded curtains, and after suitable preparations were made for not disclosing more of the form or features of the princess than court etiquette allowed, he was permitted to see her burns and her little pink tongue. Curious to relate, he was able to effect a cure speedily. Shah Jehan the Magnificent, in his most magnificent mood, offered the discreet doctor a camel-load of gold, the rarest flowers of his harem, rubies unpriced. . . . The Great Moghul simply slobbered with gratitude. Anything in reason, from a bushel of pearls to a dozen Circassian concubines, could have been demanded and obtained from him by that lucky medico. But Dr. Gabriel Boughton cared for none of these things. He wanted permission for his company to trade on the River Hughli, a trifling request, which the Great Moghul immediately granted, not without a sigh of relief at getting off with so light a fee. A charter was made out there and then: the Great Moghul impressed it with his sign manual and—that was the beginning of British India.

A woman began it. A woman began the Taj. Back of everything that happens in India is the influence of its women. Women made the mutiny of 1857. Women are causing the unrest of to-day. The India of to-morrow will be founded on the welfare of the family. The climate of India makes its inhabitants, both Muhammadans and Hindus, a uxorious people. Although *less than one per cent* of India's women are literate (there are 105,-000,000 Hindu women who cannot read or write) they all have a great influence on affairs, except the widows, of whom there are between five and six million. A Hindu widow must sometimes wish that the British had not forbidden her to burn herself on the funeral pyre of her husband. Forbidden to remarry, with her hair cut short, clothed in rags, and made to do all the household work, her life is one long round of misery and degradation, whose only release is death.

The average age of marriage is fifteen, but according to the latest census figures there are no less than nine million wives under that age.

The beauties of womankind chiefly admired can be gleaned from the past and contemporary poets of Hindustan. No more direct method is available to the Western inquirer, owing to the privacy that shrouds all domestic affairs in the East. But we can gather a fair idea of the ideal from their phrases:

"Thy well-combed hair, thy splendid eyes with their arches curved almost to thine ear, thy two rows of teeth,

entirely pure and regular, thy breasts adorned with
beautiful flowers."

"Thy body annointed with saffron, and thy waist-belt
that puts the swans to shame."

"Moon-faced, elephant-hipped, serpent-necked, an-
telope-footed, swan-waisted, lotus-eyed. . . ."

These are some of the expressions of the romanticists
of India to describe the beauty of its women. The terms
may seem strange to us, and some (but not those quoted)
are actually repellant.

But there is age-old wisdom in their aphorism from a
prince of the golden age of Sanskrit:

"The true object of amorous intercourse is the uniting
of the hearts of the lovers, and when this need is not accomplished the marriage might be that of two corpses."

There is little of our latter-day wisdom and our latter-
day cults that the sages of the Sanskrit age have not
committed to writing.

Frankness in sexual matters, which is preached nowadays as a species of modern ideal, is an old thing in India.
The Hindus are exceedingly uxorious, and treat the subject of relations between men and women with realism
and candor. Sex education, commonly rated as another
of the lofty goals toward which we are striving, is an
Indian commonplace. It is a part of the institution of
child marriage, in which wedded children, upon becoming adolescent, receive instructions from parents in the
nature of their relation toward each other. A system of

hygiene pertaining to connubial intercourse and childbirth is inculcated and enforced.

Romance in India is not limited to marriage any more than it is here, there, or the next place. There are varieties of courtesans. There is the famous nautch-girl, or dancing-girl, who is somewhat the equivalent of the geisha in Japan. There is the temple dancer, who frequently follows the rites of sacred prostitution. In ancient civilizations sanctified harlotry has a gaudy place, and India here, as in other things, goes to flamboyant extremes. Then there are the miscellaneous kinds of light ladies, such as you will find all over the world. In all of these amorous matters the Hindu is his realistic self. A school-boy may visit a bawdy house with no more scandal than an American high-school lad would arouse if he went to a haberdashery store to buy a necktie.

The dancing-girl has a definite and by no means frowned-upon place in society. She is not regarded as respectable, but is by no means considered a social evil. Prostitution is as inevitable in India as anywhere else. It might be supposed that early marriage would afford a negative influence, but on the other hand, there are many restrictions that hedge the married relation, such as those regarding pregnant wives, which, to the Hindu mind, make the harlot a necessity. The status of the dancing-girl compares very favorably with that of the prostitute in the West, who is hounded by police and moralists and is visited with every degradation. The

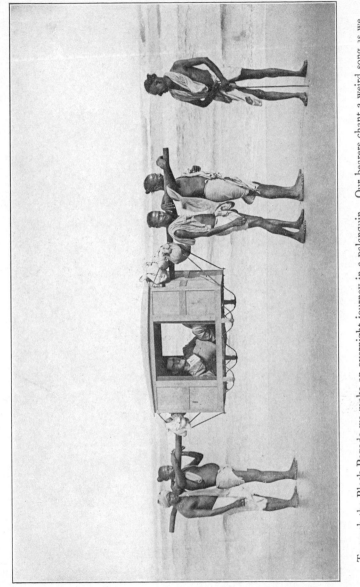

To reach the Black Pagoda we make an overnight journey in a palanquin. Our bearers chant a weird song as we bounce along.

Most of the carvings on the Black Pagoda do not bear close inspection.

nautch-girl is reared to her profession, which she is taught to accept, as any Hindu accepts his destiny or caste. She receives a certain amount of education to make her entertaining, and is schooled in hygiene such as her art requires. Her children often occupy high positions. You may liken her to the Greek hetæra, so brilliant and famous of old. Different lands, different customs.

Hindu women seem depressed to the outsider, but a closer gaze reveals that they have their compensations. In India the mother of the family is granted an amount of regard and influence seldom found elsewhere. One factor explains much here, as it explains so many things in India, and that is the importance of family. Marriage and women are regarded not from any viewpoint of individual happiness, but as instruments in the continuance and well-being of the family.

Of the India of the nautch-girl and the bayadère the Westerner sees little. He has contact with native women less perhaps than in any other part of the world. Britishers of the official class seek their diversion not at all among the dusky beauties of the land. They would be more likely to venture upon such straying in blackest Africa. In Hindustan caste is persuasive and compelling, even to the British masters, and for a white official to take up with a Hindu woman would be the equivalent of cohabiting with a woman outside of his caste, a violation of caste rules. In this, as in many other subtle ways, India conquers her conqueror.

CHAPTER XL
THE BLACK PAGODA

ALL night long we bounced in our box-like palanquins, carried on the shoulders of bearers who trotted around the curving sandy shore of the Bay of Bengal. The sun, like a molten ball, rose out of the sea from Burma as we came in sight of the Temple of the Sun at Kanarak. At last we had reached the mysterious Black Pagoda, the strange sight the British general had described to us that night in the mess tent on the edge of the desert of Sinai.

"The Desert is parched in the burning sun
And the grass is scorched and white.
But the sand is passed, and the march is done,
We are camping here tonight.

I sit in the shade of the Temple walls,
While the cadenced water evenly falls,
And a peacock out of the Jungle calls
To another, on yonder tomb.

Above, half seen, in the lofty gloom,
Strange works of a long dead people loom,
Obscene and savage and half effaced—

An elephant hunt, a musicians' feast—
And curious matings of man and beast."

Centuries ago the Moslem, Abu Fazl, wrote of this
singular architecture: "Its cost was defrayed by twelve
years' revenue of the province. Even those whose judgment is critical, and who are difficult to please, stand
astonished at its sight."

I shouldn't want to say how critical our judgments
were or how difficult we were to please, but we did stand
astonished. We saw a great, ornate pile of the general
form common to Hindu architecture, in which the
pyramid seems to be the general origin of design. It was
a species of flattened pyramid, with lines and proportions
exquisite and perfect.

As we approached, an extraordinary wealth of sculptured decoration made itself manifest, for the sloping
faces of the Black Pagoda were carved, inch by inch
over all their huge expanse, with countless figures in
deep and delicate relief. I recalled the telling phrase of
the renowned Bishop Heber, that the Hindus "build like
Titans, and finish like jewelers."

The shrine, deserted for long centuries, stands in a
waste and desolate place. But archæologists tell us that
once it was a thronged and busy site, a living and impas-
sioned Delphi or Jerusalem or Mecca, with its battalions of priests and attendants and its armies of pilgrim
worshipers. But all that is lost in a past that has gone,
with only a faint echo left—the murmur of a few naked

holy men, who cling to the ancient sacredness of the ruined shrine.

No more do the adorers of the sun troop along vanished roads to prostrate themselves in the sanctuary of the solar deity, but only occasional wayfarers, like ourselves, drawn perhaps by a prurient desire to behold what is celebrated as the most obscene building in the world. No longer do golden maharajahs dedicate their ample mite of treasure to the holy place, which is, instead, in the archæological, if not religious, care of the scholarly functionaries employed by the British Indian Government to guard and preserve the magnificent antiquities of India. That it is sufficiently valued and regarded will be apparent from the writings of Sir John Marshall, Director-General of Archæology for India, who says: "There is no monument of Hinduism . . . that is at once so stupendous and so perfectly proportioned as the Black Pagoda, and none which leaves so deep an impression on the memory."

We sauntered among broken masses of sculptured stone, where accessories of the giant structure have fallen. We walked with eyes now lowered to some delicately carved fragment, now lifted to the majestic proportions of the temple. We trod the ancient floors of lofty inner rooms and sanctuaries. The sculptures were exquisite, some of them in a green stone almost as lovely as jade.

The temple has the somewhat symbolical design of a

chariot, appropriately symbolizing the sun-god. Solar deities ride in chariots for their diurnal, fiery journey across the sky—as witness Phœbus Apollo. Great wheels are carved in the lower exterior wall to represent the proper appendages of a chariot. Dominant among the human figures is the splendid presence of Vishnu, or Krishna, in his solar guise. He is seen in perfectly sculptured effigies of stone that are models of proportion and of strength and delicacy.

Scene after scene from the life of the divinity is portrayed in an intricate bewilderment of decorative arrangement. The interior, dusky and dim as in nearly all Hindu temples, is simpler and far more austere than the exterior. Some parts perhaps were never finished. Much symbolism is there. But it is the exterior wall that catches the eye. Executed there with a splendid technique of art, is an array of unparalleled obscenity. Shaped in stony relief are seen groups of male and female figures in postures and acts of varied eroticism. To speak of frankness would be folly, for the lascivious elements are emphasized, exaggerated. They are magnified almost to caricature. And this is religion!

That exclamation goes for all of India. In a sense, the Black Pagoda stands a symbol for all of India, a symbol of its mystery, of its impenetrability to the Western eye. The things I remember best of India are the things I could not understand. I suppose the incomprehensible always beguiles us the most. A journey through India is

330 INDIA: LAND OF THE BLACK PAGODA

for the Westerner one long pilgrimage among incompre-
hensibles, and at the uttermost pinnacle of bafflement
comes the Black Pagoda.

Nothing will bewilder you more in that bewildering
land than the constant mingling of lofty religion and
what to us is debasing sensuality, and the Black Pagoda
is at the same time the most beautiful and the most obscene of Hindu temples. You know of the lofty spirituality and dizzy mystical heights of the Brahminical religion. Often they are too spiritual and unworldly for us.
How then are they to be rationally or emotionally re-
lated with these lascivious eroticisms that are so closely
mingled with them? You will ask that question and you
will not be able to answer it, as you gaze at the carnalities
in sculpture of the Black Pagoda, and you will remember that all manner of orgiastic sexual rites, such as you
will find to-day in the temples of India, must have been
performed in this magnificent shrine dedicated to the
sun.

Yet sexuality has always been more or less connected
with religion, and seems to be a part of the religious emotion. Among us to-day in our own fair United States
there are occasional outcroppings of sex irregularities
connected with religion—the love-cults, the sects that
engage in religious erotic practices. These very rituals of
fleshly desire and gratification that bewilder us in India
find a field and sympathetic votaries in our own land.
One of the characteristic minglings of mysticism and

fleshly vice in India is that of the Tantras, and you will find Tantric cults in New York and Chicago.

Moreover, in the racial and cultural background sacred eroticisms have a large place. The Bible in places is not only divinely inspired but quite divinely shocking. Ishtar in Syria (and her Hellenic form of Aphrodite in Greece) was worshiped with sexual ceremonies appropriate to the Goddess of Love. Maidens sacrificed their virginity to the goddess in a sacred act. There were holy prostitutes in the temples who sold themselves to the worshipers as a spiritual exercise. In busy, masterful, prosy Rome, in many ways so like our modern world, the women held secret religious rites of an exceedingly unedifying character. We make these reasonings upon how often lewd vices go hand in hand with sanctity, and yet we stand before the bawdy sculptures of the Black Pagoda and try in imagination to create a state of feeling in which they will combine harmoniously with the magnificent spirituality of the religious thought of India—and all we gain is a deeper sense of the mystery of that fantastic land.

We can continue to rationalize, and to meditate upon the process of evolution that connects the tenuosities of Brahminical philosophy with these manifestations of sanctified sin. We can remember that the wild pageant of religion in India is the result of an easily comprehensible process. Many centuries ago the Brahmin caste evolved a brilliant and loftily spiritual philosophy of deity. They arrived at the monotheism of an exceedingly refined and abstract thought. You will scan the catalogue of religious ideas and you will not find anything of a greater elevation and grandeur than the prime Brahminical theological conception of the timeless and changeless, supreme, only, and all-embracing Brahm, the ocean of existence, the beginning, the end.

Now comes an immediate compromise. India's lofty theologians often had to compromise. The Aryans had a pantheon of bright gods, joyous, shining gods, quite different from the gloomy and ferocious divinities of the Semites. The builders of monotheism had to take the old heavenly ones into account. Combining one with the other, regarding several as manifestations of one, they reduced the number of original Aryan deities, not an excessive number in the first place, and arrived at the familiar mystical device of a trinity, a triune godhead. Thus we have Brahma, the Creator of Forms, Vishnu, the Preserver of Forms, and Siva, the Destroyer of Forms. In this we have a philosophical distillation of the original bright religion of the Aryans. It dates from the time of the Puranas, which was the time of immense philosophic activity in India. It is the period of the early centuries of our era. Buddhism, which for a time had dominated India, had failed, and the older religion returned and conquered and formulated modern Hinduism on the ruins of the great creed founded on the teachings of Gautama Buddha.

If we were left with the Brahminical triad as the theological whole or even the larger part of the religion of India we should still have a lofty and easily comprehensible system of divinity, but the Brahmin caste, powerful and dominant as it was, had to compromise again and again. After all, Aryan race and Aryan culture were a thin veneer laid upon a huge dark ethnic and cultural mass. Below the Aryans lay tribe upon tribe of dark peoples, each with its own age-old culture and religion. Below the bright gods of the Aryans lay the dark gods of the aborigines, and in them you will find the fantastic array of deities that fills the Hindu pantheon. The Aryans might conquer the dark people, but they could not conquer the dark gods. These continued to flourish age after age, while the bright gods were being worshiped by the upper castes. The Brahmins had to compromise with the dark gods. They did as leaders of dominant religions have done in all ages. They took the older gods and the rites of the older gods into their own creed. In the same way did Christianity take northern tree-worship into its own body of customs—whence the Christmas tree. But the Brahmins were great theorists, and found a way to admit the countless aboriginal deities into their theology without destroying its formal trinitarianism.

The mechanics of the process are found in one of the oldest ideas of India—metempsychosis and the avatar idea. You can scarcely think of India without also thinking of the transmigration of souls, the rebirth of the soul into the world in different guises. This notion readily transfers itself to a god, who may appear on earth in different ages and in different forms, that is, avatars. Hence, if an aboriginal divinity was obstinate and could not be got rid of, he might be assimilated to one of the three persons of the Hindu trinity and be fitted in as an avatar of the god. Each of the three divine essences of the trinity could have an infinite number of avatars, and therefore the number of gods that could be accommodated in the system was three times infinity.

The old gods adhered to their old ways. Inevitably, if a primordial divinity was worshiped in a certain fashion and later he was identified as an avatar of one of the gods of the Hindu trinity, he would as an avatar be worshiped in his old way. Thus it came about that the bright gods of the early Aryans were worshiped in the guises and according to the strange dark rites of the dark gods. One characteristic of the Hindu temperament and of the social customs of India is what seems to us its excessive sexuality. Puritanism is unknown to Indian ideas. Extravagant asceticism flourishes, but it is for the few. For the many there is little or no denial. To us it seems like an excessive and haunting sexuality. To be sure, we are shocked, but it is well to remember that we ourselves are in bumptious revolt against the older Puritanism and that we seem to be on the way to unrestrained eroticism. The older gods of India had been worshiped with lascivious rites, and these rites were taken over into the body of orthodox Hinduism. The gods of the trinity were given wives, and to these avatars were attributed. The necessary sexual element was thereby acquired.

Of the members of the Hindu trinity Brahma, the creator, has never figured greatly in popular religion. He is too remote, too abstract. Perhaps he is identified too much with the primordial ocean of deity, the incomprehensible and unapproachable Brahm. The first member of the Hindu trinity lacks drama. The other two members have more appeal. Vishnu, the Preserver, is closer to human feelings. He is the saviour, the mediator. He has drama. And Siva, the Destroyer, has drama. That is patent. So the two gods that dominate Indian popular theology are Vishnu and Siva. The vast majority of the Hindus are divided into two cults, the Vishnuite and the Sivite. The latter has the greater following. The Destroyer seems to have been more in the mood of the dark masses, more like the dark gods. To Siva, under his many names, his many avatars, and to his goddess wife, under her many names and avatars, go the darker impulses of the soul of India. By a curious turn of mind, the Destroyer has acquired a meaning of procreation. Siva and his wife are worshiped as divinities of fertility. The symbols used are phallic, and the rites to us seem obscene. But Vishnu, the Preserver, who retains many of his characteristics as one of the ancient bright gods, has his following, too. He appears as avatars, thereby combining with the Dravidian gods, and his worship has its erotic elements—which brings us back to the Black Pagoda.

The Temple of the Sun at Kanarak is a monument of the Vishnuite cult. It is dedicated to the worship of Krishna, who is an avatar of Vishnu, and in the person of Vishnu are compounded sundry divine solar manifestations of the religion of the ancient Aryans. Vishnu, for example, connects with Mithra, the sun-god of the Persians. Surely Vishnu, who presides in the effulgent brilliance of luminous sky and solar orb, seems but incongruously commemorated by such gross and excessive sexualities as we see on the outer wall of the Black Pagoda, and indeed he and his divers avatars, whom we see in the pages of the Indian epics and myths, retain much of their early shining transcendence. The very avatar of the Black Pagoda is the knightly Krishna, the celestial cavalier quite worthy of Charlemagne's court of paladins, or of King Arthur's knights. He is a jauntier and handsomer figure than the Greek Heracles. He has, perhaps, more sparkle and verve than the peerless Roland. Yet in the divine deeds of Krishna there are incidents which, true, are common enough in any golden pantheon, but which lend themselves easily to the erotic emphasis and sensual fantasies, such as would proceed from the shadowy soul of darker India. Suffice it to say that the good knight Krishna in sundry visits to the earth engaged in sports and dalliances with the nymphs at Nanda's cow station, which romantic interludes are described with (to us) appalling minuteness of detail in some of the Puranas; and that the divine hero pursued the course of tempestuous and devoted love with the immortally beloved Radha. That clue is enough, and the lewd amours we see depicted on the walls of the Black Pagoda represent a prurient dwelling upon and expansion of the terrestrial disportings of the gay blade Krishna, which in the myths of the Greeks, for example, would probably have been given no more wantonly detailed expansion than we see in the instance of the earthly philanderings of Zeus. One shudders to think what might have happened if the hot imaginations of the Bengali artists had undertaken to depict the visits of the Father of the Gods in the form of a swan to the transported Leda.

Again we abandon the quest for the reasons why, and turn to the sculptured amours of Krishna, and vainly seek for some community with the spirit that complicated them with a lofty religious emotion, which emotion, indeed, one might readily harmonize with the brave and luminous Krishna in some of his less depraved exploits.

The legends of the Black Pagoda concern themselves with the twin miracles—that of its construction and that of its abandonment. We begin with a fanciful tale embodied in the palm-leaf chronicles, which relates that Samba, a son of Krishna, fell to quarreling with the sage

Narada, who took his spite to Krishna, informing the god that his son Samba had been playing the gallant with Krishna's sixteen hundred wives. Krishna was difficult to convince, whereupon Narada contrived, by means of a false message, to entice Samba to a tank in which his one thousand and six hundred stepmothers were bathing. They were exceedingly merry and splashed water upon one another. They were having a particularly good time, because the old chronicle describes them as "excessively flushed with wine." They saw the handsome Samba, and were instantaneously smitten with a longing for him. It was a critical moment, indeed, and who knows what might have happened? But at this moment the crafty Narada led Krishna to the place and bade him see what was to be seen. Krishna, believing that he had ocular proof of Samba's perfidy, cursed him with the affliction of leprosy.

The unfortunate Samba wandered away, a leper. After many woes and tribulations he invoked the aid of the sun-god, and through the healthful divine rays of the orb was cured of his fell malady. In gratitude, he reared a temple in honor of the divinity. This was a famous holy place for many years, and then, the shrine falling into ruin, it was replaced in the thirteenth century by the Black Pagoda. In the legend Krishna, that is, Vishnu, plays scarcely the rôle you would expect in a tale designed to account for the existence of a sanctuary dedicated to him. But the myths of Hindustan give small heed to consistent logic, as little as do the myths of other creeds, and the Temple of the Sun at Kanarak is a monument of the Vishnuite cult.

A legend that might be incorporated in the Arabian Nights explains the abandonment of the Black Pagoda. It relates that in olden times the edifice was surmounted by a great slab of stone, which had magical magnetic properties. It exerted a lodestone effect on passing ships, and drew many vessels ashore and wrecked them, until finally the crew of a Muslim craft, angered by the evil doings of the stone, came ashore, stormed the temple, and took the stone away. With that theft of the magical slab, the Hindu priests abandoned the temple.

A much more plausible tradition relates that the Black Pagoda was profaned by the Muhammadans, who took it as a religious duty to desecrate and ruin Hindu shrines and idols. For example, they might kill a cow in the most sacred sanctuary, which was profanation *par excellence.* It appears that the Hindus, once a temple was desecrated, would abandon it. Hence the desertion of the magnificent temple dedicated to the sun.

In a shed near the Black Pagoda is preserved a huge sculptured stone, which has an illuminating history. It is enormous, weighing not less than two thousand tons. Once it stood in position at a lofty height in the structure of the temple. Then it fell down. Some years ago a group of English antiquaries purposed carting it away to Calcutta to put it in the museum there. With modern equipment they contrived to move it two hundred yards through the jungle, and then gave it up. The stone was too heavy, the road too difficult. Yet the ancient builders of the Black Pagoda, with no stone anywhere near Kanarak, cut this huge block from quarries in the hills eighty miles away, and transported it across choked-up jungles and unbridged rivers, and finally hoisted it to a high position in the structure.

The Black Pagoda as a whole brings up the problem of how the ancient builders, with their poor implements, accomplished their engineering feats. This Temple of the Sun is built of giant stone blocks, the handling of which would in many cases tax the ingenuity of the modern engineer and all his technology.

Near by was a dak bungalow, ready for any sahib whose duties archæological or political might require him to make a stay at Kanarak. A book for visitors to sign lay on the table. I looked through it, and found the name of many a famous Englishman. I noticed an absence of feminine handwriting. Almost no women were to be found among the visitors to the Black Pagoda. Gentlemen apparently do not take ladies to the fabulous shrine —and no wonder.

All through the night we bounced along in our palanquins. To the rhythmic chant of our bearers the lines of the poem of Laurence Hope, the lines that the British cavalry general had recited, kept coming back

and haunting us all the way from the Black Pagoda to
Puri:

"What did they mean to the men who are long since dust?
    Whose fingers traced,
    In this arid waste,
These rioting, twisting, figures of love and lust?

Strange, weird things that no man may say,
Things Humanity hides away;—
    Secretly done—
Catch the light of the living day,
    Smile in the sun.
Cruel things that man may not name,
Naked here, without fear or shame,
    Laugh in the carven stone."

CHAPTER XLI

THE BLINKERS OF BUREAUCRACY

MOST wise are the words of Senator William E. Borah, to wit:

"It may be possible to devise some form of government more deadening to human initiative, more destructive to human progress, more burdensome to the people, than a bureaucracy, but so far God in His infinite mercy has not permitted it to curse the human family. Up to date, the worst of all human forms of government is a bureaucracy."

This curse of the human family exists in India. Some indeed may be found to glory in bureaucracy. Others declare it to be a necessary evil. Nobody will deny that it prevails and flourishes under British rule.

"We have seen in our country," writes Rabindranath Tagore, "some brands of tinned food advertised as entirely made and packed without being touched by hand. This description applies to the governing of India, which is as little touched by the human hand as possible. The governors need not know our language, need not come into personal contact with us . . ." and so forth.

There is little *human* sympathy between the rulers and the ruled. Of abstract sympathy there is aplenty: whole file-fulls and pigeonhole-loads. But in that trust, born of confidence, which touches the heart, and in that intimacy which fires the imagination of a sensitive race, and in that breadth of vision which sees the problems of the people with the eyes of the people, the British administration is deficient.

None deny that British rule in India is efficient and unsympathetic. Every one, including the rulers, admits this.

What are the reasons for this universally admitted shortcoming? What are the blinkers that narrow the vision of India's governing class? They are:

(a) Climate;

(b) Caste;

(c) Congenital antipathy; and

(d) The conspiracy of the clerks.

The climate of India is peculiar to itself, peculiar perhaps in its deadliness to northern India and the Ganges basin, where great *couches* of the population reside. Some men withstand it, it is true, but the fact remains that it makes the average individual limp and effete, so that nothing but a change of air, or the return of the cold weather, will restore him to efficiency. Other parts of the world may be hotter: Aden in Arabia, Yuma in Arizona, the Gold Coast, and Basra on the Persian Gulf. Mesopotamia has been compared to the Punjaub, to the credit of the latter. And Sir Sydney Low, going a step further, has drawn a picture of himself stifling behind inadequate blinds on a summer day in London, and invites comparison, by implication, with the dweller on the "sun-kissed" plains of India, shaded by a verandah and cooled by a fan. *Sun-kissed!* Those who have answered with their lives the call of the East will appreciate this adjective. Either the inhabitants of Arizona, Africa, and where you will are supermen, and Sir Sydney Low also, or else the northern Indian climate is one of the most trying in the world; for the fact remains that there is no other considerable region of the earth's surface where sickness and sunstroke and sudden death are so prevalent. In these stricken places, for six months out of every twelve, life is a struggle with hostile elements. Man is busy *keeping alive,* against the sun by day and the insects by night, insects that bite and strike and slay. Do you think the sallow faces and the jangled nerves of men who have done duty in the plains are due to their own indiscretion, and that you in your wisdom could keep fit if you did the work they did? Do you think Great Britain does not pay the price of empire in the blood of her sons? . . . And remember, climate affects Indians as much as it does the British.

Watch your clerk putting a postage-stamp on a letter. See him detach it slowly from the surrounding stamps, and look from it to the letter, and from the letter to it, and search for the right-hand top corner, and then look for the damper, and then look to see if the stamp and the corner are still there. Watch him for a minute or two. Compare him with a Western post-office Miss. . . . And now think of the last time you asked a question of an official. He said it was a difficult question, no doubt, and that he would refer it to a superior, and that he had no hope of getting a favorable answer. In fact, there was no answer. . . . These things are not the fault of the British Government in India. It can't find brisk babus: it can't help the fact that its higher officials sometimes feel very tired. No power on earth could order it otherwise. All the British can do is to remove their administration to the better climate of the hills, and this has the governmental disadvantage that would ensue if our Federal Government shifted from Washington to the Rockies or if the British Cabinet held their meetings in Monte Carlo. Climate! This is the blinker over the off-side eye of the off-side horse of the blundering bureaucratic barouche drawn by the civil and military team of India. The weariness, the sense of Nirvana that comes with extreme heat.

Then there is caste. See the babu sticking the envelop when he has finally affixed the stamp. Again the damper, for his lips must not touch the impure gum of aliens. And you, who sit in lordly style at the desk of authority, are as dirt to him, an unclean animal, whose breath is a contamination and whose shadow is a pollution to his food. . . . He will complain, perhaps, of your British insularity or your American or European arrogance, and ask why he is not admitted to your club. But it is impossible to describe how he really feels towards you in his inmost heart. Lord Curzon's attitude towards a cur dog would have been genial by comparison. The Indian Muhammadan is little behind his Hindu "brother" in this religious pride. He has assimilated ideas of ceremonial purity unknown to the Arabs, and frequently will not eat or drink with those who are not of his religion. Yet he is not behindhand in blaming the British for exclusiveness. Here, then, is the near-side blinker of one of the twin horses of bureaucracy. Blinded by religious pride, the steeds pull the chariot of progress all askew.

Racial antagonism is the third blinker. To pretend that it does not exist is a very poor way of tackling the problems of East and West. Congenital antipathies should be stated and faced. The West is ready to give to the East its religion, but not its daughters in marriage. Some atavism stronger than ourselves rises insurgent when we think of the admixture of our blood with theirs. And the Indians feel the same. No doubt this is prejudice—the narrow vision of prejudice.

Finally, there is the secret society of the inefficient, whose ramifications spread to every class, high and low. Their password is "Passivity." Their aim is to cripple endeavor, wet-blanket enthusiasm, and encourage six men to do the work of one. When Ghandi said that it was the sacred duty of the Hindu to non-coöperate nonviolently with everybody all the time, he was acclaimed a mahatma for formulating this delightful doctrine. The sad fact is that the average Indian does not like co-operating. He likes doing nothing. All the time he can spare he spends lying on his back on his bed. This is a generalization, of course. But look at Indian boys, when left to themselves. Look at your servants. Watch the clerks. It is the climate, doubtless. They can't help feel-ing tired. But the result is that it takes five strong men to do the work of a housemaid and three bold babus to tackle the work of a typist in her teens. No one will co-operate with the officials in India. And this is no new thing. No one has ever tried to help the rulers, through the ages. The trying has to be done by the rulers; the part of the subject is merely to submit. This idea dies hard. That it is dying is due, no doubt, to education. At present, however, the path of the administrator is a dif-ficult one.

Consider the case of Babu Ashutosh Mukerjee, who was sticking on the stamp. He earns fifty rupees ($16.50) a month, and on this pay supports a wife, a mother-in-law, three children, and two indigent cousins who have failed in their college entrance examinations. Can you wonder that if a tip comes his way he is liable to fall? Can you wonder, when you think of all those dependents, eating his pottage of pulses and nibbling his sweetmeats made of ghi, that he is a past master at *making work, not for work's sake, but in order that some one else may* be engaged to do it, the some one else being one of his relations?

So he refers back correspondence, cross-indexes, writes reams to his next-door neighbor, shunning the telephone (a base device to rob the babu of his birthright) like a thing accursed, and fattens his files on memorandums, until at last his second cousin has to be engaged to deal with the mountains of manuscript. And soon the second cousin has found work for a third.

So it goes on. Snowed under with foolscap and fixed firmly at his desk, the brutal beef-eating Briton becomes a harmless, indeed necessary creature. He has become part of the system, the signer of the pay-rolls that nepotism has created, the willing horse that babudom bestrides in the triumphal procession of bureaucracy.

Climate, caste, congenital antipathy, and the conspiracy of the clerk—these are the chief obstacles to a United India. Pride, prejudice, nepotism, and Nirvana, these are the blinkers in which bureaucracy must work. They can never be wholly removed, for this is not of the nature of things so long as bureaucracy is necessary, as we believe it to be necessary at present, for the security of India. But the blinkers can be fitted and adjusted so that the jibbing team can pull straight, or at any rate straighter, along the path of progress.

Is it democracy then, or Western science, that is keeping India for the British? Or is Britain losing India? Will the big new Parliament House that the British have recently built crumble down in a century or so, to the dust of the forgotten Delhis?

We would hazard an answer. The British will not lose India. In spite of all the talk to the contrary, they will remain, as traders and soldiers, if not as administrators, because their rule has been a success, taking it by and large. The secret of that success is simply that they do not live in India. They are not debauched by the climate like the old Aryans and Moghuls. It is the steamship lines and transports carrying tired bureaucrats to their English homes, and bringing bright, buoyant administrators back again to their bureaus, that are holding India for the British.

And not bureaucrats only. All honor to their share in the work that has been done in India, but it is the merchant, the banker, the railway executive, the engineer, and the journalist who have given India the prosperity she enjoys to-day.

These things could not have been done without the West. The West could not have done them if traveling had not been cheap and fast. The greatest need in all Asia to-day is improved communications. Movement is the heart's blood of a country, and it is the British who have stimulated a healthy circulation in India, and have brought the West to her doors. It is this constant influx of new life and new enthusiasm that India needs, and that India is getting under modern conditions of travel and trade.

There is no doubt that the British are now in the act of giving India independence. But India can never be independent of the West, nor will she want to be, nor is it at all likely that she will turn to another of the great powers for guidance and protection. A thousand agitators may say that she must, but the remaining three hundred and nineteen million and some odd people will veto the idea.

I will repeat the old reasoning that India is not one nation but several, cleft by bitter antagonisms, especially religious antagonisms, and that if the land were freed now it would be torn by civil war. Still, it is difficult to prophesy. They said that self-government for Ireland, likewise sundered by the bitterest religious feud, would mean anarchy. But the Irish, after a little trouble, seem to be getting along well enough.

India has her great qualities. The British have theirs. For centuries to come India will turn—not as a servant, but as an equal—to the wealth, the technical knowledge, and the energy of Britain to supply her needs. With this help, moral and material, India may one day rise to the proud birthright of her Aryan stock, so that the two streams of civilization that parted in the childhood of the world on the borders of the Mediterranean, one to form the European and the other to form the Indian culture, may unite in their common ancestry again, to build up a great nation of the Eastern world. . . . India a nation in fact, not in fancy.